Six Gre

Aristophanes **Birds**
Menander **The**
Euripides

Aristophanes was born in Athens probably died in 385 BC. The twenty-seven-year Peloponnesian War against Sparta began in 431 and most of Aristophanes' working career as a playwright used the hostilities as a backcloth and as a stimulus. Only the last two plays of the eleven which survive come from the fourth century and they show a marked change from the vigorous and picaresque world of war-torn Athens. Aristophanes' plays may be comedies, fantasies even, but the messages they convey frequently have a serious dimension. *Birds* (414 BC) posits a utopia created when two Athenians enable the birds to regain their ancestral power: but it is a utopia constantly threatened by the same social disorder that threatens to bring down Athens. *Frogs* (405 BC) has Dionysos visiting Hades to bring back to Athens a dead tragedian in an attempt to save the city. The political advice was too late and the Spartans finally took Athens the following year. *Women in Power* (392 BC) shows a recovering but less influential Athens and offers a new solution to the city's malaise when the women succeed in voting themselves into government.

Menander began writing for the stage some seventy years after Aristophanes' death. The social and political changes anticipated in Aristophanes' last plays have now turned Athens into a city more concerned with domestic issues than world supremacy. *The Woman from Samos* (c. 310 BC) reflects this but offers less a decline of the comic form than a change of direction. Though most of his plays have disappeared the few that are left show how and why Menander was so popular in the ancient world and how he sowed the seeds of all later comedies of manners. Little is known of Menander's personal life and the plays give nothing away about that. What they do offer is a picture of the social life of the Athens of his time, as, in an entirely different context, had the plays of Aristophanes.

Euripides was born near Athens between 485 and 480 BC and grew up during the years of Athenian recovery after the Persian Wars. His first play was presented in 455 BC and he wrote some hundred altogether. Nineteen survive, of which perhaps the best known are *Medea*, *Bacchae*, *Hippolytos*, and *Trojan Women*. It may seem odd that as a writer of tragedy any of his work should be included in a volume of comedy. Many of his tragic works do, though, contain a comic element and the two plays included here are each examples of the comic slant which could be given to a tragic structure, *Cyclops* through the satyr play, *Alkestis* as a different kind of 'fourth play' for a group submission. Euripides was a generation older than Aristophanes, but their most active creative periods overlapped. Both found the Peloponnesian War a source of stimulus and a cause for desperate concern about the way that Athens was heading. It is Euripides who appears as a character in *Frogs*, the playwright whom Dionysos goes to Hades to bring back, though, interestingly, it is Aeschylus with whom the god of the theatre returns to earth. Euripides was often controversial, an uncomfortable playwright whose signature was the subverting of audience expectations.

in the same series

SIX GREEK TRAGEDIES

Aeschylus
Persians, Prometheus

Sophocles
Women of Trachis, Philoctetes

Euripides
Trojan Women, Bacchae

FOUR ROMAN COMEDIES

Plautus
A Funny Thing Happened on the Way to the Wedding (Casina),
The Haunted House (Mostellaria)

Terence
The Eunuch, Brothers

Six Greek Comedies

ARISTOPHANES

Birds
Frogs
Women in Power

translated by Kenneth McLeish

MENANDER

The Woman from Samos

translated by J. Michael Walton

EURIPIDES

Cyclops
Alkestis

translated by J. Michael Walton

introduced by
J. Michael Walton

METHUEN DRAMA

1 3 5 7 9 10 8 6 4 2

This collection first published in the United Kingdom in 2002 by
Methuen Publishing Ltd
215 Vauxhall Bridge Road, London SW1V 1EJ

These translations of *Birds* and *Frogs* first published in 1993
by Methuen Drama

This translation of *Women in Power* published by Methuen Drama in
1994; an earlier version first published by
Cambridge University Press in 1979

This translation of *The Woman from Samos* first published
in 1994 by Methuen Drama

This translation of *Cyclops* first published in 1991 by Methuen Drama

This translation of *Alkestis* first published in 1997 by Methuen Drama

Methuen Publishing Limited Reg. No. 3543167

A CIP catalogue record for this book
is available from the British Library

ISBN 0 413 77130 X

Typeset by Wilmaset Ltd, Birkenhead, Wirral
Printed and bound in Great Britain by
Cox and Wyman Ltd, Reading, Berkshire

CONTENTS

INTRODUCTION

Comedy in Athens

As good a way as any of testing the temperament of a people is to look at what makes them laugh. For ancient Greece the comedies of their theatre provide a unique view of a culture at a time before anyone, with the single exception of Herodotus, had seen any reason to write about, never mind catalogue, the details of everyday behaviour. The first depictions of domestic life are to be found on vase-paintings; the first portraits of Athenian society are to be found in the plays of Aristophanes, who wrote eleven comedies which have survived, dated between 425 and c.392 BC. For, as Edith Hamilton put it in *The Greek Way to Western Civilisation*, 'To read Aristophanes is in some sort like reading an Athenian comic paper. All the life of Athens is there: the politics of the day and the politicians; the war party and the anti-war party; pacifism, votes for women, free trade, fiscal reform, complaining taxpayers, educational theories, the current religious and literary talk – everything, in short, that interested the average citizen. All was food for his mockery. He was the speaking picture of the follies and foibles of his day.'

Menander was not born until over forty years after Aristophanes' death. The society that he portrays had changed greatly with the decline of Athens as a world power in the face of the rise of Macedon. Athens had become more provincial in the new cosmopolitan era and Menander's plays reflect this. Aristophanes took his greatest stimulus from the Peloponnesian War between Athens and Sparta. He is political in the broadest sense of the word. In his early plays, known collectively as Old Comedy, many of the characters are contemporary figures who are lampooned and ridiculed with a joyous irreverence for authority: his heroes may influence trials in the lawcourt, build a new city of birds in mid-air to starve the gods into submission, or go down to Hades, as does Dionysos in *Frogs*, to bring back a recently deceased playwright.

Birds is a supreme example of imaginative flair inspiring

serious satirical comment. The mix of real characters, some of whom may have been in the first audience, fictional Athenians and gods, is typical of his inventive exploration of what can be achieved in a comic drama. *Frogs* is, perhaps, the best example of Aristophanes' skill in blending fantasy and farce through manipulation of the conventions of the stage. The gags are anarchic without being inconsistent, and miraculously freed from the tyranny of period. His later plays, often labelled Middle Comedy and produced after the defeat of Athens by Sparta, are less obviously party political. Less exuberant too, they deal, suitably in the age of Plato, with more philosophical issues, the curing of the blind god of wealth or, as in *Women in Power*, the possibilities of a genuine democracy created when women take over the state Assembly. The fact that this is achieved via opening scenes of complex cross-dressing serves to emphasise Aristophanes' control of that strange balance between audience and players essential in any comedy from any period.

The seeds of the European comedy of manners were sown in the world of New Comedy. Menander's concerns are parochial, day-to-day existence and getting on with the neighbours, life and love. *The Woman from Samos* is a family comedy, based on a series of misunderstandings which result from people trying to avoid causing distress to those they care for most. If this sounds a flimsy model for the future comedy of manners, a more careful look at Menander reveals a subtle awareness of the proximity of tears to laughter. Comedy may have lost some of its teeth since Aristophanes, but the awareness of individual circumstances and the portrait of people whose day-to-day problems are recognisable, set up a comic structure which would prove the basis of the whole European comic tradition through Terence, Molière, Goldoni, arguably to Chekhov, Shaw and Ayckbourn.

That accounts for four of the six comedies here – the other two are by Euripides whom Aristotle in *Poetics* called *tragikôtatos*, 'most tragic' of all the Greek playwrights. *Cyclops* is the only satyr play to have survived. Greek tragedians submitted their plays in groups of four. The first three of these were tragedies, the fourth a comic afterpiece. Though the satyr play was in part a send-up of some aspect of the tragic story or theme that had been tackled in the earlier three plays, it is not linked to our word 'satire'. Satyrs were part of the entourage of the god Dionysos, upright though animal creatures with human features, but also sporting *phalloi* and horses' tails. Representations of them appear on a large number of classical vases where they are usually engaged in drinking or chasing Bacchantes, Dionysos' female votaries. For reasons that probably have more to do with the necessary restorative power of laughter than with Horace's bald remark in the *Ars Poetica* that the satyr play was presented 'when the audience were good and drunk and in a lawless mood', this comic coda is still something of an anomaly. Without more examples it is difficult to generalise about the linking features between satyr and tragedy. Aristotle thought the form preceded tragedy and that tragedy grew out of the satyr play, but Aristotle was no theatre historian.

If that explains the inclusion of *Cyclops*, what of the other Euripides play? *Alkestis* has tended to fox critics and historians alike because it fits comfortably into no clear mould. Greek plays are often difficult to date. *Birds* and *Frogs* almost date themselves by references to contemporary events. *Alkestis* is fixed from accurate records and is the earliest of those included in the present volume. It was performed in 438 BC in a group of four Euripides plays, none of the other three of which has survived. An inscription even informs us that the group won second prize to Sophocles in that year. The oddity is that *Alkestis* was fourth in the group, the satyr position, and that, therefore, according to the assumed pattern, it should have been a satyr play. Clearly it isn't. Any resemblance between *Alkestis* and *Cyclops* amounts to no more than a short drunken scene in which Herakles makes an exhibition of himself under the impression that the death in the household is of some minor relation, not of Admetus' queen. The play is just as hard to classify as a tragedy. The one death is resolved with Alkestis being brought back to life and the mood of the piece is much more that of a romance along the lines of Shakespeare's *The Winter's Tale*, down to the restoration to life of the 'dead' wife. At most it is a potential tragedy, a serious story but a story of redemption and renewal. In 438 BC this was a new kind of play, one which to this day defies pigeon-holing but has much more the feel of Menandrian comedy than of tragedy.

There was a strong argument for including in the volume one of Euripides' 'genuine' tragedies, several of which more closely resemble the world of Menander than that of Aeschylus. *Ion* certainly looks forward to New Comedy in its tale of an exposed child brought up as a foundling; a visit to the Delphic oracle; a series of misunderstandings and revelations resolved through recognition tokens; a mother and son finally united. Substitute daughter for son and you seem to have yet another version of *The Winter's Tale*. The play was presented as a tragedy but is again a fringe play where old definitions cease to work. The same is true of Euripides' *Helen*, a version which exonerates Helen from responsibility for the Trojan War by having her physically removed to Egypt while Paris canoodles with a lookalike fashioned out of wind; and *Iphigeneia in Tauris*, a similar story, where it is Iphigeneia who has been spirited away instead of dying at the hands of her father Agamemnon, and who nearly kills her brother Orestes. Disasters threaten but fail to materialise and all ends happily – relatively. All these plays have specifically comic moments, but then so do all the plays of Euripides, even the most grim.

That it should be possible to juxtapose six such different examples of comic drama from the classical period would be less surprising were it not for the philosopher Plato. Plato was born in the year that Aristophanes presented his first comedy. He probably saw some of the plays of Euripides and Aristophanes at their first performance. His celebrated hostility towards the theatre is exhibited in a major work, *The Republic*, where, through the mouthpiece of Sokrates, he argues for the excision of drama from his ideal state. Part of the argument used revolves around specialities, 'what people do best'. The two disputants in the dialogue are in agreement that the same actor cannot play in comedy and in tragedy: more tellingly, that the same man cannot write both tragedy and comedy. To the Athenian mind, apparently, the genres were separate: comedy was comedy; tragedy was tragedy; and the satyr play was part of tragedy. Today, when such categories are less rigid, the plays of Euripides in particular can be treated with more of an open mind. Then, the performance of each form was strictly divided.

Plays and festival

Plays in Athens were presented in competition. The winter festival of the Lenaia – the Greek and Julian calendars do not coincide – and the spring festival of the Great Dionysia were occasions when all manner of celebrations took place, sacrifices, eulogies, presentations, processions, largely in the name of civic pride. The playwrights whose work was to be performed were selected in late summer of the previous year. The process was known as 'being granted a chorus'. The successful candidates – and no one was guaranteed a slot whatever his reputation – were allotted to a *choregos*, a private citizen selected to perform some state service according to his perceived wealth. It was a sort of semi-compulsory patronage, not necessarily unwelcome for the ambitious who could thereby make a name for themselves.

The *choregos* paid for the selection, recompense and training of a chorus, and for incidental production costs. The state hired and allocated the actors. The upkeep of the theatre and management of the festival was assigned by tender to a theatre manager, the *architekton*. From strictly amateur beginnings acting became professionalised. A jury was chosen, one man from each of the ten tribes of Attica. They voted for best playwright and best actor, only in tragedy initially, but eventually in comedy too. To ensure that even at this stage the lot, or the favour of the gods, was still a factor, a haphazard five votes out of the ten were picked and the prizes awarded accordingly.

Performance

All the plays included here were written for the same theatre space, the Theatre of Dionysos, part of the precinct of Dionysos below the south-east corner of the Acropolis. The *theatron* for the spectators was rather more than a semicircle, facing inwards towards the *orchestra*, or dancing-place. A stage-building at the rear framed the actors and gave them somewhere to enter from and exit to, in addition to two side-entrances or *parodoi*. The shape and detail of this theatre space is likely to have changed over the years from the flexible wooden scenic background of its earlier years when *Alkestis* was performed, to the larger and more permanent stone theatre built by Lycurgus a hundred years later. That changes should have taken place in the theatre is no surprise. That the theatre structure should have apparently become more rigid is harder to understand.

The actors were male and wore masks from the earliest times but, even within that graphic and physical acting tradition, it is not easy to see how subtle the playing could have been. By the time of late Aristophanes, the chorus was largely in decline and had become in Menander no more than a way of passing the time between scenes. There is no direct evidence that Greek comedy was restricted in the number of actors employed, but there are seldom more than four used in any scene and it is usually assumed that there was a lot of doubling in Aristophanes. Menander's *The Woman from Samos* has a cast of six speaking characters, four of whom appear in each of the five acts. A fifth character appears in four acts, the sixth and last in the one act from which number five is absent. Circumstantial evidence suggests a regular company for comedy of five, plus non-speaking extras.

There are virtually no stage-directions in Greek texts but there are indications of location. In these six plays a variety of settings range from the countryside outside Athens to mid-air (*Birds*); Athens, the River Styx (complete with frog chorus) to Hades (*Frogs*); a street in Athens (*Women in Power*); outside two adjacent houses in Athens (*The Woman from Samos*); outside Admetus' palace in Pherai (*Alkestis*); and outside a cave in Sicily (*Cyclops*). Opinion is divided as to the extent to which settings were indicated by some emblematic painting or left wholly to the imagination of the audience. What seems to be clear is that all the playwrights, tragedians and comedians, from quite early, understood the subtleties of stage space and the way in which a scene or effect may be enhanced by physical presentation. Upper levels, surprise entrances, prolonged entrances, flying entrances, positions to hide, to eavesdrop, to talk to the audience, dance and movement, mask, colour, costume, tableaux, properties and sound effects, confrontations, threats, slanging-matches: the existence of all these is implicit in the way the plays are written. Comedy offers the additional dimensions of physical business, routines, chases, playing the space and playing the house, takes and double takes, *lazzi* and routines. There is no way of going back to find out what the original performances were like. It is possible that these plays were performed as though they were radio drama. It isn't likely.

Aristophanes

Birds

All the nine Aristophanes plays written during the Peloponnesian War between Athens and Sparta have a quality of escapism. Many show the desire simply to get away from the war. When Edith Hamilton writes of the 'war party' and the 'anti-war party', she highlights a political split in Athens that the plays of the period reflect, both tragedy and comedy. The war lasted from 431 to 404 BC. *Acharnians* (425 BC) is about a man who makes his private peace with Sparta, and gets away with it. *Peace* (421 BC) has a farmer fly up to heaven to rescue the goddess Peace who has been thrown down a well by Ares, god of war. *Lysistrata* (411 BC) shows, often anatomically, the effect of the women of Greece going on a sex-strike until the men agree to stop the fighting. In each and all of these there is little doubt whose side Aristophanes is on. In the same period Euripides produces some of his toughest tragedies about the effects of war, *Hecuba* (date uncertain) and *Trojan Women* (415).

This last was written in the aftermath of one of the atrocities of that war, the siege and subjugation of the island of Melos, after which the men were slaughtered, the women and children sold into slavery. Euripides' play is straight parable, using the Trojan War as its context. Aristophanes' method is different, less concentrated but more direct. *Birds* is a fantasy about the creation of a new state in mid-air between earth and heaven. At one moment in the play, the two disenchanted Athenians who are initiating the idea try to sell the advantage to Tereus, king of the birds. Peithetairos suggests building a wall in the sky, 'a large, fortified nest' so that they can lord it over the whole human race:

> ... Not to mention starving out the gods.
> It worked with the Melians. (ll. 184–5)

This at a moment of purest whimsy is a wonderful example of Aristophanes' hard edge. This is not escapism. It is rather the setting up of a fantastical set of circumstances through which to draw attention to serious issues of state. Many of the laughs in Aristophanes are belly-laughs, created through all manner of jokes about sex and bodily functions. Alongside such are the serious jokes, about social and political ideals, all those other aspects of life in Athens that made it so lively and alarming.

At the opening of *Birds* two Athenians, Euelpides and Peithetairos, are engaged on a search for Tereus, legendary king of the birds. They have had enough of Athens, not because of the war, but because of lawyers. Perhaps there is a clue here to Aristophanes' caution. The names have a meaning in Greek, Euelpides 'Son of the man of good hope' or 'Optimist'; Peithetairos, 'Persuader of his companions'. If the Optimist takes the initiative early in the play it is the Persuader who emerges as the leader of the new state. They find Tereus and are given the opportunity to put their case to the whole chorus of birds. The birds are initially hostile but are won over and the two humans are given the chance to become birds themselves.

Work starts on the new city which is to be called *Nephelococcygia*, Cloudcuckooland. The place is immediately invaded by a series of self-servers, parasites and bureaucrats. Each of these is sent packing but, when the building work is complete, a watchman announces that a stranger has slipped through the defences. This turns out to be Iris, messenger of Zeus, who is told in no uncertain terms what she and Zeus can expect from now onwards – nothing less than a holy war. Cloudcuckooland starts to become fashionable, an excuse for the arrival of another selection of undesirables and a lot of local gossip, much of which passes us by today.

Prometheus then turns up, the rebel who gave mankind fire, and advises that the gods are indeed starving and suggests what peace terms Peithetairos should make. A deputation of three gods arrives, Poseidon, Herakles and Biggun (in Greek 'a Tri-ballian'). Peithetairos conducts negotiations while cooking a sumptuous dinner. Biggun, who speaks unintelligible Greek, is differently interpreted by each of the others and Peithetairos prevails. Not only do the gods agree to hand back the birds' sceptre, their right to self-govern, but they will also hand over the beautiful Sovereignty for Peithetairos to marry. It is at this juncture that the play takes on a probable level of political statement. Peithetairos, the persuader, 'marries' sovereign power and effectively becomes dictator of the state. The play ends with a wedding feast but an uneasy feeling that there may be a serious warning here to the Athenian people about the dangers of vesting too much power in the hands of an individual.

Birds was produced in 414 BC, the year after *Trojan Women*. It might have been expected to be a much more blatant political piece but this was a sensitive time and even Aristophanes may have thought twice about ridiculing the city at war when so many of its citizens were becoming involved in what was to prove an ill-fated military expedition to Sicily. This is, indeed, one of the few plays that has no *parabasis*, a feature of Old Comedy where the Chorus, or one of the characters, address the audience direct on topics of the day, speaking as though they were the playwright himself. On the other hand, a more generalised warning about the direction of power within the state is easy enough to detect in the play. It was, as it turned out, only three years before there was an oligarchic revolution in Athens, which, but for the intervention of the navy, might well have seen the premature end of democracy.

Frogs

In 406 BC the Peloponnesian War was nearing its end. The previous twenty-five years had sapped Athenian resources and resolve. Not a family could have escaped bereavement. Internal political struggles had savaged the processes of democracy and no one seemed sure where to turn for salvation. Much of the controversy raged over what should be done about Alcibiades, a brilliant but self-destructive military campaigner with a record of betrayal on the grand scale. Recalled to Athens by the restored democracy after the failed oligarchic coup in the city, he had then lost the battle of Notium before retiring to the north. The elderly Euripides had already departed from Athens for the court of King Archelaus of Macedon and news now came through of his death.

An unexpected victory in a sea-battle at Arginusae resulted in the enfranchising of the slaves who rowed in the battle but the arraignment of six of the successful eight generals for making too little effort to pick up survivors.

And Aristophanes started to write one of his most brilliant comedies, a comedy featuring Dionysos, god of the theatre, concerned that without Euripides the theatre would die. Consider the cast-list: the god Dionysos; Xanthias, an ordinary slave; a donkey; Herakles, the demi-god, the only man who had ever gone down to the abode of the dead and returned to tell the tale; a corpse whom Dionysos wants to carry his bags for him; Charon, the ferryman of the dead who, for a fee, rows the dead over the Styx; the all-singing, all-dancing frog chorus which gives the play its title; Plouton, god of the underworld; another chorus, this time of mystics; the recently dead Euripides and the long-dead Aeschylus, locked in verbal combat to see who is the better playwright, a decision eventually decided not on dramatic merit but by who gives the better advice over what to do about Alkibiades. If that wasn't complicated enough, half way through writing *Frogs*, Aristophanes was to hear that Sophocles, now so old that it had seemed he would live for ever, had also died, and there was no room for him in the play as well as the other two tragedians.

All of these events found their way into the play which was presented at the Lenaia of 405 and was so well received that it was called for again at the next opportunity, presumably the Great Dionysia, two months later, a festival made extra special in 405 because at it the last plays of Euripides were performed posthumously, winning him a belated fifth first prize. In Hades he must have chuckled.

As an example of how Aristophanes could pick and mix contemporary people and events with the world of myth and the fantastic, *Frogs* is as good as anything he wrote. It is also a play about the stage, about acting and about disguise, a play about pretence, a play about theatre. The god Dionysos, disguised as Herakles by putting on Herakles' lion skin, has to submit to all manner of threats and indignities from people that the real Herakles had cheated on his earlier visit. So he demands that Xanthias swap clothes and Xanthias now picks up all the goodies from those who had adored Herakles last time. Eventually Dionysos claims to be a god: so does Xanthias, and they set up the beating scene to establish which one of them feels no pain. All of this is pure theatrical conceit. If Dionysos is really the god, then he won't feel pain. He does. But then it is not the god who is being beaten, it is an actor, and he won't feel pain anyway as the whole scene is being staged. It is a scene which might come straight from a British Christmas pantomime.

If this is a scene of pure slapstick then what happens in Hades by contrast is extraordinarily sophisticated. Dionysos has come to take back Euripides. Aeschylus disputes Euripides' claim to the Chair of Drama and the god of the underworld institutes a contest between them. This is an extended scene where the two combatants compare their dramatic methods, their versification, their prologues, their sense of theatricality. It is quite unique. We have no contemporary accounts of what the Greeks thought of the productions they attended beyond the driest of records. There are no critical reviews, no indications even of whether what seems today to be theatrically or dramatically powerful is any more than the application of a modern sense of theatre to a culture that thrived twenty-four centuries ago. Aristotle was the first to give any kind of indication of what dramatic values might entail and he was not even alive at the same time as Euripides and Aristophanes, never mind Aeschylus. As dramatic criticism from someone who had at least seen Euripides on stage and probably Aeschylus too in revival,

Frogs is all we have. It turns out to be a liberating account. By a close scrutiny, albeit a comic one, of language, versification, prologue and exposition, characters, choruses, stage effects and, above all, 'realism', Aristophanes identifies many of the features of both playwrights which today might be used to evaluate their relative dramatic methods.

Then there is the politics. Some of those whose names crop up in the play are long gone; others may be more familiar but the topical references mean nothing to a modern audience. What does mean something is the playwright's burning concern. Aeschylus, Sophocles and Euripides may be the writers of serious tragedy but the comedy of Aristophanes, it often seems, is every bit as serious. *Frogs* was written almost in the bunker, performed first with the Spartans virtually at the door. The frustration of wanting to find solutions and having only the theatre as a medium to do so has been shared by generations of playwrights ever since. But, if Aristophanes' sense of the ridiculous and the fantastical was without compare, no one should ignore the passion which underpinned it.

Women in Power

Several of Aristophanes' earlier plays (*Acharnians*, *Knights* and *Birds*) are centred on the processes of government and the effect on the individual; others (*Thesmophoriazousae* or *Festival Time* and *Lysistrata*) concentrate on the effect that women can have within a male-dominated society where the place of citizen women was certainly the home and where non-citizens of either gender had no voting rights. All these plays were produced during the Peloponnesian War and, whatever other issues might be featured, the backcloth of war was never wholly absent. *Frogs*, presented little more than a year before the final defeat by the Spartans, marks the demise of comedy that was aimed at specific individuals. *Women in Power*, from only thirteen years later, gives new life to the concept comedy, a single fanciful idea which is mooted and put into practice, the rest of the play being taken up with considering the ramifications and side-effects.

Women in Power is recognisably Aristophanes, but a

slightly muted Aristophanes with no grotesque choruses of clouds or wasps, and firmly rooted in contemporary Athens. The opening offers a classic comic situation. The women of Athens, led by Praxagora, are so fed up with the way that the state is run by men that they have got up early to go in disguise to the Assembly to vote themselves into power. They are successful and the remainder of the play is taken up with the results of their new regime. But, as with *Lysistrata* and *Festival Time*, though the play revolves around female issues, they are issues filtered through a male gaze. Not only is the writing by a man, so is the playing. *Women in Power*, like *Lysistrata*, is a drag play, and a drag play intended for an audience which was, if not exclusively, certainly primarily, male. The women of Athens who enter with Praxagora are male actors, playing women who have dressed up in their husbands' clothes in order to take their place in the Assembly. As soon as they have gone off, their husbands appear, dressed as women. They have had to put on their wives' clothes: they couldn't find their own because their wives are wearing them.

The cross-dressing reversal becomes a central image for the rest of the play as the women set up a new system of government based on total equality of opportunity. There is topical satire here as the upheavals of the last twenty years had led to much speculation about what form of government could ever work. Aristophanes, born into the democracy fostered and developed under Pericles, had witnessed at first hand both the abuses of empire which the Athenian state had depended on for its wealth and fire-power, and, at home, the power of the demagogues and rabble-rousers to influence the Assembly. The fall of Athens in 404 BC and a subsequent reign of terror had led to the execution of Sokrates and eventually to the restoration of democracy. But it was a system under challenge. Plato, for whom Sokrates was the mouthpiece in most of his philosophical dialogues, was propounding ideas about the disposition of the ideal state in and around 392 BC when *Women in Power* was first staged.

Once the women have gained power they waste no time in instituting a 'communal' system with:

No more envy, no more greed; no poverty,
No despair; no pay-up-or-else, no arguments . . . (ll. 566–7)

Aristophanes may be a cynic but he can be a romantic too. The utopias he proposes in *Acharnians* and *Birds* do overcome their initial difficulties. Here, though, human nature ensures that envy and greed are not abolished by decree. Only the gullible hand in their personal possessions, while the legal entitlement of any woman to have any man plays havoc with the lives of the young lovers. Praxagora's husband Blepyros resists for a while but it all ends up in a party, of course, because Aristophanes' plays do, and this is as true for Old Comedy as it is for the transitional Middle Comedy.

There is a real difference, though, between Aristophanes at this late point in his career and the young man who took on, and fell foul of, politicians like the rabble-rouser Kleon. So risky was it to antagonise such a powerful figure that, according to one story, the mask-makers in Athens refused to make a Kleon mask for use in *Knights*. This was comedy, as is *Frogs*, with a genuine bite, comedy that could hit and hurt and which offered genuine advice over the course of action the state might take. In Middle Comedy this immediate engagement has passed. Old Comedy was part of the Athenian democracy but the writer was not necessarily protected by that. Kleon had Aristophanes successfully prosecuted for 'ridiculing the state in front of foreigners' after his second play, *Babylonians*, produced at the Great Dionysia of 426 BC. Nobody would have been greatly offended by *Women in Power*.

The play is still an issue play. Some sort of political stance was central to all his work, and, as far as we can tell, to that of his rivals and contemporaries too. None of their plays survive, sadly, for a proper comparison to be made. Often it is through the choruses, or the eccentric mix of gods, real-life and fictional characters that Aristophanes best exposes the vices of his age. The Chorus in *Women in Power* virtually fades out after the first five hundred lines and none of the characters are from real life. In his later years, if the few post-war plays we have are properly representative, then some of the fire has gone and the satirical targets pose no danger. That is probably what is lost, once the war with Sparta has gone – the sense of danger. This may have been the century of the philosophers and the orators, Plato, Aristotle and Demosthenes, but for many it is the century of decline. Political comedy will not be the same again.

Menander

The Woman from Samos

Until comparatively recently, Menander was one of the great literary mysteries. He was born some forty years after the death of Aristophanes and, apart from Aeschylus, Sophocles, Euripides and Aristophanes, is the only Greek playwright of ancient times any of whose plays have survived. His work was respected, revered, rather, in the ancient world to such an extent that one Byzantine scholar considered him a poet second only to Homer. Julius Caesar thought of him as the comic writer against whom all others had to be judged, while Plutarch wrote a celebrated essay comparing Aristophanes and Menander where he suggests somewhat pompously that:

> The uneducated and the commoner will be delighted by what Aristophanes has to say, but not the man of refinement . . . Menander's diction, on the other hand, is so smooth and consistent that he manages to adapt it to the whole range of emotions, personalities and character traits.

In conclusion he asks 'Why, if the truth be told, should any man of education ever go to the theatre except to see Menander?'

Until the present century the answer was simple. For two thousand years it had not been possible. Not a single one of Menander's reputed one hundred plays had come down to us. There were bits and pieces and lots of quotations, some identifiable to specific plays known by title. A series of chance discoveries in the twentieth century began to change this: jars full of legal documents in Egypt, enclosed for safe keeping in what turned out to be Menander manuscript; more bizarrely, a mummy in Paris wrapped up in pages from his plays. It was not till 1957 that a whole play, *Duskolos* (*The Malcontent* or *The Bad-Tempered Man*), was published having emerged in somewhat mysterious circumstances from Switzerland, to be followed in 1969 by *The Woman from Samos* which is 85 per cent complete.

The Malcontent was a disappointment to many of those who had waited so long to rediscover a masterpiece. It appeared at first sight to be a bit obvious and certainly no better than comedies of the Latin playwright Terence, a hundred years later than Menander, which were, by his own admission, based on Greek New Comedy. *The Woman from Samos* was more to the critics' liking but even this seemed to be simple in structure and characterisation. Such apparent simplicity is misleading.

The play is a far cry from the world of Aristophanes, though one of the Euripides plays contained in this volume offers a more obvious transition from the fifth century to the fourth. The setting is Athens, but not the Athens of Aristophanes' politicians, rebels, intellectuals and play-wrights. This is the Athens which reflects the preoccupations of the latter part of the fourth century when commercial acumen and family life are of greater importance than changing the world. That job had been left to Philip of Macedon and his son, Alexander the Great but, if people were writing plays about them, they have disappeared without trace. Instead we have what is almost a paradigm for a situation comedy.

In two adjacent houses live a merchant, Demeas, who is doing rather well in the world, and his down-at-heel neighbour, Nikeratos. These two have been away on business in the Black Sea area for the best part of a year and are now expected home. Their domestic situations are different too. Demeas has never married but has an adopted son, Moschion and lives with Chrysis, the Samian woman of the title. Nikeratos is married and has a daughter, Plangon, but neither mother nor daughter is anything but an off-stage presence until the wedding scene with which the play concludes. The only other characters are Demeas's slave, Parmenon and a cook who is hired to prepare the wedding banquet.

When Demeas went abroad, Chrysis was pregnant but he had left instructions that she could not keep the baby. While he and Nikeratos are away, Moschion has seduced Nikeratos' daughter and she has had a baby. Chrysis agrees to pretend that this baby is hers, having earlier lost her own, until such time as the petrified Moschion can get round to confessing to his father and the neighbour what he has been up to. Demeas and Nikeratos, as it happens, have already decided that Moschion should marry Plangon but don't know how to put it to Moschion in case he is upset. Everything is set up for a happy outcome, just so long as everyone tells everyone else the truth.

This they steadfastly refuse to do. In each act Demeas thinks he has managed to sort things out, only to be confronted with something off-stage which throws his whole world into chaos. He becomes convinced that the baby does belong to Chrysis but that Moschion is the father and has betrayed him. He has his slave whipped; throws Chrysis out of the house; disowns his son; and has a fight with his neighbour. All is, of course, resolved and ends with the wedding, preparations for which continue backstage for most of the play.

If the plot is slight, the plotting is not. The action behind the scenes, often as related in direct address to the audience, is one of the most revealing pictures of domestic life and attitudes to be found in classical literature. The conventional views of domestic tyranny exercised by the head of the household acquire a different dimension when filtered through the eyes of Demeas, a believable mix of affection, jealousy, passion and compassion. His rejection of Chrysis is brutal, disarmed only by the presence of the Cook who manages, though only just, to keep the play within the bounds of comedy. The relationship of adopted son and adoptive father is handled with great subtlety and both men learn from their experience. What Menander does do is give the first stage picture of people as they really are, learning about themselves in all their foolishness and with all their mistakes. His craft as a playwright is to juggle characters and audience, laughter and pathos with consummate skill.

Euripides

Cyclops

The satyr play, *Cyclops*, has no context, political or social. It is what it is, bold and brassy. No firm date is known and, as there is so little with which to compare it, even stylistic or linguistic considerations are inappropriate. As the only surviving play within a genre it must be both typical and unique. There is, though, one other satyr fragment, Sophocles' *Ichneutae* (*Trackers* or *Searchers*). This opens with Apollo informing the audience that he has lost his cattle and is offering a prize for their recovery. Silenus and the satyrs enter and discover tracks which they realise are back-to-front. The cattle have been dragged off backwards into a nearby cave to fool pursuers. A noise from the cave turns out to be the infant Hermes who, at six days old, has already invented the lyre which is covered with cow-hide, making him prime suspect as a cattle-rustler. At this point the fragment breaks off.

In Euripides' *Cyclops*, Odysseus' encounter with Polyphemus, the one-eyed giant, is based on one of the adventures related in Homer's *The Odyssey*. Though Greek tragedy is often assumed to take most of its plots from Homer, only Euripides' *Rhesus* and this play cover incidents directly from within either *The Iliad* or *The Odyssey*. In Euripides' *Cyclops* the satyrs are inserted into the story to provide dramatic continuity. Dionysos, whose attendants they are, was captured by pirates and they had set out to free him. When their boat was shipwrecked, they were forced to become servants to the Cyclops, Polyphemus, and they now look after his sheep. Odysseus arrives with his men in search of provisions and expecting the hospitable welcome due to strangers. He offers Silenus and the satyrs some of the extra-strong wine he has with him and, in the absence of his master, Silenus offers some of the Cyclops' sheep and cheese in exchange.

At this moment Polyphemus arrives and immediately Silenus denies everything. Odysseus asks for assistance but tells the giant that his name is Nobody. This is a joke which works rather better in Homer when his fellow-Cyclopes arrive to ask who is troubling him. The play can only cope with a single giant. Polyphemus drives Odysseus and his men into the cave. After a brief song and dance from the satyrs Odysseus emerges from the cave to tell how Polyphemus has killed and eaten some of his men. The rest are trapped inside though Odysseus cannot quite explain how he has got out and his men are unable to. He has given the Cyclops some of his special wine and plans to get him thoroughly drunk before putting out his single eye with a burning brand. The Chorus offer enthusiastic help. The Cyclops returns, unsurprised, it seems, to find Odysseus outside the cave, but perhaps already too drunk to notice. Odysseus plies him with more wine until he carries off a reluctant Silenus into the cave to have sex with him. The Chorus encourage Odysseus but when it comes to helping him with the blinding they all find excuses not to: one has twisted his ankle, another hurt his back. Odysseus succeeds in putting out the Cyclops' eye while the Chorus offer encouragement from a distance:

> Exercise, exorcise. Make his eye water.
> Pulverise, cauterise. Give him no quarter.
> Miserable animal,
> Man-mangling cannibal,
> Grind up his cornea with pestle and mortar. (ll. 660–4)

When the blinded Cyclops returns to the stage, the Chorus mock him and Odysseus admits who he really is. Odysseus and his men depart, accompanied by the Chorus, with Polyphemus' curse ringing in their ears.

The plot follows Homer quite closely but the tone is farcical and very stagey. The opening with the Chorus chasing sheep suggests some kind of dance routine but elsewhere the Chorus set the spirit of the scene. When Polyphemus returns to the stage blinded, it is their mockery that makes the scene comic. One suggestion over dating is that this play was produced in the same group as Euripides' *Hecuba*, a stark tragedy set after the fall of Troy in which Hecuba, former Queen of Troy, takes revenge on Polymestor who has killed one of her sons, by enticing him into her tent, killing his two sons and blinding him. Polymestor's return to the stage evokes pity from the Chorus and it is the Chorus who establish the tragic tone by the way that they react. This would account for Plato's assumption that the same actors cannot play in tragedy and comedy (see page x above) when the same actors probably did play in tragedy and the satyr afterpiece. The satyr play, comic as it was, was one part of tragedy and required, at least from the main actors, the skills of the tragedian, not of the comedian.

This seems to be born out by a closer look at the role of Odysseus and even of Polyphemus. The language of the set speeches is more formal than might be expected, with Odysseus' self-importance revealed primarily through a mock-heroic style which only becomes bathetic/comic at the end of a speech. Polyphemus' long justification of his attitude to life (ll. 314–44) may belong more to *antimasque* than *masque* but it does reveal a philosophy, albeit an ultimately selfish one. There are the sex jokes, about Helen and about Silenus; with the Chorus and possibly Polyphemus too sporting the phallus, these would have proved an opportunity for physical business; there are the drunk jokes and some word play. But for the most part this satyr play does offer an alternative view of a situation from myth.

Without social comment or political statement of any kind it would probably be wrong to pay too much attention to the satyr play. That it remained throughout the classical period a regular element of the theatre diet in Athens is not in doubt. As an absurd appendage tied round the waist of tragedy, the satyr play does help to pin down the nature of what made the Athenians laugh and suggests that after tragedy proper some antidote was considered necessary so as never to end on a note of despair.

Alkestis

This has often seemed an oddity of a play, if only because it defies pigeon-holing. It is certainly not a comedy as Plato or Aristotle would have defined 'comedy'. Nor, as explained above (page ix), is it a satyr play. There are no satyrs in it. It may be an experiment: it is still the earliest Euripides play to survive, the last from a group of plays performed in 438 BC. It is in a category of its own but recognisably Euripides and constructed on the same principles as his other surviving eighteen plays. Aristotle, in the *Poetics*, suggested that the two most effective elements of the dramatic plot were reversal of expectation (*peripeteia*) and recognition (*anagnorisis*). Though Euripides was writing many years before Aristotle was even born, the formula is one to which he would surely have subscribed. Greek tragedies and the satyr plays were based, for the most part, on stories from myth. These myths had been handed down by word of mouth, often through the epic poems whose sagas related complex stories of families and cities – Troy, Mycenae, Thebes – or individual heroes and heroines – Herakles, Odysseus, Agamemnon, Helen, Elektra, Antigone. Because the myths were fluid and malleable, only the outlines were fixed. There were as many versions of the story of Oedipus as there were playwrights and poets to write them. Marianne McDonald, researching her book on Greek myth in opera, discovered over fifty operatic versions of the Medea story. The skeleton remained the same. Each new writer supplied fresh flesh and blood.

Euripides' method was to take a story with whose outlines the audience might think they were familiar and to subvert it. Villains may be justified, heroes and their heroic actions questioned and often debunked. *Alkestis* works closely to this formula. The story is of Admetus, King of Pherai, who had received Apollo as his servant for a year when Apollo had been punished by Zeus for murdering the Cyclops (presumably including the blind Polyphemus). Admetus had treated Apollo well and Apollo gave him the reward that, when his time came to die, he could choose someone else to take his place. His wife Alkestis does so, but when Herakles hears what has happened, he goes to wrestle with Death and brings Alkestis back to life.

If you are literal-minded about fairytales this one suggests a number of awkward questions. Euripides asks most of them. What sort of a benefit would it be to be able to choose someone else to die on your behalf? What sort of man would ask his wife to die for him? What sort of reconciliation and future prospects would they have? The picture that is built up of Admetus is hardly an attractive one. He has, we discover, asked all the other members of his family first but all of them have refused. In an extraordinary scene over the coffin he disowns his father and mother for their selfishness. Alkestis' farewell to her children is moving but her farewell to her husband concentrates on the extraction of an oath that he will never remarry. Only when he has agreed, will she entrust the children to him. When Herakles arrives, Admetus denies that the death in the house is of anyone important. Herakles as a result gets drunk and only finds out about Alkestis when a servant reveals it, stung by his boorish behaviour. Herakles, when drunk, is a figure of fun and this is the only satyric element in the play. He sobers up fast enough when he discovers the truth.

On his return to the scene, he is accompanied by a veiled figure, a girl he says he has won in a competition, and whom he asks Admetus to receive into his house. Admetus refuses but is eventually persuaded. Only then is the woman with him revealed as Alkestis and the family restored.

What is unusual about the play is the changes of mood from tragic to comic with a lot of unexpected twists to the plot. In addition, there are the characters themselves: Alkestis, deeply loved by all her household, but quite steely about why she has agreed to be a substitute for her husband; Herakles, good friend, roustabout and real hero; the chorus of locals who, though they accept Admetus' original decision, are openly critical of his lying to Herakles; and Pheres, the aged father who, when spurned at the funeral by his son, is goaded into telling Admetus what no one else dare:

> It's a clever scheme you've worked out, I must admit.
> How to cheat death, permanently. All you have to do
> Is marry yet another wife and she'll do your dying for you.
> Then you can always blame the family, can't you,
> For refusing to do what you're too frightened to?
> (ll. 698–702)

After all this the resolution of the play in reconciliation could seem hollow but Euripides is more subtle than that. His Admetus may seem initially to be both selfish and thick-skinned, but the grief he shows after Alkestis's death is genuine enough. It is as though not until she has actually gone does he appreciate what he has lost. The scenes of mourning are filled with touching detail and the self-pity that characterises his early scenes is transformed into something far more worthy of sympathy. His change of heart is truly tested by Herakles and the sense of renewal at the end turns the initial story from rather dubious morality into uplifting fable.

As a play that is ahead of its time *Alkestis* has no parallel in the classical world. It looks forward not only to the more domestic tragedy of later Euripides, but also to the social comedy of Menander and to the romances of the Hellenistic, and later the Roman, world. This is achieved through a myth which is itself one of the few to have a happy ending, but the dramatic achievement and the dramatic novelty lie in the creation of characters whose motives and behaviour patterns are both plausible and understandable. Euripides may have changed the face of tragedy. He also reinterpreted and gave a new face to the expectations of comedy.

J. Michael Walton
University of Hull, 2001

Transliteration of Greek words and, in particular, proper nouns, into English presents problems of consistency. These translations follow different conventions according to the volumes from the Classical Greek Dramatists in which they were first published. The Greek alphabet contains a 'k' rather than a 'c', a 'u' rather than a 'y'. Full Anglicisation has been followed only in Euripides' Cyclops.

Line numbers alongside the text refer to the Greek originals rather than to these translations.

ARISTOPHANES

Birds
(*Ornithes*)

translated by Kenneth McLeish

Characters

EUELPIDES
PEITHETAIROS
AIDE
TEREUS
PRIEST
POET
ORACLE-SELLER
METON
INSPECTOR GENERAL
LAW-SELLER
WATCHMAN
MESSENGER
IRIS
YOB
KINESIAS
INFORMER
PROMETHEUS
POSEIDON
HERAKLES
BIGGUN

silent parts:
BIRDS (ruddy-rump, Arabian stork, hairy hoopoe, yellow streak)
CHAIRIS (flute-player)
SLAVES (Xanthias, Manodoros, Manes and others unnamed)
SOVEREIGNTY
WITNESS

CHORUS OF BIRDS

The foot of a cliff in the desert. There is a tree at ground level, and thick undergrowth higher up. Enter EUELPIDES *and* PEITHETAIROS. *Each has a bird perched on his arm.*

EUELPIDES (*to his bird*).
What? On? You *do* mean 'On'? To this tree here?

PEITHETAIROS (*to his bird*).
You're asking to get stuffed.

(*to* EUELPIDES)

She's cawing 'Back!'

EUELPIDES (*to his bird*).
Look, birdbrain. I'm telling you: we're lost.
And whichever way we go, we just get loster.

PEITHETAIROS.
I've had enough. I've walked a million miles
To please a bloody crow.

EUELPIDES.
I've worn my toes to stumps,
For this ... this raven. I must be. Ravin'.

PEITHETAIROS.
Don't look at *me*. *I* don't know where we are.

EUELPIDES.
You mean you can't get home again from here?

PEITHETAIROS.
No. What d'you think I am? A boomerang?

EUELPIDES.
Oh god!

PEITHETAIROS.
Never mind 'Oh god'. Come *on*.

EUELPIDES.
I blame Philokrates. That bastard in the market.
That bird-seller, yesterday. Swore blind these two
Would take us to Tereus, His Hoopoeness,
King of the birds, 'Who used to be a man,
Until, hey presto, he changed into a bird.'

I *thought* it sounded odd.
All he was after was unloading these:
His little feathered friends. Just look at them.
They're rubbish. All they know is bite.

(*to his bird*)

Yes? Something else? A message winging through?
On? Not again! How can we? It's solid rock.

PEITHETAIROS.
It's the same this side. There's nothing.

(*to his bird*)

Pardon, darling?

EUELPIDES.
Aha! Sense at last? About the road?

PEITHETAIROS.
Not exactly.

EUELPIDES.
What then?

PEITHETAIROS.
She's peckish. Wants a finger. Now.

EUELPIDES.
Why do I always listen? Why do I never learn?
'Go to the birds,' you said. 'We're unemployed;
We're starving. Let's pack, and flit, and fly.'
Go to the birds! We could have stayed at home,
Stuffed the birds, gone directly to the dogs.

(*to the audience*)

Ladies and gentlemen! Haha! I see you came.
We've got a problem here. We're sick – I mean,
We're from Athens, The Cradle of Democracy,
The Glory That Is Greece, and *still* we're sick.
Honest citizens . . . lifetime of service . . .
And we want to leave. It's not that we hate the place.

It's big, and fine, and free ... The trouble is,
Grasshoppers hop in the grass and sing
For a couple of months, and then that's that.
But Athenians perch in the lawcourts and twitter
Their whole existences, their lives away.
That's what inspired this little expedition.
We took our basket, our firepot, our bits of twigs,
And set out to find somewhere else to put down roots,
A place where lawyers are a pest unknown.
That's why we need Tereus. His Hoopoeness.
He flies about a lot. He'll tell us where
To find the kind of place we're dreaming of.

PEITHETAIROS.
Hey.

EUELPIDES.
What now?

PEITHETAIROS.
She's off again. Pointing up, this time.

EUELPIDES.
So's mine.

(*to his bird*)

It's no use gawping at the sky. What d'you mean,
'Birds are here. Make a noise. You'll see'?
What sort of birds? What sort of noise?

PEITHETAIROS.
You could kick the rock.

EUELPIDES.
You give it a head-butt.
Twice the noise.

PEITHETAIROS.
Oh, knock it with a stone.

EUELPIDES.
If you really think I should.

He knocks on the rock.

Hello. Hello.

PEITHETAIROS.
What d'you mean, Hello?
To call a hoopoe, one says, 'Yoohoo'.

EUELPIDES.
Yoohoo? One's to knock again, and say 'Yoohoo'?

He does. A door is flung open in the rockface, and the AIDE-BIRD *comes out.*

AIDE.
Who went 'Yoohoo'? Was it you? Was it you?

EUELPIDES.
Apollo, what a break.

AIDE.
Bird-catchers! Aaargh!

EUELPIDES.
That's not very nice.

AIDE.
Oh? Tough.

EUELPIDES.
I see your mistake. You think we're mortals.

AIDE.
Aren't you?

EUELPIDES.
Birds. I'm an African Squirtitout.

AIDE.
There's no such thing.

EUELPIDES.
Then what's this puddle, here?

AIDE.
He's not a bird.

PEITHETAIROS.
Of course I am: a Dungyrump.
It's a kind of ousel.

EUELPIDES.
And what are you? In god's name what are you?

AIDE.
A tweenytwink.

EUELPIDES.
We guessed. But apart from that?

AIDE.
When His Hoopoeness undertook the Change,
He went on his knees to me to change as well,
To run his errands, like when he was a man.

EUELPIDES.
So that's what it's for, a tweenytwink.

AIDE.
Despite the Change, he hasn't really changed.
He still gets cravings. 'Sardines!' he says,
And I fetch him sardines. Or 'Soup!' he goes,
And I grab a dish and spoon and fetch him soup.

EUELPIDES.
How fetching. Fetch yourself inside, and fetch him out.

AIDE.
You're joking. He's just had lunch:
Three sunflower seeds and a brace of gnats.
He's having his siesta.

EUELPIDES.
So, wake him.

AIDE.
He won't like that.
But since you ask so nicely . . .

He goes in.

PEITHETAIROS.
So nicely! We're lucky we survived.

EUELPIDES.
My raven's scarpered. Done a runner. Flown.

PEITHETAIROS.
You let it go, you mean. You were scared
And you let it go.

EUELPIDES.
So where's your crow?

PEITHETAIROS.
Ah.

EUELPIDES.
What d'you mean, ah?

PEITHETAIROS.
Her flight came up.

EUELPIDES.
Your fright, you mean.

TEREUS (*inside*).
Unbar the bushes. Sir will take the air.

The upper undergrowth is moved aside, revealing TEREUS, *the hoopoe, on his nest.*

EUELPIDES.
Good god, what's that? A duster? An eiderdown?
A flying jumble sale?

TEREUS.
Speak up!
Who ist who summoneth?

EUELPIDES.
Good question. Here's another:
Who ist who plucketh you?

TEREUS.
That's not my fault. *I once was mortal too.*

EUELPIDES.
Your feathers aren't the joke.
No joke at all.

TEREUS.
What then?

EUELPIDES.
Your beak.

TEREUS.
You can't blame me. Blame Sophocles.
He put me in that tragedy. *Tereus*. Ever so sad.
Made me change from human being to bird – and here I am.

EUELPIDES.
You *are* His Hoopoeness! You *are* a bird!

TEREUS.
Did I say I wasn't?

EUELPIDES.
Those feathers . . .

TEREUS.
I am moulting.

EUELPIDES.
You've not been well?

TEREUS.
No, dummy. It's the time of year.
We all moult now. New feathers grow.
So, I'm a bird. So, what are you?

EUELPIDES.
We're mortals.

TEREUS.
Ah.

EUELPIDES.
Athenians.

TEREUS.
Lawyers.

EUELPIDES.
Anti-lawyers.

TEREUS.
They don't grow anti-lawyers there.

EUELPIDES.
We're special. Endangered species. Rare.

TEREUS.
But why come here?

EUELPIDES.
To talk to you.

TEREUS.
What about?

EUELPIDES.
You used to be a man. Like us.
You had your little debts. Like us.
You hated paying up. Like us.
Then you changed. You turned from man to bird.
You flew ... everywhere. Sky, sea,
You've seen it all, you know it all.
There's no human being alive, no bird, like you.
So we've come to ask: have you ever seen
A city, warm, soft, snug, like a blanket
We can wrap ourselves up in, and live in peace?

TEREUS.
Somewhere better than Athens?

EUELPIDES.
Not better. More *comfortable*.

TEREUS.
A nanny state?

EUELPIDES.
That gets my goat.

TEREUS.
Be more specific. Spell it out.

EUELPIDES.
The sort of place where nothing's ever worse
Than when a friend comes knocking at your door
And says, 'Get up, get washed, come round at once,
You and the kids. We're having a wedding feast.
Don't fail me now – or if you do, don't try
Crawling round when my luck is . . . bad.' That sort of place.

TEREUS.
You certainly know how to suffer. What about you?

PEITHETAIROS.
Same sort of thing.

TEREUS.
For example?

PEITHETAIROS.
I'm minding my own business. This chap turns up.
He's a father. Really hunky son. Dad's furious.
'You bastard!' he says. 'Just exactly what's going on?
You meet my laddie here outside the baths,
And you don't kiss him or cuddle him or bounce his balls –
What kind of friend are you, anyway?'

TEREUS.
He may well ask.
There is one place. Fits every requirement.
Beside the Red Sea.

EUELPIDES.
No, no, no, no. Far too much beach.
Have you nowhere in Greece?

TEREUS.
There's Lepreos.

EUELPIDES.
Is that a town or a tropical disease?
It always makes me think of Melanthios.
I can't think why.

TEREUS.
Opous?

EUELPIDES.
Sounds much too classical. Opus what?
Hang on. What's life like here?
What sort of life do birds lead?
You should know.

TEREUS.
Pretty cosy. No money, for a start.

EUELPIDES.
I bet that cuts the crime rate.

TEREUS.
We take what comes. This garden or that garden.
We seek out seeds, we banquet on berries,
We nibble nuts.

EUELPIDES.
Nibble nuts? Sounds painful.

PEITHETAIROS.
Got it! This is great!
It's brilliant! You birds have got it made
If you listen to me, do exactly as I say.

TEREUS.
Do what?

PEITHETAIROS.
Shut your beaks for a start. Stop twittering.
You've got a dreadful reputation. In Athens,
We're always talking about people swanning about,
Being hen-pecked, rooking their neighbours –
Not to mention 'Aren't you the flighty one?'

TEREUS.
Don't go on. What else should we do?

PEITHETAIROS.
Build one single state.

TEREUS.
One bird-state. Why?

PEITHETAIROS.
It's obvious, fool. Look down.

TEREUS.
Yes.

PEITHETAIROS.
Up.

TEREUS.
Yes.

PEITHETAIROS.
Round. No, round.

TEREUS.
What's the good of looking round if I crick my neck?

PEITHETAIROS.
What d'you see?

TEREUS.
Clouds. Sky.

PEITHETAIROS.
Precisely. Your sphere.

TEREUS.
Pardon?

PEITHETAIROS.
Your sphere. Here. This is all your sphere.
It goes round and round, doesn't it, round and round
And round? That's why it's called a sphere.
So all you have to do is build a wall.
Surround it. One fortified, enormous nest.

Who do you lord it over now? Grasshoppers, flies.
Then it'll be the whole human race. Lock, stock
And barrel. Not to mention starving out the gods.
It worked with the Melians.

TEREUS.
I don't quite follow.

PEITHETAIROS.
Look: mortals are *there*,
The gods are *there*, and the birds are here,
Right in the middle. When we take a trip
From Athens to Delphi, we go past Thebes.
We have to get a visa. We have to pay.
This is just the same. When mortals sacrifice
To the gods down *there*, it has to pass through *here*
To get up *there*. You tax it on the way.
No tax, no food. The gods fork out, or starve.

TEREUS.
Ee-oo! Ee-oo!
Nets, traps and snares, it's brilliant!
Build state ... boss human race ... starve gods ...
We'll do it. That is, we'll put it to the vote.
We'll gather the birds, and put it to the vote.

PEITHETAIROS.
Who'll explain it?

TEREUS.
You will.

PEITHETAIROS.
But I don't speak –

TEREUS.
No problem: I've taught them Greek.
They're far more cultured than they were before.

PEITHETAIROS.
But how will you call them?

TEREUS.
No problem. I step in here,
Behind this bush, and wake my nightingale.
She plays; I sing; they flock to hear.

PEITHETAIROS.
You feathery genius! Beak of beaks! Well done!
Well, don't just stand there. Step and wake and sing.

TEREUS.
Up, darling, come, wake up.
Weep now for Itys,
Our dear son, weep for him,
Pure sounds from tawny throat
Throbbing, echoing,
Echoing in the woods,
High, high to the throne of Zeus
Where red-haired Apollo hears,
Takes his golden lyre,
Fretted with ivory,
Plucks chords to answer you,
And the gods dance, dance for Itys,
Weep immortal tears
Singing for Itys,
For Itys.

A flute is heard.

PEITHETAIROS.
Lord Zeus, what a pretty sound!
Hear how it honeys all the wood.

EUELPIDES.
Hey.

PEITHETAIROS.
Shh!

EUELPIDES.
Why?

PEITHETAIROS.
He hasn't finished.

TEREUS.

E-po-po-ee, po-po-po-po-po-po-po-ee,
Ee-oh, ee-oh, ku-ku-ku-ku-ku-ku-
Come, all of you: come and hear me now.
Birds of rich farmland,
Swooping, soaring behind the plough,
Pecking up corn-seed, barley,
Darting, settling in the furrows,
Calling, soft voices calling:
Tiou, tiou, tiou, tiou, tiou, tiou, tiou, tiou.
Garden-birds, feasting on berries,
Swooping to secret nests
Where ivy tendrils curl;
Birds of the hills,
Whose banquets are olives, arbutus,
Hurry, fly and hear:
Triotou, triotou, totobrinx.
Marsh-birds, birds of ditch and fen,
Who plane after midges, snapping, snapping;
Birds of the water-meadows, cool and green;
Kingfisher, godwit, francolin.
Birds whose pastures are the sea,
The endless, swelling sea,
Gulls, terns, cormorants,
Fly to me, hurry, hear.
Hear what he has to say,
This shrewd old man
With his sharp new plan
And his big idea.
Hurry now and hear,
Come, come, come, come, come, come, come.
Toro-toro-toro-toro-tinx,
Kikka-baou, kikka-baou,
Toro-toro-toro-toro-lili-linx.

PEITHETAIROS.

See anything?

EUELPIDES.

Not a bloody thing. I'm standing here

With my eyes on stalks, and . . . nothing.
After all that hopping into thickets,
All those bird-impressions, all that hoopoeing –
What a waste of time.

FIRST BIRD.
Torotinx, torotinx.

PEITHETAIROS.
Just a minute. Isn't that a bird?

EUELPIDES.
Of course it's a bird.

Enter FIRST BIRD.

Or is it?

PEITHETAIROS.
What is it?

EUELPIDES.
His Hoopoeness will tell us. Oi. What's that?

TEREUS.
That's one of our rarer species. A migrant.
Salt-pan habitat.

EUELPIDES.
Never mind its habit, look at its tail.
What a ruddy marvel!

TEREUS.
It *is* a ruddy-rump.

Enter SECOND BIRD.

EUELPIDES.
Look, look, look!

PEITHETAIROS.
Stop shouting. What?

EUELPIDES.
Another one.
What is it? A ladder? A drainpipe? A man on stilts?

TEREUS.
An Arabian stork.

EUELPIDES.
You're joking. Arabian?
It can't be. No camel.

Enter THIRD BIRD.

PEITHETAIROS.
Hey!
Another one. I've seen that sort before.
Well, almost. It's not . . . ? I thought you were unique.

TEREUS.
Not quite. This is my cousin. My distant cousin.
The Hairy Hoopoe. We try to keep it quiet.

PEITHETAIROS.
It must be hell to pluck.

TEREUS.
Don't use that word!
You've done it now. He'll not come out for weeks.

Enter FOURTH BIRD.

EUELPIDES.
Gods, not another one! What's this one called?

TEREUS.
The yellow streak.

EUELPIDES.
There can't be two of them.
We've got Kleonymos.

TEREUS.
That's not Kleonymos. No shield to shed.

PEITHETAIROS.
I wish I followed this. Do birds shed shields?
I wish I could say that.

EUELPIDES.
Don't bother now.

They're all here. A swarm, a stageful: look!
Fluttering and flapping. No room! No room!

Enter CHORUS.

TEREUS.
Partridge, francolin, mallard, kingfisher,
Pansy –

EUELPIDES.
Pansies are flowers, not birds.

TEREUS.
Take another look.
Swallow. Second swallow.

EUELPIDES.
I suppose they're trying to make a summer.

TEREUS.
Wheatear, reed-warbler, cuckoo, nuthatch, lark,
Pelican, cormorant, albatross, sea-eagle, wren,
Parrot, canary, ostrich, sparrow, stork,
Falcon, kestrel, merlin, buzzard, kite,
Woodpecker –

EUELPIDES.
Birds! Birds! Twittering, whirling, diving . . .
Just a minute. Diving? Are they friendly?
Their beaks are open. They're coming this way.

PEITHETAIROS.
Get down!

CHORUS.
Hoo-hoo-hoo-hoo-hoo-hoo-hoo-hoo-hoo
Who-hoo-hoo ko-ko-ko-ko-ko-called?
Where is he?

TEREUS.
Here. I called. This way.

CHORUS.
Dee-fe-dee-fe-dee-fe dear friend,

Te-te-te-te-te-te-te-te tell us,
Tell us why.

TEREUS.
I've news to share: fat, juicy news.
Two mortals have come, with bulging brains –

CHORUS.
Who? Where? Why?

TEREUS.
Two brilliant, wise old men,
With a mighty, magnificent idea.

CHORUS.
Traitor! I've never heard of such a thing!
Since I was a chick in arms . . .

TEREUS.
No need to panic.

CHORUS.
What have you done?

TEREUS.
Two strangers came, asking for asylum.
I welcomed them.

CHORUS.
Welcomed them?

TEREUS.
Welcomed them.

CHORUS.
You mean they're here, now? *Here?*

TEREUS.
As here as I am.

CHORUS.
Ee-ah, ee-ah,
Betrayed and cheated,
Tricked, defeated.
He grew with us,
Flew with us,

Gave us his word
He was truly a bird –
And then, and then,
Handed us to men:
Our enemy, our curse.
What could be worse?

We'll deal with him later. First, for *them*.
May I suggest – kill them? Peck them to pieces?

PEITHETAIROS.
We've had it.

EUELPIDES.
It's all your fault.

PEITHETAIROS.
You wanted to come.

EUELPIDES.
But not to come to grief.
We'll be crying for mercy.

PEITHETAIROS.
Of course we won't.
How will we cry, with our eyes pecked out?

CHORUS.
Ee-oh, ee-oh.
Charge them, barge them,
Peck them, wreck them.
Diminish them,
Then finish them.
Don't let them hide,
Peck your prey with pride.
No peak, no wave
Their lives will save.
If they try to fly
Make 'em cry, make 'em die.

Why are we waiting? Action stations!
Poking and pecking. Where's the wing commander?

EUELPIDES.
Oh well, that's that. 'Scuse me.

PEITHETAIROS.
What is it now? Stand still.

EUELPIDES.
And be torn to bits? No thanks.

PEITHETAIROS.
So where are you going to run?

EUELPIDES.
How should I know?

PEITHETAIROS.
No running. Stay and fight. Take this.

EUELPIDES.
A ladle?

PEITHETAIROS.
An owl-club. Look. If those owls
Come closer, bop them. *Make* them 'owl.

EUELPIDES.
Never mind owls. There's eagles.

PEITHETAIROS.
Kebab-sticks. Ha! On guard!

EUELPIDES.
What about my eyes?

PEITHETAIROS.
Here. Wear this sieve.

EUELPIDES.
And what d'you suggest I do with *this*, or *this?*

CHORUS.
Chocks away, chaps. Take the air.
Rip, rend, bite, beak, tear.

TEREUS.
Hang on. What's *wrong* with you?

You can't do that. These are Athenians,
Her Ladyship's cousins. You can't beak them.

CHORUS.
Athenians? The worst. They're cats,
They're ferrets. Of course we'll beak them.

TEREUS.
Not ferrets. *Friends*.
They've come to help, with good advice.

CHORUS.
Good advice? You're joking.
My feathered father's fearsome foes?

TEREUS.
Exactly. All of that. If you've any sense.
Don't people keep telling you, 'Be prepared'?
Well, who d'you prepare against, friends or foes?
Do cities build watchtowers because of friends or foes?
Not to mention warfleets and long, long walls,
To protect their wives, their children, all they own.

CHORUS.
'Be prepared', you say. 'Learn from your foes.'
'Wives, children, all they own.' All right. We'll listen.

PEITHETAIROS (*to* EUELPIDES).
They're calming down. Relax a bit.

TEREUS.
That's better. You'll thank me later.

CHORUS.
Don't we always? Whatever you suggest?

PEITHETAIROS.
They're calm at last. Take off the sieve.
Put the saucers down.
Hang on to your spear,
Your kebab-stick, here.
Patrol the pots,
Peer over the pans.

'On guard!' Be hard.
Don't flinch. Don't give an inch.

EUELPIDES.
But if we die,
Where will we lie?

PEITHETAIROS.
Where d'you think?
We're bold and brave.
In a hero's grave
By the kitchen sink.

CHORUS.
OK, chaps. Down!
Don't frown.
Be cool, be calm.
Break out the charm.
Let's get it plain.
Let's hear them explain.
Suggestions, questions ...
Your Hoopoeness, please speak.

TEREUS.
First question, then.

CHORUS.
Who are these men?

TEREUS.
They're wise. They're Greek.

CHORUS.
So why come here?

TEREUS.
That's very clear.
They're in love, they *care:*
Your little ways,
How you spend your days ...
They want to share –

CHORUS.
You can't be serious.
They told you *that?*

TEREUS.
Much more than that.
It *is* mysterious.

CHORUS.
Say that again.
Two *men?*
Just ask yourself: what
Has bird-life got
For *them?* Yummies for chummies
Or woes for foes?

TEREUS.
You've got it wrong. It's this:
He's offering you bliss
Beyond belief, beyond compare.
You're lords, he says, of there,
And *there*, and over *there* –
Of everywhere.

CHORUS.
A loony.

TEREUS.
Sane as sane.

CHORUS.
A bulging brain?

TEREUS.
Not puny.
He's nifty, shifty,
Fly, dry, sly,
And as for bright –
Quite out of sight.

CHORUS.
You've done it now. I'm weak
At the knees, I'm shaking;

I'm quivering, I'm aching
To hear him speak.

TEREUS (*to* SLAVES).
You ... you ... take this hardware
And hang it in the kitchen.
On the what's-it, yes. Now, you:
Tell them what we summoned them to hear.

PEITHETAIROS.
Not a chance.
I want a treaty first. Like the marriage contract
That knife-grinder made with his great big wife:
No biting, no tearing, no scratching,
No pecking the pectorals,
Tearing the testicles,
Shoving sharp objects up the –

CHORUS.
Stop!

PEITHETAIROS.
Nose, I was going to say.

CHORUS.
We wouldn't *dream* –

PEITHETAIROS.
So swear.

CHORUS.
We swear. On one condition: you guarantee
That we win first prize. Unanimous.

PEITHETAIROS.
I guarantee.

CHORUS.
And that if we break our word, we lose –
Nothing. One vote's enough to win.

TEREUS.
ALL FIGHTING BIRDS, STAND DOWN.
ALL WEAPONS TO THE STORES. GO HOME.

PERCH BY FOR FURTHER ORDERS.
MESSAGE ENDS.

Bustle as the military formation disintegrates. Meanwhile:

CHORUS.
Who trusts the human race?
They're an absolute disgrace.
None the less, speak out,
With your wit surprise us.
What have we missed?
Give us the gist.
Say what it's all about.
What is this news? Advise us.
What's on your mind? This is your moment: take it.
We gave our word to be good, and we won't break it.

PEITHETAIROS.
I'm bursting to start. I've kneaded the dough,
And it's rising, rising. Fetch me an ivy-wreath,
And some water to wash my hands.

EUELPIDES.
Going to have dinner, are we?

PEITHETAIROS.
Dinner, no. A feast of words, fat and sumptuous.
It'll knock them for six. Aherrm. My friends,
How I grieve for you. Once you were kings –

CHORUS.
Us? Kings? Who of?

PEITHETAIROS.
Everyone. Me, him, Zeus himself.
You were here before the gods, before the giants,
Before the Titans, before Mother Earth –

CHORUS.
Mother Earth?

PEITHETAIROS.
Mother Earth.

CHORUS.
Impossible.

PEITHETAIROS.
Oh, I'm sorry. You never went to school.
Never learned to think. Never heard of Aesop.
Don't you remember his Fable of Miss Lark?
'Once upon a time, before time began,
Before Mother Earth existed, there was Miss Lark.
Her poor old Daddy died. No Mother Earth,
No place to dig a grave. She laid him out,
She thought about it for four long days,
Then she dreamed of a grave, and buried him
Inside her head.'

EUELPIDES.
Isn't it clever? What a lark!

PEITHETAIROS.
The point is, if you were here before the gods,
You're older than they are, and you should rule.

EUELPIDES.
Beak-sharpeners, that's all you need.
Lord Zeus won't like you perching on his throne.
Mind you: two woodpeckers, he won't have a throne.

PEITHETAIROS.
In the good old days, birds ruled the human race.
Not gods: you birds. I'll give you an example.
In Persia, who used to be King of Kings?
Darius? Xerxes? Megabates? Mr Cock.
He strutted up and down, he swished his tail, he
crowed.

EUELPIDES.
And he still has that red thing on his head,
And keeps a harem. They're all the same.

PEITHETAIROS.
He was Beak of Beaks, the Voice Supreme.
When he spoke, they jumped. And we still do.
Every morning, he opens his beak and we're off:
Blacksmiths, potters, tanners, armourers,
Bakers, carpenters, cobblers – we grab our shoes,
We're off.

EUELPIDES.
You're telling me. It's all his fault.
I used to have a cloak, a woolly cloak,
But thanks to him ... I'd been to a party,
Wet the baby's head, know what I mean,
And I was dozing off, when out of the blue
He started crowing. The Voice Supreme!
It wasn't even dinner-time. But up I jumped,
Stuck my nose outside, and *bam!* Mugged, stripped,
Decloaked – and all because of *him:*
Mr Beak of Beaks who never could tell the time.

PEITHETAIROS.
When Cock retired, a buzzard ruled the Greeks.

CHORUS.
A buzzard?

PEITHETAIROS.
He taught them that song. You know:
'Let's all sing like the birdies sing ...'

EUELPIDES.
Don't remind me. I once knew all the words:
'Tweet-tweet-tweet', all the actions.
I was walking home. No purse. Coins in my mouth,
For safety. Buzzard appears. 'Tweet-tweet-tweet'.
Swallow the lot. No dinner.

PEITHETAIROS.
The Egyptians were cuckoo for cuckoos.
Whenever a cuckoo went 'Cuckoo!', they rushed
To the paddy-fields and grabbed their tools and –

EUELPIDES.
This *is* a family show.

PEITHETAIROS.
You've heard of Agamemnon? Menelaus? Names like that?
Warlords, Sceptre-swingers. In battle, big.
And what was always on the end of their sceptres?
Birds, keeping watch on Their Majesties' greasy palms.

EUELPIDES.
We should give Lysikrates one of those.

PEITHETAIROS.
It's exactly the same with gods.
Zeus is a king – and who guards him?
An eagle. Athene has an owl; Apollo has a hawk.

EUELPIDES.
So they have. I've always wondered why.

PEITHETAIROS.
Ancestral custom, idiot. Sacrificial custom.
Well, *someone* has to be on guard to snatch the meat.
Another thing: in the good old days, no one swore
By gods, they always swore by birds.

EUELPIDES.
Like Lampon now. Not 'by Zeus': 'by Goose'.

PEITHETAIROS.
Ah, the good old days! When you were kings,
Respected as you deserved,
Not like idiots or slaves.
Now they pelt you with stones,
Now they net you and trap you and snare you –
Protected species? Don't make me laugh.
They sell you in bundles, by dozens.
They poke you, they pluck you,
They spit you, they roast you,

They stuff you with herbs,
They serve you in sauce,
In sweet-and-sour sauce,
Wine, vinegar, oil,
Smothering, scalding,
As though you'd no rights,
No rights at all.

CHORUS.
What a distressing story!
To lose such ancient glory!
Thank goodness fate
Has sent you here to lead us.
It's up to you.
Tell us what to do.
Only you can make us great:
Instruct us, guide us, feed us.
Tell us what to do. What do you suggest?
If I can't be king again, I'll be *so* depressed.

PEITHETAIROS.
First, build one single city for all the birds.
Then stick up a wall, right in the middle of the sky,
All round. Use huge big bricks, like Babylon.

TEREUS.
Like Babylon! Big bricks! That's what I call a wall.

PEITHETAIROS.
When it's finished, demand that Zeus abdicates.
And if he won't, if he wriggles and sulks,
Declare a holy war, and close the wall. No road.
No more pussy-hunts down to Earth from Heaven,
No more Alkmenes or Semeles or Alopes:
No more godultery. Penalty for non-observance:
An official bulldog-clip, right where it hurts
Send a second messenger to mortals: BIRDS RULE STOP.
NEW ORDER OF SACRIFICE STOP.
(1) BIRDS, (2) GODS STOP.
Before they honour each god with offerings,

They must honour a bird appropriate in rank and function
Before Aphrodite (ex-sex-goddess): a turtle-dove.
Before Poseidon (washed-up-sea-god): an albatross.
Before Herakles (big god, ate anything): an ostrich.
Before Zeus On High, Her Majesty the Wren:
He gets a rampant ram; she gets a muscly midge.

EUELPIDES.
Old Thunder-guts is going to be *so* cross!

CHORUS.
But how will they know we're gods, not birds,
If we still flap about, if we've still got wings?

PEITHETAIROS.
No problem. Doesn't Hermes flap about? Hasn't *he*
Got wings? They all have. It goes with the job.
Victory, Eros – you must have seen the statues.
Iris, buzzing about like a demented bee.

EUELPIDES.
And Zeus' thunderbolts have wings. I'm scared.

CHORUS.
Suppose they're too stupid to *see* we're gods?
Suppose they prefer Zeus, Demeter and the rest?

PEITHETAIROS.
Send seed-gatherers to strip their cornfields.
Then let them ask Demeter for a free delivery.

EUELPIDES.
Too corny. She'd never take the call.

PEITHETAIROS.
Send crows to peck out the eyes of their oxen,
Their sheep, their cattle – then let them beg
Apollo the Healer to help. Can they afford vet fees?

EUELPIDES (*to the audience*).
That reminds me: cows for sale.

PEITHETAIROS.
On the other hand, if they *do* bow down,
If they put *you* up there with Mother Earth,
Old Father Time, Poseidon, what blessings will be theirs!

CHORUS.
What blessings?

PEITHETAIROS.
No more locusts guzzling their grapelets:
One squadron of owls, and that's the end of them.
No more blowflies filching their figlets:
We'll have a battalion of thrushes on pest control.

TEREUS.
But how can we give them wealth? That's what they *want*.

PEITHETAIROS.
Aerial surveys. Tell 'em where the goldmines are.
Map out their trade routes in advance. Thanks to you,
They'll never lose a ship.

TEREUS.
Why not?

PEITHETAIROS.
Weather forecasting.
'It's stormy ahead; don't sail.' 'Fair winds today:
You should do very nicely.'

EUELPIDES (*to the audience*).
Wanted: a merchant ship.

PEITHETAIROS.
All over the world, there are treasure-hoards,
Buried by their ancestors. Only you know where.
And, as you *also* know, 'A little bird told me ...'
You can spill the beans.

EUELPIDES (*to the audience*).
Stuff merchant ships. Who's got a spade?

TEREUS.
What about good health? Only gods grant that.

PEITHETAIROS.
No problem. If they're wealthy, they're healthy.

EUELPIDES.
No cash: that's what really makes them sick.

TEREUS
But they die so *young*. We can't extend their lives.

PEITHETAIROS.
Of course you can. Three hundred years each.

TEREUS.
Where from?

PEITHETAIROS.
You live much faster lives than they do.
One of your years equals dozens of theirs.
So hand a few over. It's in all the books.

EUELPIDES.
They'll be far better kings than Zeus.

PEITHETAIROS.
Exactly.
You won't have to build
Huge stone temples
With gorgeous golden gates.
Birds live in thickets, shrubs:
To them, an olive-twig's a shrine.
You won't have to make
Pilgrimages
To Delphi or Ammon to sacrifice –
Make offerings wherever you are:
A handful of barley,
Chucked in the bushes,
A word or two of prayer
And whatever you want is yours.

Goodies for barley-seeds:
That has to be a bargain.

CHORUS.
What a master-plan!
What a wise old man!
How did we ever misjudge him?
I give you my word –
That's my word as a bird –
That we'll do as you say,
That we'll do things your way:

We'll tackle Lord Zeus and we'll budge him.
We'll hustle and bustle,
We'll shoulder the strain.
We'll supply all the muscle,
If you bring the brain.

TEREUS.
Right. No more wittering and twittering.
Nikias can see to that.
It's time for action. Step inside my nest –
A few twigs and branches, but it's home to me.
Wait a minute: we haven't been introduced.

PEITHETAIROS.
I'm Peithetairos –

EUELPIDES.
Persuader.

PEITHETAIROS.
And he Euelpides –

EUELPIDES.
Optimist.

TEREUS.
You honour my humble home.

PEITHETAIROS.
How kind.

TEREUS.
Step this way, would you?

PEITHETAIROS.
After you.

TEREUS.
No, no, I insist.

EUELPIDES.
Hang on. Just a minute. What I mean is,
How can we live with you? We don't have wings.

TEREUS.
No problem.

EUELPIDES.
You're joking. Don't you know
What happened to the fox that tried to fly?

TEREUS.
It's easy. Wing-wort.

EUELPIDES.
Pardon?

TEREUS.
Wing-wort.
Inside. One nibble, you'll be as high as kites.

EUELPIDES.
In *that* case ... Xanthias, Manodoros, pick up the bags.

CHORUS.
Sir, sir, your Hoopoeness, oh sir.

TEREUS.
You called?

CHORUS.
Take these gentlemen inside, and give them lunch.
But send us out our nightingale, our darling,
Our own beloved Muse, to play with us.

PEITHETAIROS.
Please do. The little darling!
Call inside, and ask her out.

EUELPIDES.
Oh, please, the nightingale, oh please.
We're dying to see her, to feast our eyes.

TEREUS.
All right, if you say so. Prokne, darling,
We've visitors. Come out and say hello.

The flute-player CHAIRIS *comes out, in nightingale-mask and costume.*

PEITHETAIROS.
What a gorgeous creature! Those feathers!
So soft! So fine!

EUELPIDES.
So ripe for ruffling!

PEITHETAIROS.
Look at all that gold, like a virgin bride.

EUELPIDES.
I think I'll give her a little kiss.

PEITHETAIROS.
You fool!
There's a pecker under there. Beware!

EUELPIDES.
It's easy, look: just like shelling an egg ...

He takes off CHAIRIS' *mask, and kisses him.*

TEREUS.
Come on, come on.

PEITHETAIROS.
My dear chap, *after* you.

Exeunt TEREUS, PEITHETAIROS *and* EUELPIDES.

CHORUS.
Oh darling, tawny-throat,
Nightingale,
Beloved, come to us,
Come, sing with us.
Melting as honey,
Soft as spring,
Beloved, sing for us,
Play and sing for us.

Flute music. Then, over it:

Listen. You down there. Mortals. Leaves. Dreams.
Shadow-creatures. Mud-puppets. Pay heed
To your masters, the birds of the air,
The immortals, the favoured, the ever-young.
We'll explain. Pay attention and learn:
How the universe came into being:
Birds, gods, rivers, emptiness, dark –
Chuck your schoolbooks away. This is IT.
First of all there was nothing. No light,
No existence. Just emptiness, space.
In that fathomless, featureless dark,
Night mated with Storm, laid an egg,
And began all creation. Desire,
Golden-winged, iridescent, aglow,
Hatched and mated with Emptiness; birds
Were their nestlings, first creatures of light.
Soon the rest of the universe hatched:
Mother Earth, Sky, Sea, gods above.
We're the oldest powers, heirs of Desire,
And we'll prove it. Just picture the scene:
Blushing virgin, a little alarmed,
Not quite certain – till lover-boy sends
One of *us*, pigeon, partridge, goose, cock.
We're your friends. We're essential. We *help*.
For example, the seasons. Each year
When the cranes start migrating, you know
Winter's coming. No sailing; sow seeds;
Put warm clothes on. When kites fill the sky,

That's a signal it's spring. Shearing-time.
When the swallows of summer appear
Shed those winter clothes, wear something light.
And another thing. Forecasts. Forget
Holy pilgrimages, oracles, shrines:
We'll advise you. Big business, love, sex,
Family problems: we cover them all.
You're besotted with omens and charms:
When you both speak at once, or you sneeze
It's good luck; when a slave sings a song
Or a donkey ee-aws, it's good luck.
Well, in future *we're* lucky. Choose us.

We're available, friends,
Not aloof like the gods.
Zeus up there never bends,
Never dozes or nods.
We won't hide in the sky
With a snooty expression;
We'll accept every cry,
We'll make every concession.
Peace, happiness, wealth,
Smiling fortune, long lives
In the pink of good health
For your good selves, your wives
And your kids: all you need,
Milk and honey,
Piles of money,
Guaranteed.

Woodland Muse,
Tiou, tiou, tiou, tiou, tiou, tiou, tioutinx,
All birds who sing with us
In forests, on hillsides,
Tiou, tiou, tiou, tioutinx,
As we perch among the leaves,
Tiou, tiou, tiou, tioutinx,
Singing from tawny throats,
As we weave our songs for Pan,
For Kybele, Mother of All,

Toto, toto, toto, toto, totinx,
Sweet songs, like nectar sipped
By the poets of old,
A garland, the good old songs.
Tiou, tiou, tiou, tioutinx.

Ladies and gentlemen, you are *happy?*
Problem-free? If so, good luck. If not,
May I recommend: life with the birds?
For example, in trouble with the law?
You beat up your Daddy? No problem here.
It's *expected* here. Every fighting cock
Must challenge his dear old Dad to win his spurs.
You, over there. You're too conspicuous:
Arrow-suits, on humans, give the game away.
But here, who'd notice? You've heard of
  jailbirds . . . ?

Ah! Spintharos. How are things at home?
Another application for citizenship?
Come to us. We've a twig and a perch for everyone –
I mean, we take Karians, we'd take Exekestides.
Who's that cowering there? Not *Peisias*' little boy?
What d'you say? Scared? Want to run away
Like Daddy did? No need for that: join us.
We know all there is to know about ducks and
  quails.
So once they sang,
Tiou, tiou, tiou, tiou, tiou, tiou tioutinx,
Swans sang for Apollo,
There by the riverside,
Tiou, tiou, tiou, tioutinx,
As they flew on creaking wings,
Tiou, tiou, tiou, tioutinx,
Songs like mist, mist rising;
All creation pricked to hear,
Waves on the shore fell silent,
Toto, toto, toto, toto, totinx,
Olympos itself stood still,
Its lords struck dumb, as the Graces,

The Muses, echoed the rising song.
Tiou, tiou, tiou, tioutinx.

There's nothing better than a pair of wings.
If you had wings – yes, you, or you, or you –
And you suddenly felt peckish sitting there,
I mean *really* peckish, you could flap off home,
Fix yourself a sandwich and swoop right back.
It's the middle of the play, you're taken short –
Soar up, drop your load, fly down again:
Don't even *think* about clean underwear.
Or say you fancy someone's else's wife.
You see him here: in the posh seats, there,
Wedged in with his party. You spread your
  wings –
The ones *we* gave you – you flutter off,
Find his old lady, fuck and flutter back.
Wings are *worth* it. Need more proof?
Shall I mention Dieitrephes? Last year?
The basket-maker? Wove wicker wings,
Flew to the polls, got elected –
And's been feathering his own nest ever since.

Music, and a short dance. Then PEITHETAIROS *and* EUELPIDES *come out. They are now equipped with wings.*

PEITHETAIROS.
Well, there we are then. My god,
I've never seen anything funnier.

EUELPIDES.
What d'you mean?

PEITHETAIROS.
You and your wonderwings.
What *do* you look like? Old Mother Goose?

EUELPIDES.
What about you? A half-plucked duck?

PEITHETAIROS.
Only a bird in a gilded cage –
Isn't that Aeschylus?

EUELPIDES.
Can we please get on? What's first?

PEITHETAIROS.
First, we give the place a name. A good name,
One to roll round the tongue. Then we sacrifice.

EUELPIDES.
Name . . . sacrifice. OK by me.
What shall we call it, then?
Something impressive . . .
Sparta!

PEITHETAIROS.
Sparta! *Sparta?*
I wouldn't call a dog-blanket Sparta. I hate that word.
You call *Sparta* impressive?

EUELPIDES.
It impresses me.

PEITHETAIROS.
It ought to be something light, airy,
Billowing like clouds –

EUELPIDES.
Deceptively spacious –

PEITHETAIROS.
Cloudcuckooland?

EUELPIDES.
That's it! Cloudcuckooland.
Cloudcuckooland, where castles in the air are built:
Where Aischines is a financial colossus,
Theagenes a billionaire.

PEITHETAIROS.
Where gods outboasted giants:
Cloudcuckooland, on the Windy Plain of Brag.

EUELPIDES.
It rolls off the tongue: Cloudcuckooland.

PEITHETAIROS.
Now, we need a patron god. Any suggestions?

EUELPIDES.
Athene? She's got the shield.

PEITHETAIROS.
You're joking.
The last time *she* was in charge of a city –
Named after her, it was – you saw what happened.
Role-reversal. Think Kleisthenes. Think knitting.

EUELPIDES.
We're going to have battlements, aren't we?
A big stockade? We'll need a patron god.

PEITHETAIROS.
A patron bird, you mean. Storkade, you said.
Well, *I* say cock.

EUELPIDES.
Beg pardon?

PEITHETAIROS.
Cock.

EUELPIDES.
Ah, cock.
Perched high on the city rock: a cock.

PEITHETAIROS.
Good.
It's time, then. You've got to fly. High.
Up there. In the air. Give the builders a hand.
Hump hardcore, mix mortar, bring breezeblocks,
Scale scaffolding, fall,
Check the nightwatch,

Bank the brazier,
Take a bell and beat the bounds,
Bed down on the battlements –
Oh, and send off two messengers.
One up *there*, one down *there*.
When they come back, they must see me personally.

EUELPIDES (*crossly*).
See you personally in Hell?

PEITHETAIROS.
Don't argue. Don't grumble. Just go.
Who else can I trust? Who else knows all the ropes?

Exit EUELPIDES.

Right. Time to sacrifice. To the powers on high,
The new ones. What do we need? We need a priest.
But first ... Slave! Fetch me a basket, a water-jug.

A SLAVE *sets up an altar and prepares for the sacrifice. Meanwhile:*

CHORUS.
That's very good.
We think you should.
A sacrifice.
That's *very* nice.
Eeto, eeto, pray for us.
Chairis, Chairis, play for us.

Enter CHAIRIS, *now dressed as a crow, and playing suitably raucous flute-music.*

PEITHETAIROS.
Hang on, hang on. Stop that. What are you?
A fluty crow? What's the ... caws ... of that?
There has to be a cause.

Enter PRIEST.

Ah, there you are. We want to sacrifice,
To the new powers that be. Can you manage that?

PRIEST.
My son, no problem. Where's the basket-bearer?
Let us pray. Nest-Hestia, O Kite of Might,
Immortal cocks, cockesses everywhere –

PEITHETAIROS.
O Puffin of Piety, fish-faced and water-winged –

PRIEST.
O Sacred Swan of Prophecy, of Delos, of Delphi,
O Bunting Artemis, O Leto, Quail-mother –

PEITHETAIROS.
Hail, quail.

PRIEST.
O Winter Finch, O Ostrich Mother of All the World –

PEITHETAIROS.
Especially Kleokritos. Have you *seen* him?

PRIEST.
Grant health, wealth and happiness
To Cloudcuckooland, not to mention the Chians –

PEITHETAIROS.
I won't if you won't. How did *they* get in?

PRIEST.
Come hero birds, and the birdlets they begat,
Come pelicans, come shags;
Come coots, come cranes;
Come sparrows, magpies, wrens;
Come gannets, swallows, hens;
Come eagles, hawks,
Come vultures, kites –

PEITHETAIROS.
Hang on! Vultures, kites? Have you *seen* that sheep?
One swallow and it's gone, never mind a kite.
Oh, go away. I'll do the job myself.

He shoos the PRIEST *out.*

CHORUS.
Yes, good idea.
We'll help. We're here.
We'll kill the beast,
We'll make a feast –
Hardly, hardly. Take a look.
Skin and bones. Too small to cook.

PEITHETAIROS.
As we make this sacrifice, we pray
To bird-gods one and all –

Enter POET.

POET.
Haunts of coot and tern! Cuckoo-echoing,
Lark-charmed, rook-racked!
Cloudcuckooland! Elysium!

PEITHETAIROS.
Who the Hell are you?

POET.
A poet. One of Dame Nature's craftsmen.
I flit; I pluck; I serve.

PEITHETAIROS.
A long-haired freak.

POET.
No, no, no.
One of Dame Nature's craftsmen –
As I think I said.

PEITHETAIROS.
You've not come *here* to flit, and pluck, and serve?

POET.
I've composed an ode celebrating your city,
And a sonnet-sequence, and a limerick
In the style of Simonides:
There once was a town in the sky . . .

PEITHETAIROS.
All that? Since when?

POET.
Since days of yore, as we poets say.

PEITHETAIROS.
Days of yore?
It was only born five minutes ago.

POET.
Poetic licence. When the Muses come
It's like horses galloping, galloping.
Just a moment, something's arriving now.
He rules the mighty mountains,
He rules the soggy sea;
He's generous and kindly
To artists, such as me –

PEITHETAIROS (*to the* SLAVE).
He'll go on like this all night, unless ...
Look: you don't need *all* that gear.
Strip off, and make a donation.

(*to the* POET)

Oi. Will this do? Warm up your limericks?

POET.
Ah! *Lineaments of gratified desire.*
Excuse me: another inspiration.

PEITHETAIROS.
He *will* go on all night.

POET.
Blow, blow, thou winter wind,
When icicles hang by the wall,
A cold coming we had of it ...
Something about *Snow had fallen,*
Snow on snow ... you know the one?

PEITHETAIROS.
I know we're talking underwear.

(*to the* SLAVE)

Divest. We must all support the arts.

(*to the* POET)

Take this, and go.

POET.
I will, I will.
'Tis nearly morning; I must needs begone;
Oft have I travell'd in the realms of gold,
Not to mention the forests, the forests of the night –
Oft in the stilly night . . . the rest is silence.

Exit.

PEITHETAIROS.
I should think so, under all those clothes.
Who invited him? How did he sniff us out?
Never mind. Time to get on. Pick up
The holy water, and walk round the altar.
In the name of . . .

Enter ORACLE SELLER, *loaded with scrolls.*

ORACLE SELLER.
STOP! Don't gut that goat.

PEITHETAIROS.
Who are you?

ORACLE SELLER.
The oracle man.

PEITHETAIROS.
Bye bye.

ORACLE SELLER.
Don't be like that. Respect the Other Side.

He rummages among his scrolls.

I've a message here from Bakis. An oracle
Directly concerning Cloudcuckooland.

PEITHETAIROS.
Why didn't you say so before?

ORACLE SELLER.
The Powers prevented me.

PEITHETAIROS.
Get on with it.

ORACLE SELLER (*reading*).
WHEN WHITE-HEADED RAVENS AND WOLF-PACKS
COME TOGETHER 'TWIXT SIKYON AND KORINTH –

PEITHETAIROS.
Beg pardon, Korinth?

ORACLE SELLER.
It's what they call the air on the Other Side.
FIRST OFFER MOTHER EARTH A BAALAMB,
THEN OFFER MY SPOKESMAN THESE PRESENTS:
A NICE NEW CLOAK, A PAIR OF SANDALS –

PEITHETAIROS.
Excuse me. Sandals?

ORACLE SELLER.
See for yourself.
– AND SOME WINE AND A PLACE AT THE BANQUET.

PEITHETAIROS.
I'm sorry. Banquet?

ORACLE SELLER.
See for yourself.
IF YOU LISTEN AND DO AS I TELL YOU
YOU'LL SOAR IN THE SKY LIKE AN EAGLE.
IF YOU DON'T, THEN YOU WON'T. NOT AN EAGLE,
NOT EVEN A PIGEON, A SPARROW –

PEITHETAIROS.
That's in there?

ORACLE SELLER.
See for yourself.

PEITHETAIROS.
That's funny. Look at *this* one.
A BEGGAR WILL COME OUT OF NOWHERE
DEMANDING A SEAT AT THE BANQUET.
A CONMAN, A PAIN IN THE BUM.
GIVE HIM ALL HE DESERVES –
A KNUCKLE SANDWICH, A BUNCH OF FIVES.

ORACLE SELLER.
Excuse me, Fives?

PEITHETAIROS.
See for yourself.
HE MAY PRATTLE OF BAKIS
OR FUSS ABOUT FAKIS.
IT'S PHONEY, BALONEY –

ORACLE SELLER.
That's in there?

PEITHETAIROS.
See for yourself.

(*hitting him with scrolls*)

See? See? See?

ORACLE SELLER.
Ow!

PEITHETAIROS.
Find a home for your Bakises somewhere else.

Exit ORACLE SELLER. *Enter* METON.

METON.
One could begin just here.

PEITHETAIROS.
Another of them!

Excuse me, what can I do for you?
This *is* a professional visit, one assumes.

METON.
Indeed. Project Middle Air. Two priorities:
One: three-dimensional survey;
Two: cubic allocation.

PEITHETAIROS.
But who *are* you?

METON.
Meton, geometer, cartographer,
Estate agent. My card.

PEITHETAIROS.
And what is *that?*

METON.
An air-surveyor. Look.
The concept's simple. Our latest thinking
Is that space is, how shall I put it, *nightcap*-shaped.
I take my instrument, put one leg here,
Another here, and move the arm like *this* –
You see the principle?

PEITHETAIROS.
No.

METON.
If you calibrate with care,
You can square each circle, which simplifies
The whole equation. I'm envisaging
Town centre *here*, streets *here* and *here* and *here:*
It's a radial alignment, patterned on the rays
Of that other celestial sphere, the Sun.

PEITHETAIROS.
Pythagoras rides again! Excuse me.

METON.
Of course.

PEITHETAIROS.
I'm sorry to interrupt, I mean ... I like you,
The way you think ... But you really ought ...

METON.
What?

PEITHETAIROS.
To bugger off.

METON.
Pardon?

PEITHETAIROS.
Before it's too late.

METON.
You mean, there's trouble here?
Some socio-political unrest?

PEITHETAIROS.
Not exactly.

METON.
What then?

PEITHETAIROS.
They just like beaking frauds.

METON.
Beaking?

PEITHETAIROS.
Frauds.

METON.
I think I get it.

PEITHETAIROS.
I think you do. Hey! What was that?
Did *you* hear wing-beats?

METON.
Yike!

Exit.

PEITHETAIROS.
I thought so. Bye.
Make a straight line somewhere else.

Enter INSPECTOR GENERAL.

INSPECTOR GENERAL.
Where's the welcoming committee?

PEITHETAIROS.
A walking tailor's shop!

INSPECTOR GENERAL.
Aren't you ready for inspection?
This *is* Cloudcuckooland?

PEITHETAIROS.
Inspection? Who by?

INSPECTOR GENERAL.
We represent the majesty of the Athenian state.
We were otherwise engaged, but were snatched away –
Emergency proposal, that hothead Teleas ...

PEITHETAIROS.
Suppose I slip you something to go away?

INSPECTOR GENERAL.
We'd be grateful. We were halfway through
An *absorbing* piece of work when the summons came.
The Pharnakes file. A motion before the People.

PEITHETAIROS.
I understand. Suppose I slip you ... this?

INSPECTOR GENERAL.
Ow! What's that?

PEITHETAIROS (*gesturing at the audience*).
A motion before the people.

INSPECTOR GENERAL.
You can't hit State officials.

PEITHETAIROS.
Can't I? Out!

He chases him out.

What are they doing? Inspectors?
I haven't even sacrificed.

Enter LAW-SELLER.

LAW-SELLER.
PARAGRAPH THREE. TORTS AND MISDEMEANOURS.
SUBSECTION FORTY-NINE.

PEITHETAIROS.
Not more paper! Well?

LAW-SELLER.
You're in the market for some laws. Try these.
Full constitution, by-laws . . . take your pick.

PEITHETAIROS.
Give me an example.

LAW-SELLER.
WEIGHTS, MEASURES, COINS.
CLOUDCUCKOOLANDISH MEASURES WILL CONFORM
TO THOSE PREVAILING NOW IN OLOPHYXIA.

PEITHETAIROS.
Olo-fix-ya? Not a bad idea.

LAW-SELLER.
What's the matter?

PEITHETAIROS.
Out!
Take your laws and . . . out!

Enter INSPECTOR GENERAL *with* WITNESS.

INSPECTOR GENERAL.
I summons Peithetairos for assault and battery –

PEITHETAIROS.
That's right. And here's some more.

LAW-SELLER.
For G.B.H. against an officer of state –

PEITHETAIROS.
Are you still here?

INSPECTOR GENERAL.
I demand restitution. Ten thousand drachs.

PEITHETAIROS.
Ten thousand whacks. Just watch me.

LAW-SELLER.
WHEREAS LAST NIGHT YOU CRAPPED IN COURT –

PEITHETAIROS.
Keep him away from me. And you, get out!

He chases them out.

I've had enough of this. I'm going. Here, goat.
We'll see to the sacrifice, inside.

He goes in.

CHORUS.
Soon mortals everywhere
Will sacrifice to *us*, will pray to *us*,
All-seeing, all-ruling, the birds of the air.
Their world is our concern:
In fields, in orchards,
We patrol their crops:
We pick off the pests that swarm there,
Nibbling, sucking the swelling seeds,
Buds on the bough.
Destroyers of sweet-smelling gardens
We dive-bomb:
Stingers, creepy-crawlies –
We swoop from on high; they die.

Did you hear that announcement the other day?
WANTED FOR BLASPHEMY: DIAGORAS OF MELOS,

DEAD OR ALIVE. REWARD: SIX
  THOUSAND DRACHMAS.
Well, we've a counter-announcement of our own.
WANTED FOR BIRD-SELLING:
  PHILOKRATES OF MARKET STREET.
SIX THOUSAND FOR HIS CARCASS,
  TWENTY THOUSAND
IF YOU BRING HIM IN ALIVE. You want to
  know why?
He sells finches on strings, a dozen a drach.
He sells thrushes, blown up to look like grouse
(Not much fun for you, and none at all for them).
He sells blackbirds with straws up their noses,
Stool pigeons, netted and caged, to be decoys.
That's enough about him. But there's this as well.
If anyone here keeps a budgie, let it go
Or be sorry. We'll string you, we'll sell you,
We'll budgie you. D'you want to go cheap?

How lucky we are, we birds,
How blessed in our feathers, in our wings.
We need no winter cloaks to cosset us;
No blazing summer sun
Ever scorches us, stifles us.
We sit in the shade,
In leafy woods, in lush green grass,
While cicadas, drunk on sunshine,
Giggle and shriek.
In the high hills we winter, snug
In dark caves;
In spring we banquet on berries,
White myrtle, the Graces' feast.

A word in the judges' ears. It'll do you no harm
If you give *us* first prize. Remember Paris,
That beauty contest? Peanuts, compared to *this*.
To start with, drachmas: coins in the pocket.
Just have a quick look. Which bird's on the back?
Owls. Exactly. Owls and drachmas go together.
You'd like them swooping round your houses,

Nesting in your purses, hatching little ones?
It could be arranged. Are you ambitious –
A career in politics, perhaps? We'll send you
Eagles to soar overhead and impress the neighbours,
Hawks to help anyone who wants to grease your palm.
Going out to dinner? No need for a doggy-bag:
Our friendly local Pelican has a surprise for you.
If, on the other hand, we *don't* win, we suggest
A tin helmet, and never go out in new clothes.

Dance. When it ends, PEITHETAIROS *comes out.*

PEITHETAIROS.
That's that, then, Birds. One sacrifice.
I'm surprised we haven't heard what's going on
Up there. No, here's someone. Heavens!
What does he think this is, the Olympic Games?

Enter MESSENGER.

MESSENGER.
Whey pey, whey whey pey, whey whey whey pey,
Where's Peithetairos? Where's Himself?

PEITHETAIROS.
I'm here.

MESSENGER.
The walls's ... hoo, arrgh ... finished.

PEITHETAIROS.
Marvellous.

MESSENGER.
The very word, Marvellous. Hoo. Magnificent.
Big enough for chariot races, Proxenides
And Theagenes even, the Trojan Horse.

PEITHETAIROS.
That's big.

MESSENGER.
And high. Hoo, high. I measures it myself.
Six hundred feet.

PEITHETAIROS.
That's high. Who built it that high?

MESSENGER.
Birds.
No one else. No brickies from Egypt,
No stonecutters, no pyramid-erectors.
Birds, just birds, with their own bare claws.
I stood like this, hoo, haa, and watched.
Thirty thousand cranes flew in from Africa
With cropfuls of stones, and handed them
To stonebills for cornering. Sand martens mixed
Cement, and dippers and waders and spoonbills
Kept the water coming.

PEITHETAIROS.
Six hundred feet . . .
Who carried the mortar?

MESSENGER.
Herons. In hods.

PEITHETAIROS.
And how did they fill those hods?

MESSENGER.
You'd have liked that.
Geese stuck in their feet like this, and shovelled it.

PEITHETAIROS.
What a feat.

MESSENGER.
A duck-line passed the bricks along.
Swallows darted about like apprentices,
Pecking the cement in place.

PEITHETAIROS.
What a production-line.
Who did the carpentering?

MESSENGER.
Who d'you think? Woodpeckers.
They tapped and split and planed and drilled
Those gates. Tock, tack, thwock, thwack,
It was as noisy as a shipyard. Well, it's done.
It's gated, it's barred, it's bolted.
Watch set, patrols, bells, beacon fires.
It's up to you now. I'm going to have a bath.

Exit.

CHORUS.
What's wrong with you? You're looking sick.
They built a wall, and they built it quick.

PEITHETAIROS.
Exactly. Sounds like castles in the air to me.
Here's someone else. A watchman from the wall.
But why the war-dance? There's something wrong.

Enter WATCHMAN.

WATCHMAN.
Eeoo eeoo, eeoo eeoo, eeoo eeoo.

PEITHETAIROS.
What's wrong with eeoo?

WATCHMAN.
Disaster! On the wall.
Some god, some messenger from Zeus slipped past
The crow-guard. Flew through the gates, flew *here*.

PEITHETAIROS.
The cheeky sod. Which god?

WATCHMAN.
It had wings, that's all we know.

PEITHETAIROS.
Call security. Send out a posse.

WATCHMAN.
We have already.
A phalanx of falcons,
A squadron of sparrowhawks,
The entire beak-and-hook brigade,
Every osprey and eagle and kite in sight.
They're beating bounds, they're combing clouds.
Wings whirring, beaks banging, claws clattering –
Can't you hear them? Whatever it is, it's *near*.

PEITHETAIROS.
Slings, bows, stones! To arms!
Send the squadron-leaders here.
Where did I put that catapult?

CHORUS.
War, war, that dreadful word,
Between every god and every bird.
Man the sky,
On guard!
Low and high,
Look hard.
Don't let immortals through:
They're fighting *you*.

The whole air's humming.
Something's coming.
Make a circle. Peer.
There's someone here.

Enter IRIS, *with rainbow wings and elaborate helmet. She flies in on the theatre crane.*

PEITHETAIROS.
Hey. Here girl, here girl, here girl.
Stop flapping. There now. Steady.
Who are you? You have to say. Where from?

IRIS.
From high Olympos' halls I come, the gods.

PEITHETAIROS.
What's your name? What are you – messenger
Or sailing boat?

IRIS.
Iris the fleet.

PEITHETAIROS.
The fleet's in, lads!

IRIS.
What's here afoot?

PEITHETAIROS.
Quick, grab her: she's off again.

IRIS.
Unhand me. DON'T DO THAT!

PEITHETAIROS.
You've had it now.

IRIS.
Outrageous.

PEITHETAIROS.
Quite. Which gate did you fly through?

IRIS.
Great Zeus on high! One recognised no gate.

PEITHETAIROS.
'Great Zeus' . . . 'One recognised no gate' . . .
You *did* see the customs crow? The visa stork
Did prick your permit?

IRIS.
What impertinence *is* this?

PEITHETAIROS.
They didn't? You didn't?

IRIS.
You're out of your mind.

PEITHETAIROS.
Officially, then, you've not been entered?

IRIS.
Of course not. One would like to see them try.

PEITHETAIROS.
So there we are. Illegal entry . . .
You force our frontier, violate our air-space –

IRIS.
One *is* an immortal god. One flies where one likes.

PEITHETAIROS.
Not here, one doesn't. One's well out of order.
If we're talking punishment that fits the crime,
Iris or no Iris, you're dead. Quite dead.

IRIS.
But I'm *immortal!*

PEITHETAIROS.
That's no excuse.
There are no exceptions. Why should everyone else
Bow down, and you gods turn up your noses,
And refuse to acknowledge your betters? No
chance.

IRIS *flaps her wings for take-off.*

Now what are you doing? What *is* all this?

IRIS.
One can't stay here all day. One flies
From Zeus on High to mortals. Urgent orders.
YOH!
START SACRIFICE. BASH BULLS, GUT
GOATS, SLAY SLEEP.
LET EVERY HIGHWAY, BYWAY, STEAM
WITH SMOKE.
THE POWERS ON HIGH ARE PECKISH.

PEITHETAIROS.
Powers on high?
What powers on high?

IRIS.
Us. Gods. *The* gods.

PEITHETAIROS.
Ye gods!

IRIS.
Who else would you suggest?

PEITHETAIROS.
I see you haven't heard.
They sacrifice to birds now. Birds are gods.
Not gods. Our feather in Heaven. Stuff Zeus.

IRIS.
Fool! Fool! Rouse not immortal rage,
Lest Zeus almighty curse thee quite,
Lest Justice, mattock of the gods,
With vengeful violence hoe thy house,
Lest baleful blasts of flaming fire –

PEITHETAIROS.
Do shut it. Do stand still.
Just who d'you think you're scaring?
Vengeful violence? Mattock of the gods?
It's mumbo-jumbo. Anyone can do it.
Tell Zeus to put a sock in it –
Unless he wants his palace purged
With eagle-fire, a fearsome force
Of firecrests, zooming up with zest
To kindle chaos and dish out doom
I've got six hundred here, on standby,
Tawny as leopards, grim as giants –
That's right, giant trouble, just like he had before.
And as for you, young lady ... Zeusogram ...
Any more of you, and I'll clap on sail,
Open up your shipping-lanes, and give you a big
surprise.

IRIS.
You dirty old man. How dare you?

PEITHETAIROS.
Fly away. Go on. Shoo.

IRIS.
I'll tell my Daddy. He'll see to you.

PEITHETAIROS.
I'm scared. Show some other little boy
Your fireworks. Shoo. Shoo. Shoo.

Exit IRIS, *by crane.*

CHORUS.
This air is closed. No way
For Olympian gods, as from today.
Don't expect
Friends here.
Show respect,
Keep clear.
No sacrifice, no joke:
No holy smoke.

PEITHETAIROS.
I thought I sent a messenger to mortals.
Where is he? Is he ever coming back?

Enter MESSENGER.

MESSENGER.
Peithetairos! Magnificence!
O Excellence, O Wisest of the Wise,
O Thrice Renowned, O Brain of Brains,
Oh ask me what I want.

PEITHETAIROS.
What is it?

MESSENGER.
Mortals.
They want to give you this golden crown,
For bulging brains, for services.

PEITHETAIROS.
I'll take it. What services?

MESSENGER.
You mean you don't know? You founded Cloud-
cuckooland
And you've no idea what it means to them?
They love it. They can't get enough of it.
Until you built Cloudcuckooland
They were mad for all things Spartan:
Spartan haircuts, Spartan diet, Spartan pong
(They saved on baths. Like Sokrates),
Spartan walking-sticks. Now that's all gone.
They're bird-mad. Some even *think* they're birds:
Up with the lark each morning, and flit away
To perch in the lawcourts, to cluck and peck.
The madder ones have even changed their names.
That one-legged stallholder: he's 'Flamingo' now.
Menippos is 'Swift'; Opountios is 'Crow';
Philokles is 'Lark'; Theagenes is 'Stork';
Lykourgos is 'Ibis' and Chairephon is 'Bats'
(I know bats aren't birds, but you know
Chairephon);
Syrakosios is 'Popinjay' and Meidias –
He's 'Shite-hawk'. That's right, 'Shite-hawk'.
What d'you mean what's new, you're not surprised?
The good old songs have never been so popular:
'Lullaby of Birdland ...', 'A Nightingale Sang ...'
'There'll be Blue Birds Over ...', 'Swannee ...',
'O for the Wings of a ...'. That reminds me. Wings.
You'd better get a stock in, fast.
Wings, claws, beaks, all that.
They're flocking here in millions.
To join you. They're on their way.

PEITHETAIROS.
No point standing here, then. You go in,
Stuff all the baskets and boxes you can find
With wings. Manes, help him. Bring them out here.
I'll wait. I'll see these would-be birds myself.

Bustle of preparations.

CHORUS.
Cloudcuckooland, sublime –

PEITHETAIROS.
We're short of time.

CHORUS.
No grief, no worry –

PEITHETAIROS (*to* SLAVE.).
Why can't you hurry?

CHORUS.
A lovely land. Desire is here,
Wit, Wisdom, Charm and Grace;
Here Quiet smiles,
And Calm –

PEITHETAIROS (*to* SLAVE).
Come on! Be quick!
You make me sick.

CHORUS.
Here. Put the basket down.

PEITHETAIROS.
Get on, you clown.

CHORUS.
Be strict. Be firm.

PEITHETAIROS.
I'll make him squirm.

CHORUS.
Set out the wings, in proper piles.
They'll choose the kind they want:
Gull, songbird, swift,
Hawk, owl –

PEITHETAIROS (*to* SLAVE).
You'll feel my fist.
I can't resist.

YOB (*offstage*).
Wings! Wings! Wings!
Gimme wings!
I wanna fly.
High. Inna sky.
Gimme wings! Wings! Wings!

PEITHETAIROS.
That messenger was right.
Here's someone already, eager for eagles.

Enter YOB.

YOB.
Whee, wheeeyyy,
Gimme wings! Wings! Wings!
You've got new laws here. I like them.
Make me a bird. You heard.

PEITHETAIROS.
What laws? We've got a lot of laws.

YOB.
All of them. Specially the one
Says you can peck your Daddy's head in.

PEITHETAIROS.
We *do* think it's natural for a fighting chick
To challenge his father, test his strength –

YOB.
And choke him and chuck him out the nest.
Grab everything. Why else d'you think I came?

PEITHETAIROS.
But we've another law:
Older, much older, the Pterodactyl Code.
WHEN DADDY AND MUMMY HAVE
REARED THEIR CHICKS,
BEGAN THEM, HATCHED THEM,
FLEDGED THEM, FED THEM,

YEA VERILY, THEN SHALL THE ROLES BE REVERSED:
LOOK-AFTER-TIME BEGINS FOR EVERY CHICK.

YOB.
Look-after time? Look-*after* bloody time?
I've come to the wrong place after all.

PEITHETAIROS.
No, no. You chose to come. You want to stay.
Why not join our 'A' Team, our Do-the-Business Firm?
Forget your father. Leave him alone.
I'm telling you. I learned that years ago.
Take these wings, this battle-spur, this crest.
Join the Professionals, Take the Strain,
Rely on Yourself, Look out for Number One,
Leave Daddy alone – and if it's a fight you want,
Fly North. Away match. Tough. They need you there.

YOB.
'A' Team. Look out for Number One. Fly North.
I'll do it. You're right.

PEITHETAIROS.
I always am.

Exit YOB.

KINESIAS (*offstage*).
Away! Away! For I will fly to thee,
Not charioted by Bacchus and his pards,
But on the viewless wings of Poesy ...

PEITHETAIROS.
We'll need a ton of wings for this one.

Enter KINESIAS.

KINESIAS.
Already with thee! Tender is the night,
And haply the Queen-Moon is on her throne ...

PEITHETAIROS.
Kinesias. What d'you want? What is it?

KINESIAS.
My heart aches, and a drowsy numbness pains
My sense –

PEITHETAIROS.
Stop quoting and tell us what you want.

KINESIAS.
I want some wings. I want to fly,
Stopping through a fleecy cloud,
Plucking up inspiration on the wing.

PEITHETAIROS.
Inspiration. You pluck it up *there?*

KINESIAS.
Of course. It hangs there,
On a sort of *heaventree of stars.*
It's all up there:
The fleeting, the darkling, the purple, the plain –
Let me show you.

PEITHETAIROS.
It's all right.

KINESIAS.
No, no.
It's the least I can do. A guided tour.
Look at the stars! Look, look up at the skies!
O look at the fire-folk sitting in the air!

PEITHETAIROS.
Just a minute.

KINESIAS.
My heart in hiding
Stirred for a bird –

PEITHETAIROS.
I think I'll do some stirring of my own.

He selects a wing.

KINESIAS.
The achieve of,
The mastery of the thing!
Ow! Critic! That wasn't nice at all.

PEITHETAIROS.
I thought you wanted wings.

KINESIAS.
I don't have to put up with this.
In Athens they queue to hear me.

PEITHETAIROS.
Stay here. We'll queue as well –
To get away.

KINESIAS.
You cheeky devil.
Don't think you've heard the last of this.
I want those wings!

Exit.

INFORMER (*offstage*).
'Is it weakness of intellect, birdie?' I cried,
'Or a rather tough worm in your little inside?' ...

PEITHETAIROS.
Another warbler. It's a flock, a plague,
A migration. What's the *matter* with them all?

Enter INFORMER.

INFORMER.
O swallow, swallow, flying, flying south,
Ti-tum-ti-tum-ti-tum-ti something something eaves,
And tell her, tell her, what I tell to thee ...

PEITHETAIROS.
Don't ask her to swallow it, that's all.
Has something been nesting in your cloak?

INFORMER.
There's a free handout of wings going on. Who?
Where?

PEITHETAIROS.
Me. Here. What exactly do you want?

INFORMER.
Wings, fool, wings. Some kind of joker, are you?

PEITHETAIROS.
Don't tell me: you're trading-in that cloak.

INFORMER.
Undercover work. Or ground-cover, rather.
I cover a lot of ground. I go round the islands,
Delivering summonses, collecting evidence,
Sniffing out offenders . . .

PEITHETAIROS.
Public Benefactor Number One.

INFORMER.
Exactly. The point is, if I had wings,
I could scare them witless twice as fast.

PEITHETAIROS.
Dump them with summonses from up above?

INFORMER.
There are some real crooks out there. Pirates.
I could slip in and out in a flock of cranes,
With a cropful of summonses for ballast.

PEITHETAIROS.
Aren't you a little *spry* for this kind of work?
A little *husky* to be putting the bite on strangers?

INFORMER.
What else d'you suggest? Not . . . go *legit?*

PEITHETAIROS.
There must be something. Decent, clean –
Well, anything's cleaner than hatching lawsuits.

INFORMER.
Look, pal, I came here for wings, not sermons.

PEITHETAIROS.
I'll give you wings: word-wings.

INFORMER.
What's that mean?

PEITHETAIROS.
Words are wings. Everyone knows that.

INFORMER.
They do?

PEITHETAIROS.
Haven't you heard people talking? Fathers,
For example, in barber's shops. 'I'll kill
Dietrephes.
All that talk of chariots. My boy's flown off
To learn to drive.' 'With mine, it's poetry.
One ode and he's off. Head in the clouds. Away.'

INFORMER.
You've lost me, squire.

PEITHETAIROS.
It's simple. Words inspire.
They give you uplift, make you rise
To higher things. In your case, I hope,
An honest job of work.

INFORMER.
Not interested.

PEITHETAIROS.
Pardon?

INFORMER.
It's genetic, what I do. It's in the blood.
Father, grandad before him. I can't disgrace
The family. Just give me wings – executive type,
Hawk's, falcon's, I'm not fussy – so I can zoom

To the islands, deliver the summonses,
Whizz back to Athens, give evidence in court . . .

PEITHETAIROS.
So that everything's despatched and decided
Before the defendant even gets there?

INFORMER.
That's how it works.

PEITHETAIROS.
So while he's sailing *out*, you're flying *in*
To pick up his goods and chattels.

INFORMER.
That's right.
You need speed in this job, to stay on top.

PEITHETAIROS.
Top. Top. I've got it. Here are some wings.
Try these.

INFORMER.
Those aren't wings, they're whips.

PEITHETAIROS.
That's right.
Words inspire the mind. *You* mentioned tops.

INFORMER.
Ow! Oo!

PEITHETAIROS.
Speed, speed, you said you needed speed.
Get whizzing, then. Get zooming – somewhere else.

He chases him out.

We'll take the rest of the wings inside.

He and the SLAVE *take the wings, and go in.*

CHORUS.
We've been on mystery flights,
And seen some funny sights.
The oddest of all must be

The K-K-Kleonymos-tree.
It's big, and thick, and yellow.
Hear it stammer, lie and bellow.
In spring it never fails:
Its buds are fairy tales.
When autumn comes, it yields
A crop of little shields.

It's the darkest place we know,
Where the Sun's afraid to go,
Where the Moon holds back her light
And it's always dead of night.
Strange creatures wail and moan there.
Don't wander on your own there.
You'll be jumped on, bumped and bashed,
Stripped naked, mugged and mashed.
That's Orestes' cunning plan.
The hero? The highwayman.

Enter PROMETHEUS, *cloaked.*

PROMETHEUS.
Oh dear, I do hope Zeus doesn't see me.

(*to* PEITHETAIROS, *as he passes in and out*)

Psst. Where's Peithetairos?

PEITHETAIROS.
A walking duvet. Who are *you?*

PROMETHEUS.
Are there any gods about? Behind?

PEITHETAIROS.
No. Who *are* you?

PROMETHEUS.
What time is it?

PEITHETAIROS.
Afternoon. Just. *Who* are you?

PROMETHEUS.
How much after noon?

PEITHETAIROS.
I'm getting tired of this.

PROMETHEUS.
What's Zeus doing? Is it dark or sunny?

PEITHETAIROS.
Dear, dear!

PROMETHEUS.
All clear? In that case . . . there.

He unwraps himself.

PEITHETAIROS (*overjoyed*).
Prometheus!

PROMETHEUS.
Shh! For heaven's sake, not so loud.

PEITHETAIROS.
What's wrong?

PROMETHEUS.
Don't shout my name all over the place.
If Zeus gets to hear I'm here . . . I've come
To tell you what's going on in Heaven.
I tell you what. Get under this.

He puts up a sunshade.

Hold it up, so the gods can't see us.

PEITHETAIROS.
I do like you.
You always have everything worked out.
Come under. What's going on?

PROMETHEUS.
Listen.

PEITHETAIROS.
I'm listening.

PROMETHEUS.
Zeus is done for.

PEITHETAIROS.
Since when?

PROMETHEUS.
Since you closed the air.
The human race stopped sacrificing, on the spot.
We haven't had a sniff of offering for yonks.
Emergency rations. It's worse than the annual fast.
The Olympian gods are fine: stiff upper lip.
But some of the out-of-towners are turning nasty,
Threatening to chuck Zeus out and start again
If he doesn't reopen the trade-routes
And get the gravy-train on the move again.

PEITHETAIROS.
Out-of-towners? You don't have gods from out-of-town.

PROMETHEUS.
Of course we do. From beyond the stars.
We've a god for everyone – even Exekestides.

PEITHETAIROS.
And what d'you call these out-of-towners?

PROMETHEUS.
Bigguns.

PEITHETAIROS.
Why Bigguns?

PROMETHEUS.
Because they *are*.
Anyway, they're sending down a mission,
Zeus and the Bigguns. To ask for terms.
And what *I* came to say is, stand your ground.
Don't budge till Zeus agrees to two conditions:
(1) The birds get total, universal power;
(2) You get to marry Sovereignty.

PEITHETAIROS.
Who?

PROMETHEUS.
Sovereignty.
She's a kind of . . . personal assistant.
Knockout to look at. She polishes
His Nibs' Ultimate Weapon, his thunderbolt.
She's got a bunch of keys *this* big.
You name it, she dishes it out:
Life, Liberty, Pursuit of Happiness,
Naval Bases, Political Debate, the Welfare State –

PEITHETAIROS.
She's got key to all those?

PROMETHEUS.
Marry her, control the lot.
That's my advice. That's what I came to say.
You know how I dote on the human race.

PEITHETAIROS.
Who gave us the barbecue?

PROMETHEUS.
I never *did* like gods.

PEITHETAIROS.
I think it's mutual.

PROMETHEUS.
There must be a play in there.
Now I really must run. Look, take the sunshade,
And walk in front. That way, if Zeus looks down,
He'll think I'm part of some procession.

PEITHETAIROS.
Good idea. You carry this deckchair:
That'll make it look more natural.

Exeunt.

CHORUS.
In the land of the Darkyfeet
Where shadows flit and bleat,
A man with dirty knees
(They call him Sokrates)

Gives classes to the spooks there.
Peisandros comes and looks there.
'Please help me find my soul.'
'Pour camel-blood: one bowl.
But watch out for Chairephon:
He'll drink it on his own.'

Enter POSEIDON, HERAKLES *and* BIGGUN.

POSEIDON.
This is the place. Cloudcuckooland.
Fancy *us*, ambassadors to a place like this!

(*to* BIGGUN)

What're you *doing?* You don't wear that like that.
Over the *other* shoulder. For heaven's sake,
Who do you think you are, Laispodias?
Is that what advanced democracy means,
That we have to put up with clowns like this?

BIGGUN.
Yarrup.

POSEIDON.
Thanks. Oh thanks. That's very nice.
Gods, what a specimen! I thought I'd seen it all ...
Well, Herakles, have you got it straight?
Our plan of campaign?

HERAKLES.
Find the mortal bastard
Who built the wall, and throttle him.

POSEIDON.
No, no, no, no.
We're a *peace* mission.

HERAKLES.
So make peace first, *then* throttle him.

Enter PEITHETAIROS *and* SLAVE. *They bring cooking implements, to prepare for a feast.*

PEITHETAIROS.
Give me the grater. Where's the garlic?
I've lost the cheese. That fire needs air.

POSEIDON.
You. Mortal. The Embassy from Heaven presents
Credentials. We've come to kiss hands.

PEITHETAIROS.
Better not. I'm grating garlic.

HERAKLES.
What meat is this?

PEITHETAIROS.
Jailbirds.
They plotted High Treason, they paid the price.

HERAKLES.
You garlic them first, then spit them?

PEITHETAIROS.
I *thought* you were Herakles. How's tricks?

POSEIDON.
Harumph. The Embassy from Heaven presents –

PEITHETAIROS.
We're short of oil.

HERAKLES.
That's bad. I like my poultry oily.

POSEIDON.
Our position is: this war is getting us nowhere,
And peace could get *you* somewhere. For example:
Rain-butts full, permanent supply. Summer weather,
Whenever you want. We've full authority,
Full power to negotiate, my colleagues and myself.

PEITHETAIROS.
We didn't start the war. It's not our fault.
We'll make peace gladly, any time you like.
All we ask is our rights. And our rights are these:

Lord Zeus must hand our sceptre back. If that's
Acceptable, I invite the Embassy to lunch.

HERAKLES.
Acceptable? I'll say. That gets my vote.

POSEIDON.
You brainless oaf? You gutbag! Think, for once.
Lord Zeus' sceptre? You can't be serious.

PEITHETAIROS.
You don't understand. Let birds rule here,
You'll be far better off than you were before.
You've had a hell of a time with mortals – up
Till now. It's because of the clouds.
They skulk underneath the clouds. They laugh
At you. They take your names in vain. Not any
more.
Come in with *us*, when mortals swear 'By Jove'
They'll have to add 'By Jay' – and then,
If they break their word, a jackdaw slips down,
And pecks their eye out.

POSEIDON.
Poseidon! Yes! That's clever.

HERAKLES.
I agree.

PEITHETAIROS.
And what do *you* say?

BIGGUN.
Ploog.

PEITHETAIROS.
He's with us all the way.
And there's something else we can do for you.
Suppose a mortal makes a holy promise –
'Grant this wish, and I'll sacrifice a sheep' –
And then delays, thinking 'The Gods are immortal,
They can wait'? We can deal with that.'

POSEIDON.
Oh can you? How?

PEITHETAIROS.
We'll wait till he's otherwise engaged,
Counting his money, say, or lying in his bath,
Then *Woof! Shoof!* We'll send a kite
To snaffle you up the price of two fat sheep.

HERAKLES.
Two sheep?

PEITHETAIROS.
Double-dealing, double penalty.

HERAKLES.
That gets my vote. Give them back their power.

PEITHETAIROS.
Right. What does Biggun say?

HERAKLES (*to* BIGGUN).
Oi. Bunch of fives?

BIGGUN.
Sinoffeta snakko. Blap.

HERAKLES.
Yes, he agrees.

POSEIDON.
If that's the majority decision, I accept.
You. Mortal. That sceptre: request agreed.

PEITHETAIROS.
– Which brings me to the second thing I had
To ask. I don't want Hera: Zeus can keep her.
But you must hand Sovereignty, his . . . handmaiden
To me to marry.

POSEIDON.
Come on, you two.
He doesn't want peace at all.

PEITHETAIROS.
It's all the same to me.

(*to the* SLAVE)

How's the sauce? I told you sweet *and* sour.

HERAKLES.
Poseidon, lovey. I mean, Poseidon, sea-lord,
We're not going to argue over a bit of skirt?

POSEIDON.
What else do you suggest?

HERAKLES.
Make peace, of course.

POSEIDON.
You haven't the brains you were born with. Clown!
They're swindling you. Say yes, it's you that suffers.
If Zeus gives these people all his sovereign power,
What's left for you? Your father, right? His son?
When he shuffles off, *you* stand to get the lot.

PEITHETAIROS.
Don't listen to him. It's a three card trick.
Come over here a minute. Let me explain.
Don't listen to uncle. He's got it wrong.
You won't get a penny when your old man dies.
When your old *god* dies. The problem is,
You're a bastard.

HERAKLES.
What did you say?

PEITHETAIROS.
Not me, the law.
Olympian father, yes, but mortal Mum.
Legitimate heirs take precedence –
Athene, in this case. She gets the lot.

HERAKLES.
Unless he makes a will leaving all to me.
I could arrange that.

PEITHETAIROS.
No use. Another law.
Try anything like that, and *he'll* contest it:
Your uncle Poseidon, who's so hot for you right now.
He'll have you up in court: his Lordship's brother.
Next of kin. He'll grab the lot. You know the law:
WHEREAS IF THE AFORESAID TESTATOR DIETH INTESTATE
THE ESTATE,TOGETHER WITH ALL MESSUAGE, CHATTELS, GOODS
THERETO APPERTAINING, SHALL PASS, *DUSTIBUS FUSTIBUS*,
(1) TO LEGITIMATE ISSUE, (2) TO NEXT OF KIN.

HERAKLES.
I don't get a penny?

PEITHETAIROS.
Dustibus, fustibus.
Unless, of course, he passed a separate law
Making you legitimate.

HERAKLES.
He never did. What a bastard!

PEITHETAIROS.
Like son, like father. Don't grind your teeth.
Stay here with us, you're made. Captain of Crows,
Duke of Dodos, throne of your own, best pigeon's milk . . .

HERAKLES.
I said it before and I say it again,
She's yours. Hand her over. That's *my* vote.

PEITHETAIROS.
Poseidon?

POSEIDON.
Never.

PEITHETAIROS.
It's up to Biggun, then.
You've got the casting vote. Well, what d'you say?

BIGGUN.
Sovrankro, burdi handle. Heap.

HERAKLES.
Well, that was clear enough.

POSEIDON.
'Sovrankro'? 'Sov-*ran*-kro'? You call that clear?

HERAKLES.
It seemed clear to me. 'Sovran crow, birdie handle. Heap!'

POSEIDON.
Oh, settle it yourselves. I've nothing more to say.

HERAKLES (*to* PEITHETAIROS).
Right, it's agreed. Exactly as you asked.
She's ready and waiting, up in Heaven.
Come along with us, then. Walk this way.

PEITHETAIROS.
Those jailbirds will come in really handy.
Wedding-banquet.

HERAKLES.
Wedding-banquet? Ah.
You three go on. I'll stay and roast the meat.

POSEIDON.
'Stay and roast the meat' ... That's all you're fit for!

HERAKLES.
Who's complaining?

POSEIDON.
Walk *this* way.

PEITHETAIROS.
Someone fetch my wedding suit. I won't be long.

Exeunt PEITHETAIROS, POSEIDON, HERAKLES.

CHORUS.
In Lawcourt Land, behind
The water-clock you'll find
The grimy, slimy nest
Of the Creepy-crawly pest.
It's a tongue on legs. It wriggles,
Slobbers, nudges, niggles.
It tends its crop of lies
Till they tower to the skies.
So before it gets too fat,
Lift a foot and squash it, flat.

Enter MESSENGER.

MESSENGER.
Happiness! Happiness! Blissful race,
Flap happy wings, receive your king.
He comes to claim his rightful place,
The golden, the star-bright, wide of wing.
He dazzles the Sun; he rides the sky;
His glory glitters, wide and high.
And at his side, his shining queen,
His lovely lady, and in his hand
Fire-wings, the thunderbolt. Be seen!
Be welcome! Grace this happy land!
He comes. Play music, loud and long.
Burn incense. Sing the wedding song.

Music. Enter PEITHETAIROS *and* SOVEREIGNTY, *in procession.*

CHORUS.
Make way! Draw back! Stand clear!
Our king is here.
Fly round his head with pride.
Serenade his bride.

Hymen, Hymenaios, O!
Hymen, Hymenaios, O!
Oh happy man, oh saviour-king,
With pride we sing.
For you, your Queen, our songs we raise,
Our hymns of praise.
Hymen, Hymenaios, O!
Hymen, Hymenaios, O!

As now, so then, the Fates once led
Zeus and his bride to bed,
His lordliness,
Her loveliness.
Hymen, Hymenaios, O!
Hymen, Hymenaios, O!

Young Cupid, golden-winged and fair
With blessings showered the pair,
The king, the queen,
Joy to be seen.
Hymen, Hymenaios, O!
Hymen, Hymenaios, O!

PEITHETAIROS.
Your song is pleasing; sweet your voices.

CHORUS.
Now, while Heaven with Earth rejoices,
Wake Zeus' thunder. Let it roll,
Let it terrify each living soul.
Golden thunder, Heaven-cleaving,
Echoed from the sea-swell's heaving;
It shakes the Earth, makes rain-clouds weep,
It gives all power, on Earth, in Air –
Like Sovereignty, Zeus' consort fair,
That once was his, and now is yours to keep.

Thunder.

Hymen, Hymenaios, O!
Hymen, Hymenaios, O!

PEITHETAIROS.
Birds of the air, salute my royal bride.
Come with us now, inside.

CHORUS.
Hymen, Hymenaios, O!
Hymen, Hymenaios, O!

PEITHETAIROS.
Give me your hand, my love, and wing to wing
We'll lead the way,
To end the play,
While nightingales our wedding-chorus sing.

CHORUS.
Alalala-ee, ee-ay, pay-ohn,
Lead the way,
Sing today,
Sing for the king.
Hymen, Hymenaios, O!
Hymen, Hymenaios, O!

Exeunt omnes.

ARISTOPHANES

Frogs
(*Batrachoi*)

translated by Kenneth McLeish

Characters

XANTHIAS
DIONYSOS
HERAKLES
CORPSE
CHARON
AIAKOS
SERVANT GIRL
LANDLADY
PLATHANE
EURIPIDES
AESCHYLUS
PLOUTON

silent parts:
CORPSE-BEARERS
EURIPIDES' MUSE
MUSICIANS
SLAVES

FROGS
CHORUS OF HOLY ONES

A large open space. On one side, the door of HERAKLES' *house. On the other, the gateway of the Underworld. Enter* DIONYSOS, *wearing a yellow costume covered with a lion-skin, and carrying a club. Behind him, loaded with luggage, enter* XANTHIAS *on a donkey.*

XANTHIAS.
Hey, sir, shall I start with one of the old routines?
They never fail.

DIONYSOS.
Yes, if you must.
So long as it's not 'I've had this up to here'.
Not that again. I've had that up to here.

XANTHIAS.
Something more upmarket?

DIONYSOS.
'I'm knackered'? No.

XANTHIAS.
The Mother of all Funnies?

DIONYSOS.
Good idea –
Unless it's the one I think it is.

XANTHIAS.
Which one?

DIONYSOS.
When you shift your bags about, and shout
'I've got to dump my load'.

XANTHIAS.
Not quite. I had in mind,
'Won't someone relieve me – before I relieve myself?'

DIONYSOS.
Not now. I'll tell you when. When I want to puke.

XANTHIAS.
So what's the point of carrying all these bags,
If I can't get a laugh with them? They're all at it:
Ameipsias, Phrynichos, Lykis.
There's *always* a baggage scene.

DIONYSOS.
Except this time.
Leave all that clever stuff to them. I come away
From their plays years older as it is.

XANTHIAS.
Poor old shoulders. They've had it up to here –
And that's no joke.

DIONYSOS.
The whole thing's no joke. Here am I,
Dionysos, son of Juice, walking, on foot,
Left, right, left right, while you sit there in style –
Just to save you carrying half a dozen bags.

XANTHIAS.
You mean I'm *not* carrying them?

DIONYSOS.
How can you be? You're riding.

XANTHIAS.
I'm bearing the baggage.

DIONYSOS.
How, bearing it?

XANTHIAS.
Grin-and-bearing it.

DIONYSOS.
How can someone be bearing something,
When something's bearing *him?*

XANTHIAS.
Oh, I don't know.
All I know is, I've got to dump my load.

DIONYSOS.
So, dump it. If the donkey's doing you no good,
Let *him* carry it. *You* carry *him*.

XANTHIAS.
Ha! Very funny. I wish I'd served at sea.
I'd be a free man now, and you could –

DIONYSOS.
Shh! We're here. We've reached ... the door.
The door I was making for. This door.
I'll knock. Hello-oh. Anyone at home?

HERAKLES *opens the door.*

HERAKLES.
Who's that hammering? Who d'you think you are?
My god! What is it? Who *do* you think you are?

He goes inside, bursting with laughter.

DIONYSOS.
You saw that?

XANTHIAS.
What?

DIONYSOS.
You took that in?

XANTHIAS.
What in?

DIONYSOS.
How scared he was –

XANTHIAS.
That you were a loony. Yes.

HERAKLES *opens the door again, still convulsed.*

HERAKLES.
I'm terribly sorry. I couldn't help it.
I'm all right now. I'm biting my lip. Oh god, oh god.

DIONYSOS.
That's quite all right. Don't be alarmed. Approach.
I want to ask you something.

HERAKLES.
Excuse me a moment.
A lion-skin ... a yellow dress ... a *club*... ?
Are you ... going somewhere?

DIONYSOS.
I served with Kleisthenes.

HERAKLES.
Ooh, sailor . . .

DIONYSOS.
We sank twelve or thirteen of them.

HERAKLES.
You and him . . . *between* you?

DIONYSOS.
Ask anyone.

XANTHIAS.
Then I woke up.

DIONYSOS.
The point is, I was sitting on deck,
Reading Euripides' *Andromeda*,
When I felt a sudden prick. Of desire.

HERAKLES.
How big?

DIONYSOS.
This big.

HERAKLES.
For a woman?

DIONYSOS.
No.

HERAKLES.
A boy, then?

DIONYSOS.
No.

HERAKLES.
A man?

DIONYSOS.
Don't be daft.

HERAKLES.
Not . . . Kleisthenes?

DIONYSOS.
This isn't a joke. It's serious.
It's eating me away. I just can't cope.

HERAKLES.
There, there. What are the symptoms?

DIONYSOS.
How can I explain?
Make it simple . . . ? Use words you'll understand . . . ?
Have you ever craved, really craved, pea soup?

HERAKLES.
A million times. Pea soup!

DIONYSOS.
Is that quite clear? Shall I try again?

HERAKLES.
No, no. Pea soup's quite clear. If you see what I mean.

DIONYSOS.
Well, that's the kind of craving that's eating me.
For Euripides.

HERAKLES.
But he's a corpse.

DIONYSOS.
I *know* that.
I'm going to see him, and no one's going to stop me.

HERAKLES.
But he's . . . Down There. In the Underworld.

DIONYSOS.
I *know*.
I'll go as low as I have to. Lower.

HERAKLES.
But *why?*

DIONYSOS.
I need a classy poet, fast.
Where are the snows of yesteryear? Not here.

HERAKLES.
You're joking. There's Iophon.

DIONYSOS.
Oh, really?
You're really recommending Iophon?
Some yesteryear. Some snow.

HERAKLES.
What about his Daddy?
Sophocles? If you must bring someone back,
Bring Sophocles. Who needs Euripides?

DIONYSOS.
Not fair to Iophon. Such a Daddy's boy.
Can he hack it on his own – or were those Daddy's plays?
In any case, he won't. Not Sophocles.
He's easy. He liked it here. He'll like it there.
Not like Euripides. He's such a scamp!
Give him half a chance, he's out of there.

HERAKLES.
Just a minute. What's wrong with Agathon?

DIONYSOS.
He's gone. Good friend,
Good poet, and now he's good and gone.

HERAKLES.
Gone where?

DIONYSOS.
The Banquets of the Blest.

HERAKLES.
What about Xenokles?

DIONYSOS.
To Hell with him.

HERAKLES.
Pythangelos?

XANTHIAS.
What about *me?*
Won't someone relieve me, before I relieve myself?

HERAKLES.
There are millions more of them out there:
The younger generation. Scribbling away,
Miles more words to the minute than Euripides.

DIONYSOS.
Barren leaves, dregs, chattering starlings.
They get one play put on, cock their legs once
Against Tragedy, you never hear of them again.
No, no, I want a really ballsy genius –

HERAKLES.
How d'you mean, ballsy?

DIONYSOS.
Technical expression.
Someone who gives inspiration a bit of welly.
'Air, Zeus' garden shed'; 'the foot of Time';
'My tongue it was that promised, not my brain.'

HERAKLES.
You go for that?

DIONYSOS.
I'm mad for it.

HERAKLES.
You're joking.
It's load of old –

DIONYSOS.
Steady. Who's god of drama here?

HERAKLES.
It's just my opinion.

DIONYSOS.
Do *I* lecture *you* on food?

XANTHIAS.
They've forgotten I exist.

DIONYSOS.
Anyway, that's why I'm here. With all this stuff.
Dressed like you. I want you to tell me everything.
I mean, you've *been* there, the Underworld ...
That time you went to steal Kerberos. *You* know.
I want you to tell me everything about the place:
Harbours, snack-bars, whore-houses, dosshouses,
Water-holes, roads, bed-and-breakfast joints
With the fewest bugs ...

XANTHIAS.
They *have* forgotten I exist.

HERAKLES.
I don't believe this. You're *going* there? *You?*

DIONYSOS.
Don't start again. Just tell me a quick way down.
One that's not too hot, and not too cold.

HERAKLES.
There's such a lot to choose from. H'm. I know.
There's Kick-Chair-Slipknot Alley. Hanging yourself.

DIONYSOS.
Too much of a strain.

HERAKLES.
Stay-Out-in-the-Rain?

DIONYSOS.
Freeze to death, you mean?

HERAKLES.
Exactly.

DIONYSOS.
I'd get cold feet.

HERAKLES.
You want a short cut?

DIONYSOS.
Please. I'm not much of a walker.

HERAKLES.
Right. Straight up the road,
Turn left into Potter's Row . . .

DIONYSOS.
Then what?

HERAKLES.
Climb to the top of the tower.

DIONYSOS.
Then what?

HERAKLES.
When they start the torch-race,
When you hear them shout 'Ready, steady, go!',
You go as well.

DIONYSOS.
Where?

HERAKLES.
Down.

DIONYSOS.
No thanks. I *hate* minced brain.
What about the other way?

HERAKLES.
What other way?

DIONYSOS.
The way *you* took.

HERAKLES.
Oh, that.
It's more of a cruise than a way. A bottomless lake –

DIONYSOS.
How do I get across?

HERAKLES.
There's an aged ferryman.

DIONYSOS.
Charon, you mean?

HERAKLES.
He'll take you over. The fare's two obols.

DIONYSOS.
Two obols? That's nearly half a drach.

HERAKLES.
No kidding. Once you get to the other side,
Past all the snakes and monsters –

DIONYSOS.
You can't scare me. Get on.

HERAKLES.
– you'll come to the Mud Marsh,
The Great Desolation of Dung. That's where they keep
Bastards who cheated their friends,
Or beat up their Mummies,
Or walloped their Daddies,
Or swore false oaths –

DIONYSOS.
– or quoted Morsimos,
Or danced with Kinesias –

HERAKLES.
Quite suddenly, there'll be a breath of flutes,
And it'll all turn bright and sunny, like up here.
You'll have reached the Myrtle Groves ...
The Banquets of the Blest ... men and women, feasting ...

DIONYSOS.
Who are they?

HERAKLES.
The Holy Ones, who understand the mysteries –

XANTHIAS.
Like me and this donkey. I've got to put these down.

Can't wait any longer. Going, going ... gone!

HERAKLES.
They'll tell you everything you need to know.
They'll put you right, on the road to Pluto's Place.
Good luck.

DIONYSOS.
I'll need it. Thanks.

HERAKLES *goes in and shuts the door.*

Pick up the bags.

XANTHIAS.
But I've only just –

DIONYSOS.
Don't argue. Now.

XANTHIAS.
Just a minute.

Enter a funeral procession.

Can't you get *him* to carry them?

DIONYSOS.
What if he won't?

XANTHIAS.
Then I will.

DIONYSOS.
Aren't we lucky he came along? I'll have a word.
I say. Excuse me. You, lying there.
A little favour ... ? A bag or two ... down there?

CORPSE.
What bags?

DIONYSOS.
Just these.

CORPSE.
All those? Two drachmas.

DIONYSOS.
You're joking.

CORPSE (*to* BEARERS).
On we go.

DIONYSOS.
Can't we discuss this?

CORPSE.
Two drachs or nothing.

DIONYSOS.
Nine obols?

CORPSE.
I'd rather live!

Exit procession.

XANTHIAS.
Cheeky beggar. To Hell with him. I'll do it.

DIONYSOS.
I don't know what I'd do without you.
This way. Down to the jetty.

Enter CHARON *in his ferry-boat.*

CHARON.
Avast behind!

DIONYSOS.
Pardon?

XANTHIAS.
It's that lake he was on about. That ferry-boat.

DIONYSOS.
This must be Charon, then. Ooh-ar, me hearty.
See?

CHARON.
Any more for the Ground Floor, the Dogs,
The Last Resting Place, the Lower Depths?

DIONYSOS.
Yes. Me.

CHARON.
Get in, then, quick.

DIONYSOS.
You go all the way to Hell?

CHARON.
You'll see. Get in.

DIONYSOS.
Xanthias, after you.

CHARON.
Oh, no you don't.
No slaves allowed – unless they served at sea.

XANTHIAS.
Ah. Flat feet. They wouldn't take me.

CHARON.
Tough. Start walking. The whole way round.

XANTHIAS.
Where shall I meet you?

CHARON.
At the Skull and Skeletons.
The pub by the Withered Rock.

DIONYSOS.
Have you got that?

XANTHIAS.
I've got it, I've got it.
I don't want it, but I've got it.

Exit.

CHARON.
Right. You. Sit to the oar.
Anyone else? Any more for the Die-lark?
Hey, what are you doing?

DIONYSOS.
Sitting on my oar. That's what you said.

CHARON.
You great fat ... Here, sit here.

DIONYSOS.
All right.

CHARON.
Grab hold.

DIONYSOS.
All right.

CHARON.
Now, stop fooling about, and *pull*.

DIONYSOS.
Pull? Me? I've never rowed before.
Which end did you say you hold?

CHARON.
It's simple, once you start.
They'll help you.

DIONYSOS.
Who will?

CHARON.
Frog-swans. Singing. You'll see. Are you ready?

DIONYSOS.
I suppose so.

CHARON.
Right. LEAN-and-PULL, LEAN-and-PULL ...

DIONYSOS *starts rowing to this rhythm. The air gradually fills with the sound of* FROGS. *Their song is in an entirely different rhythm, and puts* DIONYSOS *off his stroke.*

FROGS.
Brekekekex, koax, koax,
Brekekekex, koax, koax.

Children of the limpid lake,
Sing with us, till echoes break
Along the reedbeds by the shore,
Koax, koax.
Sing, as you never sang before,
For Dionysos, lord of Vine,
Who leads singing, leads laughter,
Leads revels in the shrine –

Leads fuzzy heads, the morning after.
Brekekekex, koax, koax.

DIONYSOS.
I'm getting a blistered behind,
Koax, koax,
And you don't seem to mind.

FROGS.
Brekekekex, koax, koax.

DIONYSOS.
You're going too FAR with your koax.
Is that all you ARE, koax?

FROGS.
In deep dark pools, where fat carp feed,
We plant and tend the sacred reed
For Apollo's lute. The Muses hymn us,
Expert divers, expert swimmers –
They love our song.
Horn-footed Pan agrees,
As he dances through the trees –
And he's not wrong.
Brekekekex, koax, koax.

DIONYSOS.
I'm getting sore.
My bottom's sweating,
Fretting,
Ready to roar –

FROGS.
Brekekekex, koax, koax.

DIONYSOS.
That's over the top.
Please stop.

FROGS.
In sunny, summer days,
Our song was a mist, a haze
Rising to heaven. Now, in the rain,
We sing again,
Diving and burbling,
Singing and gurgling,
For you, for you,
A bubble of melody bursting through –

DIONYSOS.
Brekekekex, koax, koax.
Ye gods, *I'm* doing it now.
I got that from you.

FROGS.
Well, give it back.

DIONYSOS.
I'm on the rack.
I'm rowing myself in two.
I'd stop, but I don't know how.

FROGS.
Brekekekex, koax, koax.

DIONYSOS.
You're driving me mad.

FROGS.
How sad.
We're a musical crowd.
All night and all day,
We open our gullets and say –

DIONYSOS.
Brekekekex, koax, koax.
How's that for loud?

FROGS.
You won't beat us.

DIONYSOS.
No fret, no fuss.
I'll shout you down. I'll yell myself hoarse.
I'll stop your koaxing, if need be by force.
Brekekekex, KOAX, KOAX.
No answer? Give in, KOAX?
I knew I'd win, KOAX.

CHARON.
Lay to! We're here. Ship the oar and step ashore.
Fares, please.

DIONYSOS.
Two obols. Here.

He steps ashore. The boat disappears.

Xanthias? Oo-oo. Xanthy.

XANTHIAS (*out of sight*).
Ya-oo.

DIONYSOS.
Come over here.

XANTHIAS (*appearing*).
Welcome to Hell, sir.

DIONYSOS.
What *is* there?

XANTHIAS.
Mud . . . dark . . .

DIONYSOS.
Did you see the Daddy-bashers and oath-breakers
He told us about?

XANTHIAS.
Can't *you?*

DIONYSOS.
Oh my god. *Now* what?

XANTHIAS.
Now we get out of here. Fast.
This is where all the nasties are. *He* said.

DIONYSOS.
He said? And you believed him? He was piling it on,
Trying to scare me. Me – Mr Brave, Mr Iron
Resolve.
Typical Herakles: all mouth and monsters.
Twelve labours! I'll have thirteen any day.

XANTHIAS.
What's that?

DIONYSOS.
What? Where?

XANTHIAS.
Behind you.

DIONYSOS (*pushing him behind*).
Get over there.

XANTHIAS.
Now it's in front.

DIONYSOS (*pushing him in front*).
Get *there*, I said.

XANTHIAS.
A huge great beast.

DIONYSOS.
T-tell me.

XANTHIAS.
It's horrible. Keeps changing. Now it's a cow ...
A mule ... a pretty girl ...

DIONYSOS.
Let's have a look.

XANTHIAS.
Too late. Changed again. She-wolf.

DIONYSOS.
It's probably Empousa.

XANTHIAS.
Fiery features.

DIONYSOS.
Is one leg made of copper?

XANTHIAS.
It is, and one of cowdung.

DIONYSOS.
Where can I hide?

XANTHIAS.
Come back!

DIONYSOS.
Is there a priest in the house?
A priest of Dionysos? Help!

XANTHIAS.
We're done for, Herakles.

DIONYSOS.
Don't call me that down here.

XANTHIAS.
Dionysos, then.

DIONYSOS.
That's worse.

XANTHIAS.
Bad girl! Shoo! This way, sir.

DIONYSOS.
What d'you mean?

XANTHIAS.
Out of this nettle, danger, we pluck this flower,
Safety.

DIONYSOS.
Eh?

XANTHIAS.
Empousa's hopped it.

DIONYSOS.
You're joking.

XANTHIAS.
I promise.

DIONYSOS.
Cross your heart.

XANTHIAS.
And spit in your eye. Sir.

DIONYSOS.
D'you know, I went quite pale.

XANTHIAS.
You went pale? You should see that priest.

DIONYSOS.
What a brute! Where *did* she come from?
Air, Zeus' garden-shed? The foot of time?

A flute is heard, offstage.

Hey!

XANTHIAS.
What?

DIONYSOS.
Can't you hear it?

XANTHIAS.
What?

DIONYSOS.
A breath of flutes.

XANTHIAS.
And a whiff of torches. Nice.

DIONYSOS.
Get your *head* down. Shh! We'll listen.

CHORUS (*offstage*).
Iacchos, O Iacchos!
Iacchos, O Iacchos!

XANTHIAS.
It's a procession. The Holy Ones. The Blest.
He told us. They sing and dance. It's them.

DIONYSOS.
Get down. Shut up. Let's see.

Enter CHORUS. *They are carrying the statue of Iacchos in a torchlit procession.*

CHORUS.
Iacchos,
Here in this holy place,
Iacchos, O Iacchos,
Dance with us,
Sing with us.
Toss your head,
Flower-crowned,
In the holy dance.
Dance with us,
Sing with us,
Your worshippers,
Your holy ones,
Come, share our feast we pray,
Come, crown this holy day.

XANTHIAS.
What's that I can smell? Roast pork?

DIONYSOS.
If you want some sausage, shush.

CHORUS.
Iacchos,
Shine in our darkness, lord.
Iacchos, O Iacchos,
Morning star,
End night for us,

Shine for us.
All dance for you,
Old men shake off
Their years and dance,
Dance for you,
Your worshippers,
Your holy ones.
Here in this place of night
Dance for us, lord of light.

If you're not one of us,
If you don't know the words,
If you don't know the steps,
Keep away.
If you can't hold your drink,
If you can't take a joke,
If you can't make a joke,
Keep away.
If it's profit you want,
If it's 'I'm all right, Jack',
If it's 'I was elected, I'm making my pile,
I'm in charge, I've a mandate,
I'll rob and I'll cheat and I'll do as I like –
And if comedy playwrights make fun of me,
Cut off their subsidies' –
Please keep away.
Keep away.
Keep away.
There's no room for you here.
Only singers allowed,
Only dancers,
Who honour the gods
And dance our dance.

Dance!
In fields of flowers advance.
Sing!
Happy voices raise,
To the goddess of spring
Sing praise.

Persephone, praise! Demeter too,
Harvest-bringer, we honour you.

Dance!
Excite, inspire, entrance.
Sing!
With laughing eyes
Bring luck, bring laughter, bring
First prize.

To Iacchos again your voices raise.
To the lord of the dance, sing praise.

Lord Iacchos, along the sacred way
Sing with us, dance with us today.
Our spirits soaring, our hearts on fire
We'll follow you, we'll never tire.
O Iacchos, lord, come lead the dance.
We revelled last night from dusk till dawn;
Shoes down at heel, clothes frayed and worn.
Wartime economy and ration.
Who cares? We're dancing – who needs fashion?
O Iacchos, lord, come lead the dance.

There was twist, there was leap, there was twirl,
And then, right beside me, this girl –
She was bubbly and bouncy and pretty,
And one proud little, pert little titty –
O Iacchos, lord, come lead the dance.

DIONYSOS.
I fancy some of that.

XANTHIAS.
Me first.

CHORUS.
Ladies and gentlemen, Archdemos.
Mr Nobody. Takes a correspondence course,
A law degree,
Next minute he's Mr High-and-Mighty,
Big cheese among the Living Dead Upstairs.

And another one: Kleisthenes.
Mr Lover-boy. Loses his fancy,
Come-Kiss-Me-Quick,
And he's sobbing and tearing his hair,
No chance now for fucking among the tombs.

Kallias comes to mind as well.
Mr Hips. Buys a lion-skin, sashays to sea –
Where else would he be? –
And bumps and grinds among the ...

DIONYSOS.
Excuse me, I wonder if you know
The way to Plouton's Place. We've just arrived –

CHORUS.
No problem. You see that door?
You're nearly there.

DIONYSOS.
Xanthias, the bags.

XANTHIAS.
What's in here anyway, the kitchen sink?

CHORUS.
On, on,
To the flower-meadows, the holy dance,
The singing, feasting.
Women eager and waiting
To see me raise the sacred torch.

Iacchos, lord, come lead the dance.

In fields of flowers,
Rose-meadows,
Guide us, lead us,
Dancing, singing –

Iacchos, lord, come lead the dance.

For us alone the Sun
Still smiles below.
We see, we know,
Your holy ones –

Iacchos, lord, come lead the dance.

DIONYSOS.
So this is the place. I wonder how to knock ...
How *does* one knock on doors down here?

XANTHIAS.
Any way you like. Get on with it.
Just remember one thing: you're Herakles.

DIONYSOS *knocks.*

DIONYSOS.
Open up! Ha-HO!

AIAKOS *throws open the door.*

AIAKOS.
Oo is it?

DIONYSOS.
Herakles the Strong.

AIAKOS.
Ho. *You* again.
Bastard. Conman. Bum.
Cheating, lowlife scum.
Ere before, weren't you?
Grabbed our Kerberos and snitched him.
Right under my nose. And now you're back.
We've been waiting for you:
The Big Black Ole of Ell.
The Gaping Gulf. Y-enas, mate.
The Grasping Gorgon oo'll grab your guts,
The Undred-eaded Unger-snake oo'll ug your eart,
The Pitiless Piranha oo'll pluck your pubes –
Oh, we've been waiting, mate. Don't go away.

He goes in.

XANTHIAS.
What's the matter?

DIONYSOS.
I've had an accident.

XANTHIAS.
Why not clear off while you've got the chance?
There may be more of them.

DIONYSOS.
You don't understand.
I've had an *accident*. Give me a sponge, quick.

XANTHIAS.
Where d'you want it?

DIONYSOS.
Put it on my heart. Oh, oh.

XANTHIAS.
Is *that* where you keep your heart?

DIONYSOS.
It slipped in the excitement.

XANTHIAS.
A right little Herakles *you* are.

DIONYSOS.
What d'you mean? I asked for a sponge, didn't I?
He wouldn't have asked for a sponge.

XANTHIAS.
He wouldn't?

DIONYSOS.
He's have stood there, oozing.
Whereas *I* asked for a sponge and bounced right back.

XANTHIAS.
I've never seen bravery like it.

DIONYSOS.
Weren't *you* afraid? All that shouting?

XANTHIAS.
Me? Hot air.

DIONYSOS.
All right, if you're so brave,

Change clothes with me.
You take the club and the lionskin.
Stiff upper lip!
I'll be you, and carry the bags.

XANTHIAS.
All right. Why not?
Xanthias, superhero. I like the sound of that.
Well? What d'you think? Do I get the part?

DIONYSOS.
Oh yes. You get the part all right.
And I get the bags. Where are they? Right.

The door opens. The SERVANT GIRL *comes out.*

SERVANT GIRL.
Herakles, darling, there you are!
Her Ladyship could hardly believe her ears, inside.
Fresh rolls, bean stew, roast ox,
And *masses* of cheesecake. *Do* come in ...

XANTHIAS.
No, really.

SERVANT GIRL.
Please ...
Roast pigeon, those *darling* little tarts,
A keg of wine. Come on.

XANTHIAS.
Well, I –

SERVANT GIRL.
I *daren't* let you slip away.
Did I mention the dancing-girls?

XANTHIAS.
What dancing-girls?

SERVANT GIRL.
Young and pretty.
The table's laid. There's shish-kebab.

XANTHIAS.
All right. Go in and tell the dancing-girls
I'll be with them right away, in person.

The SERVANT GIRL *goes in and shuts the door.*

Hey, you. Pick up the bags, and follow me.

DIONYSOS.
Just a minute, just a minute.
You didn't take me seriously just now?
I was joking. You, Herakles? I *mean* ...
Stop messing about, and get those bags.

XANTHIAS.
All change again?

DIONYSOS.
Take off that skin.

XANTHIAS.
Ye gods!

DIONYSOS.
Precisely. Have you forgotten who I am?
And who *you* are? *You,* Herakles?
Take off that skin.

XANTHIAS.
Whatever you say.
And if you need help again, don't hesitate ...

They change clothes.

CHORUS.
What a clever idea!
It's magnificent stuff!
When the sea's getting rough,
When the breaker looms near,
Just roll with the ship and avoid it.
Be a rascal, rogue, cheat,
Lying swine, politician;
Think up something neat,

Try a novel position.
Don't wait till disaster's destroyed it.

DIONYSOS.
There's a moral in this.
He just *got* to behave.
He's an ignorant slave,
He's not living in bliss,
He's not guzzling and snogging and kissing,
While his master stands by
With a tear in his eye,
With a groan and a cry,
With a sob and a sigh,
Looking on at the goodies he's missing.

DIONYSOS *is now dressed as Herakles again. Enter* LANDLADY *and* PLATHANE.

LANDLADY.
My god, it's him. Plathane, it's him.
That bed-and-breakfast bastard
Who ate sixteen loaves at a single sitting.

PLATHANE.
That's the one.

XANTHIAS.
Oh-oh.

LANDLADY.
I've got the bill here.
Twenty portions of lamb, one drachma seventy-five.

XANTHIAS.
Big trouble.

LANDLADY.
Not to mention all that garlic.

DIONYSOS.
You're babbling woman. There's some mistake.

LANDLADY.
Some mistake, all right. I suppose you thought

I wouldn't recognise you in that yellow dress.
I haven't even *mentioned* the pickle.

PLATHANE.
Or the cheese. Don't forget the cheese.
Rind and all. Don't forget the cheese.

LANDLADY.
And when I tried to give him the bill,
He looked at me all bristly and shouted 'Boo!'

XANTHIAS.
Oh, he's like that. Does that all the time.

LANDLADY.
Pulled out his sword like a maniac –

PLATHANE.
A maniac –

LANDLADY.
Chased me upstairs and locked me in the ...
Well, *you* know. Then he legged it,
Taking half the carpet with him.

XANTHIAS.
That's him all over.

PLATHANE.
So what do we do?

LANDLADY.
Ladies and gents, have you seen Kleon down here?

PLATHANE.
Never mind Kleon. We need Hyperbolos.

LANDLADY.
Give me a stone. I'll stuff it down his gob.

PLATHANE.
Chuck him in the pit.

LANDLADY.
Fetch a fish-knife. Fast.
He filleted those kippers. I'll fillet *him*.

PLATHANE.
Nah, nah, Kleon's best. We need a bit of shout.

Exeunt.

DIONYSOS.
Ahem. Xanthias.

XANTHIAS.
Don't ask. Not Herakles again.

DIONYSOS.
Oh, go on. Xanthy.

XANTHIAS.
Have you forgotten who I am? And who *you* are?

DIONYSOS.
You're right to be angry. Hit me if you want to.
But you can keep it this time. I promise.
Cross my heart and hope to die.
And if that isn't true
You can spit in my eye
And my wife's eye too.

XANTHIAS.
Oh, if you put it like that . . .

They change clothes again.

CHORUS.
Now you're back in the part
That you had at the start,
And in that yellow dress,
You must try to impress,
You must screw up your eyebrows and roar.
You must act like a god,
You must rumble and curse,
You must do nothing odd,
Or you'll end up far worse,
Humping bags as you humped them before.

XANTHIAS.
Don't tell me, I know.

I must put on a show.
I entirely agree.
But the problem, you see,
Is: my master's a cheat and a coward,
And he'll con me again.
Hey! What was that noise?
Brace up! Take the strain.
You can deal with those boys,
You can do it! Just roar, long and ... er ... loward.

AIAKOS *comes out, with* SLAVES.

AIAKOS.
There's the dognapper. Grab him, quick.

DIONYSOS.
Someone's for it.

XANTHIAS.
Back! I warn you.

AIAKOS.
Ho.
Smasher, Gnasher, Basher, out here, quick.

DIONYSOS.
Fantastic, isn't it? Steals what isn't his,
Then hits an officer.

AIAKOS.
Unbelievable.

DIONYSOS.
Worse: incredible.

XANTHIAS.
Look, I've never been here before.
I've never stolen a hair off your head.
If I have, may I go to Hell. Here's a fair offer:
Take my slave, and torture him. *Then*,
If you find I'm guilty, do what you like to me.

AIAKOS.
Torture him, eh? How would you suggest?

XANTHIAS.
Any way you like. Rack, thumbscrews, whip,
Bricks on the chest, vinegar up the nose – anything
Except oiling him with onion or lashing him with leeks.

AIAKOS.
You can't say fairer than that. But what if I ...
Break him a little? You won't want damages?

XANTHIAS.
Damages? You do like your little joke.
No, no. Take him in, do what you like with him.

AIAKOS.
Take him *in?* No, here. Where you can see.
Hey, you, come out from behind those bags.
We want the truth. You're not going to lie, now are you?

DIONYSOS.
I'm not having this. One *is* an immortal god.
Lay one finger on me, you'll be sorry.

AIAKOS.
You're raving mad.

DIONYSOS.
I'm Dionysos, son of Zeus –
And he's the slave.

AIAKOS.
Did you hear what he said?

XANTHIAS.
Of course.
All the more reason for thrashing him.
If he's a god, he won't feel a thing.

DIONYSOS.
Just a minute. You say *you're* a god.
Why doesn't he hit you too? Blow for blow?

XANTHIAS.
Fair enough. And the first to scream or yell
Or show the slightest sign of pain, isn't a god.

AIAKOS.
You *are* a gent. I can always tell.
Right. Get undressed, the pair if you.

XANTHIAS (*as he strips*).
Had you any particular method in mind?

AIAKOS.
One blow each. First you, then him.

XANTHIAS.
Fine by me.

AIAKOS *hits him.*

AIAKOS.
There.

XANTHIAS.
Ready when you are.

AIAKOS.
I've just hit you.

XANTHIAS.
You're joking.

AIAKOS.
I see. His turn, then.

He hits DIONYSOS.

DIONYSOS.
Get on with it.

AIAKOS.
I've done it.

DIONYSOS.
I'd have felt the draught.

AIAKOS.
Back to the other one.

XANTHIAS.
Ready when you – hoo!

AIAKOS.
What d'you mean, yoohoo? Felt that, did you?

XANTHIAS.
Felt what? I was waving to the audience.

AIAKOS.
Tough little specimen. Back to the other one.

He hits DIONYSOS.

DIONYSOS.
Ho-ho-ho-ho-*HO*.

AIAKOS.
Pardon?

DIONYSOS.
Ho-ho-horsemen. Look.

AIAKOS.
You're crying.

DIONYSOS.
Can't *you* smell onions?

AIAKOS.
You can't *feel* anything?

DIONYSOS.
Not a thing.

AIAKOS.
Back over here.

He hits XANTHIAS.

XANTHIAS.
Oh my god.

AIAKOS.
What's the matter?

XANTHIAS.
Thorn in my foot.

AIAKOS.
I don't get this. Back again.

He hits DIONYSOS.

DIONYSOS.
Zeus!

XANTHIAS.
He felt that all right.

DIONYSOS.
Of course I didn't. How does that song go?
'What's z-use of worrying?'

XANTHIAS.
We're getting nowhere. Hit him lower down.

AIAKOS.
Oi! Stick your belly out.

He hits him again.

DIONYSOS.
GOD! – of the misty mountains, God of the rolling plains.

AIAKOS.
This is ridiculous. How am I supposed to tell
Which one of you's the god? Oh, come inside.
The boss'll know, and Her Queasiness the Queen.
I mean, *they're* gods as well. They'll know.

DIONYSOS.
What a good idea. A little *late*, but good.

They all go in.

CHORUS.
Muse of comedy, dance with us, join in the fun.
There's a sensible crowd in today – all but one.
No, no, don't moan.
We're talking Kleophon.
The babbler,
The gabbler,

Won't say a single word if forty-nine will do.
Ignore him, Muse! Don't let him dine with you.

Now it's time to break into the play
With some serious moments, and give
You some useful advice. And today
Our prescription is, 'Live and let live'.
There's a tangle, a muddle, a mess –
And democracy's suffering. What
Are we talking about? Pain and distress
For Phrynichos' followers – that lot.
So they voted against you? They're brave,
Honest citizens, good men and true.
'But they voted against us.' A slave
Does his duty, fights fiercely – for you,
For his city – he's praised and rewarded.
'So what? It seems all right to me.'
All right? When a slave is applauded
For one noble action, set free,
And *they're* punished for just one mistake?
Why not welcome them back to the fold?
What a fine contribution they'd make
If you let them come in from the cold.

I'll read the leaves, consult my silver ball,
Tell people's fortunes – and first of all
(Don't make a face)
It's Kleigenes' case.
The tailor.
The failure.
You'll come to Assembly, you'll vote for war and
  strife –
What else should we expect, with your domestic
  life?

'What's he on about?' someone may ask.
'What's the problem? Why can't he explain?'
Well, I'll try. It's a difficult task,
Puts a serious strain on the brain,
But I'll try. We don't honour the brave.

We forget their achievements, their feats,
We devalue the service they gave,
Put them second to conmen and cheats.
It's exactly what happens with money.
Time *was*, coins were gold, bright and new,
Sleek and shiny, as yellow as honey –
And where are they now? Keeping *you?*
So, if someone's old, honest and fair
We reject him, and put all our trust
In jumped-up young orators, spouting hot air,
And surprised when their schemes all go bust.
Don't be fooled, fellow-citizens. Hail
The old stagers. Put *them* to the test –
At least then if we lose, if we fail,
We'll fail honestly, doing our best.

Dance. When it ends, enter AIAKOS *and* XANTHIAS.

AIAKOS.
He really is a gent, your boss.

XANTHIAS.
Huh! Boozing and schmoozing.
Of course he's a gent.

AIAKOS.
I mean, fancy him not mashing you to pulp
For pretending you were him and he was you.

XANTHIAS.
I'd like to have seen him try.

AIAKOS.
I love it, I love it.

XANTHIAS.
Pardon?

AIAKOS.
Talking big about the boss behind his back.
You really *are* a slave.

XANTHIAS.
What about
When he knocks you one, and you slope out muttering
And slam the door?

AIAKOS.
Can't beat it.

XANTHIAS.
And the keyhole game?

AIAKOS.
What keyhole game?

XANTHIAS.
Listening at keyholes
When he's gabbing to his friends –

AIAKOS.
My favourite.

XANTHIAS.
Then blabbing to the neighbours.

AIAKOS.
My other favourite.

XANTHIAS.
Give us your hand. Nah, give us a kiss.
We're soul-mates, mate. We've seen it all –

Noise from inside.

What was that? What the Hell was that?

AIAKOS.
Aeschylus. Euripides.

XANTHIAS.
Ah.

AIAKOS.
Rows, rows, rows.
Fighting and arguing. The Dead used to be so *quiet.*

XANTHIAS.
What's it about?

AIAKOS.
The thrones. The banqueting thrones,
Up beside His Nibs.

XANTHIAS.
I don't get it.

AIAKOS.
Look: the best artist, best singer, best playwright,
They each have a throne beside His Majesty
Whenever there's a party.

XANTHIAS.
Oh.

AIAKOS.
And if someone classier turns up,
They have to give up their throne to *him*.

XANTHIAS.
So what's making Aeschylus so cross?

AIAKOS.
He's had the Throne of Tragedy for years.
Because he's the best. No arguing.

XANTHIAS.
Till now, you mean?

AIAKOS.
Euripides, exactly.
As soon as he arrived, he started showing off.
They're a rough lot down here – muggers,
  murderers –
And when he started with his metaphors
And his hypotheses and his stichomythia
They lapped it up. Next thing, they vote
That he's the greatest, and he nabs the throne.
Aeschylus' throne.

XANTHIAS.
So kick him off.

AIAKOS.
We tried that.
The crowd turned nasty, demanded a proper trial,
To test who was best. Insisted on fair play.

XANTHIAS.
Those murderers and muggers?

AIAKOS.
It's Hell in there.

XANTHIAS.
But what about Aeschylus? Hasn't *he* got friends?

AIAKOS.
Like, people of taste? Like this lot here?

He gestures at the audience.

XANTHIAS.
So what can Plouton do?

AIAKOS.
His Nibs? He's organised a fight.
A word-fight, to sort it out.

XANTHIAS.
Just a minute.
Sophocles. Didn't *he* claim the throne as well?

AIAKOS.
As soon as he arrived, he shook his hand –
That's Aeschylus' hand – and gave him a great big kiss.
So Aeschylus budged up, made room on the throne.
But Sophocles said no. Well, not in his own voice:
He got that actor Kleidemides to read his part.
He'll act as first reserve, he says. (That's Sophocles.)
If Aeschylus wins, that's fine with him.
But if Euripides comes top, he'll challenge him
And start the whole thing off again.

XANTHIAS.
Proper little madhouse.

AIAKOS.
Wait till you see the scales.

XANTHIAS.
What scales?

AIAKOS.
For weighing the lines. False quantities.
And there's plumblines and set-squares and wedges

XANTHIAS.
It's a building site.

AIAKOS.
For poetry: that's right – and yardsticks and endstops.
Euripides insists it's all done proper,
Tragedy by tragedy, line by line, word by word.

XANTHIAS.
And Aeschylus is *taking* this?

AIAKOS.
A bull sits on my tongue, as the proverb says –
You know what he's like.

XANTHIAS.
Who's going to judge?

AIAKOS.
That was the problem.
Brains are in short supply down here.
We suggested Athenians, but Aeschylus said no.

XANTHIAS.
All those muggers and murderers? I'm not surprised.

AIAKOS.
And the rest are no better: wouldn't recognise
A poet if they fell over one in the street.
So when your boss turned up –

XANTHIAS.
The god of tragedy.

AIAKOS.
He ought to know what's what.

Fanfare from inside.

It's starting. We'd better go inside.
When the bosses get busy, stay out of their way.

He and XANTHIAS *go in. Fanfare. During the chorus which follows,* ATTENDANTS *bring out thrones.* PLOUTON *and* DIONYSOS *take their places.*

CHORUS.
Rumble of thunder. Word-warrior now
Rolls his eyes, knits his big, bushy brow,
Pawing, snorting for battle. His enemy, too.
Subtle arguments, polished and new,
Sharp as scalpels, to slice him in two.

Solemn sentiments, lofty and loud;
Massive adjectives, prancing and proud.
And the slippery, slithery sound
Of a word-wrestler wriggling around,
Twisting, turning and changing his ground.

With his word–mane contemptuously tossed
And his metaphors rough-hewn, embossed,
Hear the lord of high rhetoric roar,
Hear him rack up and stack up the score
As he grumbles and rumbles for more.

On the other side, shivers and spills,
Tongue-entanglements, mouth-mugging, thrills,
As he darts in and ducks down and dips
With a twirl and a twist of the hips
And a feather-light flick of the lips.

Enter EURIPIDES *and* AESCHYLUS.

EURIPIDES.
Oh, no. It's mine and I mean to have it.
Better poet – you, me? No contest.

DIONYSOS.
Well, Aeschylus? No comment? You did hear that?

EURIPIDES.
He heard. He's just like one of his own tragedies:
The silences are the best bits.

DIONYSOS.
That's not very nice.

EURIPIDES.
You don't know him like I do.
How can I describe him? Over-elaborate?
Torrents of verbiage? Mount-Etna-mouth?
Ask what *restraint* means, he'd have a fit.

AESCHYLUS.
Restraint? What do you know about restraint,
You . . . grocer's boy? What about the beggars you favour –
The stench, the filthy clothes, the bugs?
Don't talk to *me* about restraint.

DIONYSOS.
Hang on.
You'll have a fit if you don't hang on.

AESCHYLUS.
Hang on?
Not till I've shown this rag-and-bone man
Just what I really think of him.

DIONYSOS.
Someone bring a sou'wester.
There's going to be *such* a storm.

AESCHYLUS.
Do *I* write choruses like Cretan belly-dances?
Am *I* obsessed with incest?

DIONYSOS.
Hold your horses. Wind-lord, wait.
Stand here, Euripides, out of range.

It's a tornado, a forest fire, a wordwind.
Mind a flying phrase doesn't topple your *Telephos*.
It's getting rough. Down, Aeschylus.
We agreed on a contest, line by line.
Not blaring and flaring,
Not puffing and panting and ranting.

EURIPIDES.
Line by line? No problem *there*.
I'm quite prepared, and so are my tragedies –
Peleus, *Meleager*, and especially *Telephos:*
Lined up, ready for inspection.

DIONYSOS.
Aeschylus?

AESCHYLUS.
It's hardly an equal contest.

DIONYSOS.
What d'you mean?

AESCHYLUS.
I mean that when I died, my works lived on.
I haven't got them by me. His died with him –
You heard him: 'lined up, ready for inspection'.
Still, if we must, we must.

DIONYSOS.
Good. Bring incense, bring holy fire.
I'll have a little pray before we start.
For critical acumen, a *rigorous* approach.

(*to the* CHORUS)

And while I'm at it, *you* can sing a hymn.

CHORUS.
Muses, daughters of Zeus on high,
When it's tournament time,
When word-warriors gather and glower,
You check their equipment –
All metaphors mustered?

All adjectives polished?
All similies sharp?
They're ready. Sir Tingle-tongue,
Lord Mighty-mouth. It's art.
Are you ready? They're dying to start.

DIONYSOS.
That's better. Why don't you two pray as well?

AESCHYLUS.
Oh Mighty Mater, nurturer,
Thou seest thine acolyte. Vouchsafe.

DIONYSOS (*to* EURIPIDES).
Your turn. Here. Take the pot.

EURIPIDES.
I'd rather not.
One has powers of one's own, if you really must know.

DIONYSOS.
You're joking. Home-made gods?

EURIPIDES.
You could call them that.

DIONYSOS.
Well, pray to them, then. Powers of one's own!

EURIPIDES.
Space, fill one's brain.
Twist, take one's tongue.
It's wriggle-out-of-trouble time.

CHORUS.
How exciting! To watch while such wits
Stand displaying their glamour, their glitz!
Their razzle,
Their dazzle,
Inspires us and thrills us to bits.

This one's slippery, nifty and quick,
First off quotes that are slinky and slick

For the other
To smother
With word-blankets, woolly and thick.

DIONYSOS.
You start. And make it original.
No 'On the one hand ... on the other hand'.

EURIPIDES.
I'll come to my own work in a minute. First
I'll show how this word-monger cheats his audiences.
(They were stupid enough before. But *then*,
All they knew was Phrynichos.)
The play begins. And who's that onstage?
Hooded and wrapped, can't see the face.
Is it Niobe? Achilles? Who knows? All they do
Is sit like dummies, not uttering a word.

DIONYSOS.
I noticed that.

EURIPIDES.
The Chorus starts spouting:
Torrents, waterfalls. Achilles: nothing.

DIONYSOS.
It worked for *me*. The trouble with modern plays
Is, *everyone* speaks *all* the time.

AESCHYLUS.
It worked for you!

DIONYSOS.
What d'you mean?

EURIPIDES.
Cheap trick. Audience on edge of seats –
What's Niobe going to say? Play goes on,
And on, and on, and ... nothing.

DIONYSOS.
It *is* a cheap trick.

(*to* AESCHYLUS)

What are you *doing?*

EURIPIDES.
He's wriggling. Can't take the strain.
Then, halfway through, just when everyone's relaxed,
She whips the cloak off her head and bellows
A great long speech with eyebrows and whiskers on,
Like the Demon Queen in a pantomine.
Who understands a word?

AESCHYLUS.
Now *look* . . .

DIONYSOS.
Be quiet.

EURIPIDES.
From beginning to end, it's gibberish.

DIONYSOS (*to* AESCHYLUS).
Stop grinding your teeth.

EURIPIDES.
Scamanders, sepulchres, bronze-clad vulture-eagles,
Words like the wall of a fortress,
Impossible to batter your way into.

DIONYSOS.
He has got a point.
I spent several sleepless nights myself,
Wondering what on Earth a tawny horse-cock is.

AESCHYLUS.
It's a figurehead on ships, you fool.

DIONYSOS.
Thank God for that. I thought it meant Eryxis.

EURIPIDES.
A horse-cock! We write tragedies about horse-cocks now?

AESCHYLUS.
All right, what are *your* tragedies about?

EURIPIDES.
Not horse-cocks or goat-leopards. I leave those to you.
I don't get *my* inspiration from a Persian carpet.
When you handed me Tragedy, she was in a bad, bad way:
Bloated with adverbs, plumped-up with particles,
So stuffed with syllables she could hardly move.
I put her on a diet right away. Pure logic,
A pinch of prosody, carefully-selected metaphors,
Non-fattening similes, a touch of this, a touch of that –

AESCHYLUS.
– and more than a touch of Kephisophon.

EURIPIDES.
I didn't start in the middle, or babble on.
The first person onstage told the audience
Exactly what to expect.

AESCHYLUS.
They knew before they came.

EURIPIDES.
In *my* plays, no one stands about doing nothing.
Everyone gets a say: wife, daughter-in-law,
Slaves, even old Granny in the corner.

AESCHYLUS.
Ridiculous.

EURIPIDES.
Democracy in action.

DIONYSOS.
Oh, don't let's start on politics.

EURIPIDES.
I taught *them* –

He gestures at the audience.

– how to argue.

AESCHYLUS.
You should have been mashed to mincemeat.

EURIPIDES.
I taught them to *use* language,
Arrange words *neatly:*
Careful examination, logical argument,
Look at everything twice, no stone unturned –

AESCHYLUS.
He's *proud* of it!

EURIPIDES.
I kept to ordinary matters in my plays,
Things everyone knows, we all understand.
My audience could follow every word.
I didn't baffle them with Kyknoses and Memnons,
All horsebrasses and hippomanic crests.
You want to know what we're like? Look at our admirers.
His are Phormisios, Megainetos and Maniac,
By-the-lord-Harry merchants, Tear-em-limb-from-limb;
Mine are lean and spry: Theramenes, Kleitophon –

DIONYSOS.
Theramenes? Lean and spry?
I think you mean Mean and sly.
Rolls into trouble,
Quick change of policy,
Quick turn of the coat,
And rolls right out again.

EURIPIDES.
Question everything I taught them.
First principle in drama,
First rule in life:
Don't let anything go by.
'Why's that?
What's going on?

How? When?
Where did that come from?'
Beg pardon?
Whose idea was that?

DIONYSOS.
I know exactly what you mean.
They're all at it now.
Come home, call the slaves,
Start shouting and yelling.
'Who moved that jug?
Who scoffed that sardine?
How? When?'
Once all they did was sit
On a stool
Like *this*, and drool.

CHORUS.
Now it's your turn. He's stated his case.
Don't keep groaning. Don't make such a face.
No, don't roar,
Don't be sore,
Or you'll blow it and forfeit the race.

Play it cool. Play it safe. Play it smart.
Take your time. Take your place at the start.
When we shout
'Let him out' –
Then get *in* there and take him apart!

DIONYSOS.
Word-lord, it's time. Mighty architect, answer.
White-water arguments. Open the floodgates.

AESCHYLUS.
Rather a comedown. Not what I'm used to.
Bandying arguments. Still, if I have to . . .
Can't have him crowing and claiming I'm
  speechless.
Answer me this, then: what makes a great
  playwright?

EURIPIDES.
Clever ideas, and a clear moral viewpoint.
Open the audience's eyes and alert them –

AESCHYLUS.
What if you don't? If you drag them behind you,
Down to the gutter – ?

DIONYSOS.
Simple: you've had it.

AESCHYLUS.
Right then. Let's start with the audience I left him.
Noble, uplifted, not market-place gossips,
Public-bar chatterers. Mine dreamed of breastplates,
Proud waving helmet-plumes, gauntlets, greaves, corselets –

DIONYSOS.
Steady! We're drowning in armour already.

EURIPIDES.
That made them better, eh? How did you do it?

DIONYSOS.
Words of one syllable, Aeschylus. *Quietly*.

AESCHYLUS.
War-plays. I gave them my war-plays.

DIONYSOS.
Please name one.

AESCHYLUS.
Well, there was *Seven*.

DIONYSOS.
What seven?

AESCHYLUS.
Against Thebes. Against *Thebes*.
That got them going.

DIONYSOS.
Yes, especially in Thebes.
Started them training. Good tactics it wasn't.

AESCHYLUS.
The message was simple.
Even in Athens, you could have learned *something*.
What about *Persians*, then? Brimful of battle,
Stick-it-and-win-through. A masterpiece, *Persians*.

DIONYSOS.
AND what a ghost-scene! The Chorus all stand there,
Clapping their hands, going 'EE-a-oo-OH-ee!'

AESCHYLUS.
Teaching, instruction ... the job of the poet.
That's what we've always done. Orpheus, remember?
'Worship the gods and respect Mother Nature'.
Hesiod: farming, the seasons. Mousaios:
Oracles, cures. Then, of course, there was Homer.
Crammed with instruction: on strategy, tactics –

DIONYSOS.
Yes, and I wish Pantakles had been listening.
There he was, yesterday, on the parade-ground,
Trying to march while he fastened his helmet ...

AESCHYLUS.
Plenty of *good* soldiers learned: look at Lamachos.
Anyway, *my* plays are stuffed full of Homer.
Look at my characters: Teuker, Patroklos,
Wait-for-the-signal-then-leap-into-battle men:
Great-hearted heroes the audience could learn from.
None of your Phaidras, Medeas –
I never bothered with love-maddened females.

EURIPIDES.
You never bothered with females.

AESCHYLUS.
Of course not.
You were the expert on love-maddened females.

DIONYSOS.
Didn't you have some yourself? Quite a houseful?
Models for every emotion you showed us?

EURIPIDES.
Stories. What harm did my Phaidra, Medea do – ?

AESCHYLUS.
Plenty. They made every woman of spirit,
Woman of decency, rush and take poison.

EURIPIDES.
Phaidra, Medea – I didn't invent them.

AESCHYLUS.
No, but you put them onstage. Didn't hide them.
Children have teachers to teach them, and grown-ups
Have playwrights. To set good examples.

EURIPIDES.
Examples?
Up, up, where it spurts from highest peaks
On Caucasus, ceiling of the world. Climb here,
Rock-pinnacles beside the stars, then down –
That's an example? Do *you* understand it?

AESCHYLUS.
Towering sentiments, towering speeches.
Gods don't use language like ordinary mortals –
And they should dress better. *I* gave them costumes;
You gave them – why am I wasting my breath here?

EURIPIDES.
What?

AESCHYLUS.
Every person of stature or standing
You put in plays, comes out ragged and tatty –
Sobbing for sympathy, playing for pathos.

EURIPIDES.
So? What's the problem?

AESCHYLUS.
Is *that* an example?
Rich people dress up in rags. 'Cut my taxes,
Cold, I'm so cold, look I'm starving, I'm shaking' –

DIONYSOS.
Not underneath. Woolly underwear. Starving?
Posh little restaurant – 'Case won, let's party.'

AESCHYLUS.
Everyone's at it. You've taught them to quibble.
No one works out; they've abandoned their training;
Teenagers tongue-wrestle; sailors on warships
Answer back, question their officers, argue.
Once it was 'Hard tack, sir, Aye-aye, sir, Now, sir' –

DIONYSOS.
Now it's all fiddling and faddling and farting:
'Whoops, we're adrift, dearie, pass us your hankie' –

AESCHYLUS.
Yes, and there's more
Here on shore.
'Do you want a good time?
Over here in the shrine.'
All those unmarried mothers,
Sisters sleeping with brothers,
Crying 'Life isn't life any more'.
No one's safe in the streets:
It's all lawyers and cheats,
Politicians and loungers,
Tax-dodgers and scroungers,
All 'I'm all right, Jack',
Feeble, flabby and slack –

DIONYSOS.
The other day
I was watching that marathon, over the way,

And there, right by the start
Was a slight little,
White little
Pug of a man,
A slug of a man.
He was puffing and blowing,
He couldn't get going.
All the others were lapping him.
People kept slapping him,
Charging him,
Barging him –
Till he made up his mind
And came up from behind
With a stonking great, zonking great fart.

CHORUS.
How long can this last?
It's frantic, it's fast.
The Olympian strains
Like a colt at the reins
And the Brainbox goes bounding right past.

Play dirty, play rough.
Try some really hot stuff.
Make him sweat, make him melt.
Hit him! Pound, paste and pelt.
Below the belt!

This crowd here tonight
Is remarkably bright.
They'll follow you,
Swallow you,
Take every subtlety, feast on the fight.

They're incredibly sharp.
They won't shuffle or carp.
So don't hold yourselves back.
Get on track
With a big-brain attack.

EURIPIDES.
It's time for Round Two. Opening Speeches.
And even there, our learned friend falls down.
He's obscure and hard to follow.

DIONYSOS.
What Opening Speeches?

EURIPIDES.
Plenty.
Let's start with *Libation-Bearers.*

DIONYSOS.
Shh! Shh! *Libation-Bearers.* Aeschylus . . . ?

AESCHYLUS.
Lord Hermes, who, with ever-watchful eye
Hast ever guarded this, my father's realm,
Protect me now, and give me thy support.
I have come back, returning home at last.

DIONYSOS.
What's wrong with that?

EURIPIDES.
A dozen things.

DIONYSOS.
But he's only said four lines.

EURIPIDES.
With twenty mistakes in each of them.

DIONYSOS.
Quiet, Aeschylus! That's eighty mistakes already.

AESCHYLUS.
You want *me* to be quiet for *him?*

DIONYSOS.
It *is* his turn.

EURIPIDES.
Right from the start, he puts his foot in it.

AESCHYLUS.
Rubbish.

DIONYSOS.
I did try to warn you.

AESCHYLUS.
What foot in it? Prove it!

EURIPIDES.
Give me the lines again.

AESCHYLUS.
Lord Hermes, who, with ever-watchful eye
Hast ever guarded this, my father's realm . . .

EURIPIDES.
Orestes says this – do remind me –
At the tomb of his dead father?

AESCHYLUS.
Of course he does.

EURIPIDES.
Yes. So let's get this right.
The father comes home from the Trojan War.
His wife (who's been planning the deed for years)
Bops his napper with a chopper – and *that's*
How Lord Hermes does his guarding?
That's his ever-watchful eye?

AESCHYLUS.
I said he guards
The *realm* with ever-watchful eye. *Realm*, not *helm*.

EURIPIDES.
Oh, right. But it's his father's realm –

DIONYSOS.
– which makes Orestes a grave-robber.

AESCHYLUS.
Stay out of this.

DIONYSOS.
Sorry. Do go on.

AESCHYLUS.
Protect me now, and give me thy support.
I have come back, returning home at last.

EURIPIDES.
Brilliant, Aeschylus. The same thing twice.

DIONYSOS.
Thing twice?

EURIPIDES.
Thing twice.
I have come back, returning home at last.
'Come back', 'return' – the same thing twice.

DIONYSOS.
You're right! It's like saying to a neighbour,
'Lend me a pie-dish, or perhaps a dish for pie.'

AESCHYLUS.
You know nothing about it. He's splitting hairs.
It's brilliantly expressed.

EURIPIDES.
Oh, how?
Please show me what I'm missing.

AESCHYLUS.
Orestes has been away.
So he 'comes back'. We all do that.
But he's also been in exile, so he 'returns'.

DIONYSOS.
That's brilliant! You can't knock holes in that.

EURIPIDES.
Of course I can. Orestes came on the quiet.
Afraid of arrest. That's not 'returning'.

DIONYSOS.
Dazzling! I wish I understood.

EURIPIDES.
We'll take the next two lines.

DIONYSOS (*to* AESCHYLUS).
We'll take the next two lines.

AESCHYLUS.
On this sad grave I summon thee, grim ghost
Of my dead father. Hear me! Hearken now!

EURIPIDES.
There he goes again. 'Hear me!' 'Hearken!'
The same thing twice.

DIONYSOS.
He's talking to a corpse, you fool.
Twice, three times – he still won't get through.

AESCHYLUS.
What about you, anyway? How do you begin?

EURIPIDES.
I'll show you. And if I say anything twice,
If you find one syllable more, or less,
Spit in my eye.

DIONYSOS.
Let's hear some, then.

EURIPIDES.
A happy man was Oedipus at first.

AESCHYLUS.
He wasn't. Condemned by the gods from birth,
To murder his father and marry his mother.
Before he was even born. A happy man, at first!

EURIPIDES.
As things turned out, most miserable.

AESCHYLUS.
There you go again. 'As things turned out'.
He was miserable from start to finish.
Exposed at birth on a piece of pot,
In the cold, cold snow, in case he killed his Daddy;

Limping to Korinth on those poor swollen feet;
Marrying a woman old enough to be his Mummy,
Who actually *was* his Mummy; putting out his eyes –

DIONYSOS.
At least he never sailed with Erasinides.

EURIPIDES.
I say my opening lines are brilliant.

AESCHYLUS.
And I say they're rubbish. They're all the same.
You write them to a formula. I'll prove it, too.
I'll wreck the lot with a little saucebox.

EURIPIDES.
A saucebox?

AESCHYLUS.
A saucebox. Your openings are all the same.
Any old words do nicely: a woolly vest,
A lump of coal, a saucebox. I'll show you.

EURIPIDES.
Oh, no you won't.

AESCHYLUS.
Oh, yes I will.

DIONYSOS.
Get *on!*

EURIPIDES.
Aigyptos, as the well-known story tells,
With fifty daughters in a big, broad boat,
Sailing to Argos –

AESCHYLUS.
Lost his little saucebox.

EURIPIDES.
He didn't. This isn't fair.

DIONYSOS.
I see what he means, though. Try again.

EURIPIDES.
Great Dionysos, who in fawn-skins dressed,
Bears high the pine-torch in his holy hand,
Leading our revels –

AESCHYLUS.
Lost his little saucebox.

DIONYSOS.
Another saucebox. It's everywhere.

EURIPIDES.
Oh no. There's no sauce here, for starters.
Bewail the unhappy lot of mortals. See:
Yon prince, high-born and proud, lost all his wealth;
Yon starving beggar –

AESCHYLUS.
Lost his little saucebox.

DIONYSOS.
Euripides.

EURIPIDES.
Yes?

DIONYSOS.
Best mop up now. It's getting everywhere.

EURIPIDES.
Rubbish. I'll try another.

DIONYSOS.
All right, but beware of the sauce.

EURIPIDES.
One day Agenor's son, great Kadmos, while
Leaving the city –

AESCHYLUS.
Lost his little saucebox.

DIONYSOS.
Give up.

EURIPIDES.
Give up?

DIONYSOS.
Or take out shares in a sauce factory.
You're drowning in it.

EURIPIDES.
I've thousands more, all sauce-proof.
Once Pelops, son of Tantalos, while on
His way to Pisa –

AESCHYLUS.
Lost his little saucebox.

DIONYSOS.
Not Pelops too. For God's sake give it back.
Or buy him another one. They only cost one drach.

EURIPIDES.
I haven't finished. I said I'd thousands more.
Once great king Oineus –

AESCHYLUS.
Lost his little saucebox.

EURIPIDES.
You might at least let me finish the line.
Once great king Oineus, offering sacrifice
To the gods in Heaven –

AESCHYLUS.
Lost his little saucebox.

DIONYSOS.
In the middle of a sacrifice? Awkward.
Who snaffled it?

EURIPIDES.
Zeus, lord of Heaven, as the story goes –

DIONYSOS.
I know what's coming. 'Lost his little saucebox'.
It's like a stye on the eye, that saucebox.
Oh, change the subject. Time for a chorus.

EURIPIDES.
A chorus? This is where I really score.
He writes terrible choruses, and I can prove it.

He hurries out.

CHORUS.
What happens next?
What will he do?
I'm perplexed.
Aren't you?
We're talking genius here,
Not trash –
Has Euripides no fear?
How rash,
How brash,
To have a go at *him*,
To throw at *him*
Whatever comes to hand.
It should be banned.

Enter EURIPIDES *with* MUSICIANS.

EURIPIDES.
Terrible choruses. I'll give you a sample.
I'll lump them all together.

DIONYSOS.
I'll count them with these pebbles.

Someone plays a flute introduction.

EURIPIDES.
O clamorous clan-chief, the warfare is woeful –
Drub, drub the doom-drum, rush to the rescue.
We lake-lovers clamour for Hermes our helpmeet –
Drub, drub the doom-drum, rush to the rescue.

DIONYSOS (*shouting above the noise*).
Two thumps, Aeschylus.

EURIPIDES.
Bloodied, embattled, we wail for our warlord –
Drub, drub the doom-drum, rush to the rescue.

DIONYSOS.
Three!

EURIPIDES.
Hark, it's a heaven-sound! Choir-voices chanting –
Drub, drub the doom-drum, rush to the rescue.
With a bang, with a boom, with a bang-bang, boom-boom bang –
Drub, drub the doom-drum, rush to the rescue.

Silence.

DIONYSOS.
Zeus, what a pounding. I'm black and blue all over.
I'd love a hot bath – not to mention earmuffs.

EURIPIDES.
Hang on. There's more. With *this*, this time.
Lyre-work.

DIONYSOS.
So long as it's not that drum.

EURIPIDES.
A-winging through the welkin,
DaDUNG, DaDUNG, daDUNG,
Bird dog dogs bird birds dog,
DaDUNG, DaDUNG, daDUNG,
Spear-handed, handy-speared,
DaDUNG, DaDUNG, daDUNG,
Sky-chargers, galloping, galloping,
DaDUNG, DaDUNG, daDUNG,
To succour Ajax,
DaDUNG, DaDUNG, daDUNG.

DIONYSOS.
Oh, Aeschylus. Where did you pick that up?
DaDUNG, DaDUNG? A donkey ride?

AESCHYLUS.
Wherever I 'picked it up', I made good use of it.
One wanders the garden of the Muses. One plucks at will.
Along a slightly different path from Phrynichos.
And not like *him*. Where does he go for inspiration?
The pub, the disco, the strip-club ... I'll show you.
Someone give me a lyre. No, what am I talking about?
Who needs a lyre? Where's that girl with the castanets?
Here, puss, here, puss. Puss-puss-puss.
Ladies and gentlemen: the Muse of Euripides.

Enter EURIPIDES' MUSE.

DIONYSOS.
Thank god she didn't bring her friends.

EURIPIDES' MUSE *dances as* AESCHYLUS *sings.*

AESCHYLUS.
Kingfishers, diving, arriving
At the salt sea spray at the water's edge,
Chattering, spattering
Their wings with watery wetness,
Then flying high where spiders spin
Spi-i-i-i-i-i-i-in
Webs woven under roof-rafters,
Up there on the ceiling,
While the dolphin sings the song
Sailors smile at,
Leaping in the wavelets at the sharp ship's bows.
O grapes! O vine-leaves clustering
Round the thick, strong stem,
Unwearying woe-remover
O! O! O! Come to me!

(*to* DIONYSOS)

You noticed that bit at the bottom?

DIONYSOS (*gazing at* EURIPIDES' MUSE).
Oh yes.

AESCHYLUS.
Didn't fit the metre.

DIONYSOS.
Eh? Oh.

AESCHYLUS.
Typical. All his choruses are the same.
And this ... this bump-and-grind-merchant
Criticises me?
It's not just the choruses.
His solo songs are just the same.
I mean, for example:

A gleamy gloom of Night,
Dream-shapes, dream-messengers
You send up, send up
From Down Below, down, up,
Ghost-messengers,
Billowing, billowing,
Glaring eyes,
Blood, blood in glaring eyes
And great long talons.
Light me, light me a lamp,
Fetch water in a pot,
A droplet in a potlet,
From limpid streamlets fetch
And warm it well, that I may wash
The nasty dream away.
God! O God
Of the swelling, heaving sea,
Look here. I say, look here,
Slaves of the house, look here,
Look what naughty Glyke's done:
Grabbed hold of cock
And scarpered.
To the hills, the hills.
Mania, you see to that.

Ah me, me miserable!
I sat there spinning,
Spi-i-i-i-inning,
Busy fingers flicking the flax,
Making little balls, balls,
To creep out of the house in the dawn-light
And sell in that stall in the market.
And now he's gone, gone,
On fluttery, feathery winglets
My cock has flown.
Oh woe! Oh no!
Beat breast, breast beat,
Tears fall, fall tears.
Cretans, children of Ida,
Snatch quivers, bows,
Surround the house.
Artemis, dear, Diktynna's darling daughter,
Haste to the hunt,
Send doggies padding here,
Padding there, padding everywhere.
Hekate, come,
Zeus' thunder-torches blazing in your hand,
Light me to Glyke's house
And let's have a really good look-see.

DIONYSOS.
No more singing. Please.

AESCHYLUS.
I quite agree.
There's only one real way to settle this.
We'll weigh the lines. It's time for the scales.

DIONYSOS.
The scales! The scales!
We'll weigh those tragedies like lumps of cheese.

The scales are set up.

CHORUS.
It's amazing. It's hard to believe

What these supermen have up their sleeve.
Each one devises
A million surprises
For the other one soon to receive.

It's a good job we're here, and can view
It ourselves. For if any of you
Had outlined it,
Defined it,
We'd never have thought it was true.

DIONYSOS.
Right. Stand by your weighing pans.

AESCHYLUS.
There.

EURIPIDES.
There.

DIONYSOS.
Take hold and say a line each.
And don't let go till I say 'Cuckoo'. Right?

AESCHYLUS.
Right.

EURIPIDES.
Right.

DIONYSOS.
Ready, steady, speak.

EURIPIDES.
O why did it have to sail, the good ship Argo?

AESCHYLUS.
O river Spercheios, where cattle drink ...

DIONYSOS.
Cuckoo. Let go. Ah. His is lower.

EURIPIDES.
Why?

DIONYSOS.
He put in a river, like a wool-merchant
Wetting his fleeces to make them heavier.
You put in a fast, light sailing-ship.

EURIPIDES.
I get the idea now. Let's try again.

DIONYSOS.
Take hold of the pans, then. Right?

AESCHYLUS.
Right.

EURIPIDES.
Right.

DIONYSOS.
Ready, steady, speak.

EURIPIDES.
Persuasion builds her temples in words alone ...

AESCHYLUS.
Alone of the gods, grim Death accepts no gifts ...

DIONYSOS.
Cuckoo. Let go. His is lower again.
He threw in Death, the heaviest blow of all.

EURIPIDES.
You mean Persuasion carries no weight at all?

DIONYSOS.
Of course she doesn't. What is she? Words.
Try to remember some really *massive* sentiment,
Some really *solid* line, *immense* and *packed*.

EURIPIDES.
There are so many ...

DIONYSOS.
I know.
Achilles, threw two sixes and a four ...
No dice? Find something else: it's your only chance.

EURIPIDES.
The hero hefted his bulbous, bronze-bound club ...

AESCHYLUS.
Chariot on chariot, corpse on broken corpse ...

DIONYSOS.
Cuckoo. He's done it again.

EURIPIDES.
How?

DIONYSOS.
Two chariots, two corpses.
You'd need a crane to lift them.

AESCHYLUS.
Look, forget lines. So far as I'm concerned,
He can sit in the scales himself, with his wife,
His kids, his manuscripts, Kephisophon –
With two well-chosen words, I'll outweigh the lot.

DIONYSOS (*to* PLOUTON).
I don't know what to do. I like them both.
I want to be friends with both. How can I judge?
One's so clever ... one's so *satisfying*.

PLOUTON.
You mean you can't fulfil your mission?

DIONYSOS.
Pardon?

PLOUTON.
You came to choose a poet and a poet you must
choose.
One stays, one goes. Your mission must succeed.

DIONYSOS.
Thanks very much. Look, luvvies, it's like this:
I came to fetch a playwright, take him back.

EURIPIDES.
What for?

DIONYSOS.
To sort the city out.
To write some sensible plays and sort the city out.
Look, one more contest. Give some good advice –
Whoever gives the best, goes back with me.
All right? First problem: Alkibiades.
What's your opinion? They really need to know.

EURIPIDES.
What's *their* opinion?

DIONYSOS.
That's the problem: they can't decide.
One minute they want him out. The next they don't.
The next ... you know the sort of thing. So, speak.

EURIPIDES.
How can we trust a citizen who's slow
To help his city, quick to help himself?

DIONYSOS.
Oh, very good. Now, Aeschylus.

AESCHYLUS.
It's hardly sensible to keep a lion as pet.
But if you do, remember: lions bite.

DIONYSOS.
Well, that didn't help much. Brilliant, bright ...
I still can't choose. We'd better try again.
Some specific advice, perhaps. To end the war.

EURIPIDES.
Kleokritos could use Kinesias as wings.
The pair of them could fly across the sea –

DIONYSOS.
I'm getting it. Fly across the sea ... Go on.

EURIPIDES.
They'd be carrying vinegar, in flasks.

Then, when they reached the enemy,
Aerial bombardment.

Baffled silence all round.

Or then, again ...

DIONYSOS.
Go on.

EURIPIDES.
What you trust, distrust, and start to trust
What you distrusted heretofore.

DIONYSOS.
Brilliant!
Pardon?

EURIPIDES.
Group A, Group B. A in, B out, big trouble.
So change. B in, A out. Could work.

DIONYSOS.
Amazing!
Did *you* think of that, or did Kephisophon?

EURIPIDES.
I did. Kephisophon thought of the vinegar-flasks.

DIONYSOS.
Right, Aeschylus.

AESCHYLUS.
A in, B out. Depends.
Who's in just now? The people's choice?
Good men and true?

DIONYSOS.
You're joking.

AESCHYLUS.
Bastards?

DIONYSOS.
Well –

AESCHYLUS.
The people's choice. They *do* need help. I'm stumped.

DIONYSOS.
Oh, don't be stumped, if you want to live again.

AESCHYLUS.
I'll see for myself, up there, and then I'll say.

DIONYSOS.
Oh, no. You have to give advice down here.

AESCHYLUS.
Make enemy land your own, your land their land.
Make taxes ships. Who sails on silver coins?

DIONYSOS.
Who sails on coins? D'you think he means lawyers?

PLUTO.
It's time. Decide.

DIONYSOS.
Ah. Right. Decide. I'll choose –
The one my instinct tells me, deep inside.

EURIPIDES.
Good. Ready when you are. You promised. Me.

DIONYSOS.
My tongue it was that promised, not my brain.
I'm taking Aeschylus.

EURIPIDES.
You bastard! *Why?*

DIONYSOS.
Because he's won. I say he's won. All right?

EURIPIDES.
You dare such a deed, and look me in the face?

DIONYSOS.
What d'you mean, such a deed? The audience agrees.

EURIPIDES.
O heart of stone! You'll leave me here to die?

DIONYSOS.
You die, to sleep, perchance ... Just a minute.
You're dead already.

Exit EURIPIDES.

PLOUTON.
Step inside, at once.

DIONYSOS.
What for?

PLOUTON.
One for the road. Before you go.

DIONYSOS.
Oh, thanks. 1480
How very kind. No, no, please. After *you.*

He and AESCHYLUS *follow* PLOUTON *inside.*

CHORUS.
Well, that's that, then. The contest is done,
And the Sensible Candidate won –
Took first place
In a race
That was over before it was run.

And it's hardly a moment too soon. 1491–99
We were rapidly reaching high noon.
On the page,
On the stage,
Every lamebrain and lunkhead and loon

Who assaulted our eyes and our ears
Had reduced us to fury and tears
With their vile
Want of style
And their lunatic lack of ideas.

The entire population will gain 1487
From a poet so sound and so sane.

He'll tend us,
Defend us;
We'll all bless that bulging great brain.

PLOUTON *and* AESCHYLUS *come out.*

PLOUTON.
Bye-bye, Aeschylus.
Save our city,
Educate the fools.
There are plenty to choose from.
Please deliver these presents –
Or should I say hints:
Kleophon can have *this*,
Nikomachos *this*
And the Income Tax *these*.
Tell them to hurry:
We want them down here.
If they're chicken, I'll come up there,
Hurry them, flurry them,
Snatch them and catch them
In person.

AESCHYLUS.
You got it.
And while I'm away
Please let Sophocles see to my throne,
Be my stand-in – well, sit-in –
As long as I'm gone.
As for that other one,
Niminy-piminy,
Dazzle-'em, Frazzle-'em –
What *is* the man's name? –
Don't let *him* ever sit in it,
Even if he doesn't want to.

PLOUTON.
Lift your torches,
Lift your voices,
Make a procession,
Sing in his honour.

The CHORUS *forms up round* AESCHYLUS.

CHORUS.
Spirits of darkness, grant us your blessing.
Lead us and guide us, home with our poet.
Let his majestic brain
Help us end war and pain.
Those who like fighting, don't keep them guessing.
'Swords into ploughshares'. 'Plant it and hoe it'.
Mottoes for happiness.
End of all strain and stress . . .

Exeunt.

ARISTOPHANES

Women in Power
(*Ekklesiazousai, 'Assemblywomen'*)

translated by Kenneth McLeish

Characters

PRAXAGORA
FIRST WOMAN
SECOND WOMAN
THIRD WOMAN
BLEPYROS
PHEIDOLOS
CHREMES
TOWN CRIERESS
PRETTY GIRL
EPIGENES
FIRST HAG
SECOND HAG
THIRD HAG
SLAVE (silent part)
CHORUS of WOMEN

A street in Athens. Night. Enter PRAXAGORA, *disguised as a man, and carrying a lamp which she places on a pedestal and addresses with reverence.*

PRAXAGORA.
O eye! Bright eye! O second Sun!
O triumph of the potter's art,
O lamp, O monster born of clay
Whose nostrils breathe the Sun's own fire,
Be our beacon, our messenger, today.
We trust no one else. Only to you
Do we bare ourselves; only you
Are allowed to watch the game we play:
Love games, sweet wrestling in the night.
You watch, and no one puts you out.
You know our secret places, singe
The thickets between our thighs; you come
Down to the cellar where the wine is stored,
A silent friend who never tells.
And now, you can share our secret plans
For this Assembly, where we, today –

Oh, it's too bad! Where are they? It'll soon
Be dawn. The Assembly starts at first light.
They said they'd be here. We ought to be ready,
In our places. 'Be prepared', as someone said.
What's happened to hold them up? Is it their beards?
Or was it too hard to steal their husband's clothes?
Ah . . . there's a light.
Who's coming? I'd better get out of the way.
It might be a *man* . . . and that would never do.

Enter some WOMEN, *dressed in men's clothes.*

FIRST WOMAN.
This way, chaps. Pick up your feet, come on.
The cock crowed, y'know, just as we started out.

PRAXAGORA.
Thank goodness you're here. I've been up all night.

I'll just see if my next-door neighbour's ready.
The tiniest tap ... we don't want her husband
To hear ...

She taps on a house-door. The SECOND WOMAN *comes out.*

SECOND WOMAN.
Shh! It's all right. I heard you.
I was just trying to get these shoes on ...
My husband ... you've no *idea* what it's like.
He's a fisherman – and when we get to bed
He just wants to row all night.
I just *couldn't* get his clothes until now.

FIRST WOMAN.
Oh, look: down the road. Here come the others.

Enter more WOMEN, *all dressed as men.*

SECOND WOMAN.
Oh, do be quick! Don't you remember
What Glyke said? The last one here
Was to pay for the cakes, and *all* the drinks ...

FIRST WOMAN.
Who's that, trying to run in those boots?
Oh, it's Smikythion's wife.

SECOND WOMAN.
Must be. He always did like a loose fit.

FIRST WOMAN.
Isn't that the innkeeper's wife?
Look: the one with the enormous torch.

SECOND WOMAN.
They're all coming. Every woman in Athens ...

THIRD WOMAN (*as she enters*).
Praxagora, darling! You've simply no *idea*
How hard it was to slip away. My husband
Was at it the whole night long. Red in the face.
He *always* burps when he eats sardines.

PRAXAGORA.
I think we're all here. Gather round. Sit down.
Now, have you all done what we arranged to do?

FIRST WOMAN.
Oh yes, I haven't shaved under my arms
For *weeks*, just like we said. It's like a *wood*
Under there. And every day, when my husband
Goes out to work, I oil myself all over
And sit in the sun, to get a manly tan.

SECOND WOMAN.
Me too. I threw my razor out at once.
You should *see* the undergrowth. I don't
Look like a woman down there at all.

PRAXAGORA.
Have you all got your beards, as we agreed?

FIRST WOMAN.
Heavens, yes. What about this one, then?

SECOND WOMAN.
What about this one? Isn't he lovely?

PRAXAGORA.
What about the others?

FIRST WOMAN.
Yes, they're nodding. They've got theirs.

PRAXAGORA.
I can see you've everything else you need.
Men's clothes, and proper cloaks, and walking sticks.

FIRST WOMAN.
I got this from my husband when he was still asleep.

SECOND WOMAN.
Is *that* your husband's? How *does* he get it up?

FIRST WOMAN.
Practice. He's been doing it for years. You know him:
Picks up anything that's not tied down.

PRAXAGORA.
Ladies ... ladies ... we've got to make our plans
Now, before the stars go in. The Assembly
Begins at dawn: we've got to be ready.

FIRST WOMAN.
We'll have to get the places at the front,
On the rows just before the speaker's stand.

THIRD WOMAN.
I've brought *this*. I don't care *how* boring it is.

PRAXAGORA.
How *boring* ... ?

THIRD WOMAN.
Yes, darling. The men, you know. Arguing.
I can work away as I listen. I mean,
My little ones ... they haven't a *stitch* to wear.

PRAXAGORA.
Oh, yes. Oh, very nice. One look at you,
They'll know you're a man, all right. Put it away!
Now then, make sure your cloaks are properly on.
It would be dreadful if we got there late,
When the whole place was full, and had to climb
Over the benches to find a seat. Suppose
One of us tripped, and her cloak slipped,
And everyone saw ... ? If we get there first
We can sit down and arrange ourselves in peace.
Once you're comfortable, fasten on your beards.
If we're wearing beards, they're sure to think we're
men.

SECOND WOMAN.
She's right. Remember that pansy Agyrrios?
He grew a beard, everyone took him for a man,
And he went all the way in politics.

PRAXAGORA.
Exactly.
And that's what *we're* going to do today.
We're going to stand up, take over the state,

And run it like it's never been run before.
Women in power! We can't do worse than men.

FIRST WOMAN.
There's just one problem. Women in power ...
We've no experience.

PRAXAGORA.
Of course we have.
Just look at the young *men* in power today.
How d'you think *they* learned to argue, and talk
Till they had it the way they wanted it?
By lying down and taking it in bed, of course.
We're naturally equipped.

FIRST WOMAN.
Yes, but that's not ... *public* experience.

PRAXAGORA.
Well, isn't that exactly why we're here?
To practise what we're going to say, before
The Assembly starts? Quick, on with your beards –
Yes, all of you, however good you are.

FIRST WOMAN.
Oh, we're all *good* at it! Talking, I mean ...

PRAXAGORA.
Put on your beards, then. Turn into men.
Here are the wreaths ... proper speaker's wreaths
Like they use in the Assembly. I'll wear this one:
I may just want to make a speech myself.

THIRD WOMAN.
Oh, darling, look! It's too ridiculous.

PRAXAGORA.
What is?

THIRD WOMAN.
What *do* we look like? Hairy mops.

PRAXAGORA.
Pray silence. Let the padre come forward.
Bring in the sacrificial pussy.

FIRST WOMAN.
You mean pig, surely?

PRAXAGORA.
We'll practise on the cat.
Put it down there. Oh, do stop chattering!
Now then, who wishes to address us first?

THIRD WOMAN.
Oh, me please!

PRAXAGORA (*handing her the speaker's wreath*).
Come forward, then. Speak in good health.

Pause. The THIRD WOMAN *seems to be waiting.*

THIRD WOMAN (*at last*).
Well yes ... I'd simply *love* one.

PRAXAGORA.
One what?

THIRD WOMAN.
A drink, darling. You did say 'Good health'.

PRAXAGORA (*taking the wreath*).
Really! You've no idea at all of politics.

THIRD WOMAN.
You mean ... politicians don't even *drink*?

PRAXAGORA.
Oh, do sit down.

THIRD WOMAN.
No, I mean they *must* drink.
Look at the laws they pass.

SECOND WOMAN.
It's all *parties*, too.
How can they have parties, if they never drink?

THIRD WOMAN.
All that shouting and fighting. They *must* drink.

PRAXAGORA.
Will you sit down, and stop wasting time?

THIRD WOMAN.
I never asked for a beard in the first place.
It tickles . . . and it makes my throat so dry . . .

PRAXAGORA.
Does anyone else want to speak?

FIRST WOMAN.
Yes. I do.

PRAXAGORA (*giving her the wreath*).
Come forward, then. Perhaps we'll get somewhere now.
Speak up, like a man. That's right: lean on your stick.

FIRST WOMAN.
Unaccustomed as I am, I'd have liked
To yield the floor to a better man than me,
And learn from his experience. But still . . .
I'll give my vote to any motion about *bars:*
What we want is far less water in the wine.
I mean, good goodness me, it's *dreadful* how . . .

PRAXAGORA.
'My goodness me'? 'It's dreadful'? Oh, sit down.

FIRST WOMAN.
What's wrong? *She* asked for a drink, not me.

PRAXAGORA.
No, no, no. What man ever says 'My goodness',
Or 'It's dreadful'? Everything else was fine.

FIRST WOMAN.
Ah.

(*as a man*)

By gad, sir, somethin' must be done . . .

PRAXAGORA.
Do stop.
We've got to get it right, every detail,
Or there's no point going on with it at all.

THIRD WOMAN.
No, no, let me try. I've *got* to try again.
I've thought it out . . . I'll get it right this time.

(*as a man*)

The whole point of the thing is this, ladies . . .

PRAXAGORA.
Ladies? You'd stand up there and call them ladies?

THIRD WOMAN.
Well, you know, with some it's rather hard to tell.

PRAXAGORA (*taking the wreath*).
Do be quiet. Go and sit over there.
I'm going to speak.
God guide our words today.

My friends, we're all citizens: we take part
In the state, and its troubles affect us all.
I can see how it's going downhill; I can see
How things keep getting worse and worse.
Must I suffer in silence? Must I put up with it?
Look at our leaders: they're all fools or crooks.
They spend one day helping the state, and ten
Helping themselves. If you get rid of one lot,
The next are worse. And it's all your fault, you know.
You never listen; you adore bad advice.
If a man's on your side you throw him out;
If he's not, you crawl to him and give him power.
In the old days, we didn't need an Assembly
To decide who was corrupt and who was loyal –
But now? Now everyone's in politics;
Everyone takes a hand. Something for nothing:
If a man offers that, we vote for him;
If not, we call him a crook and throw him out.

SECOND WOMAN.
That was lovely, dear. She's awfully good.

FIRST WOMAN.
'Awfully good'? Don't you know anything?

Suppose you come out with 'awfully good' in *there*?

SECOND WOMAN.
Oh, but I'd never say it *there*.

FIRST WOMAN.
Well then,
Don't keep saying it here.

SECOND WOMAN.
Shh! She's off again.

PRAXAGORA.
Things have simply never been so chaotic.
Look at the alliance we made with Thebes
Against the Spartans. When it was up
For approval, we said it was the only way
To save the state; as soon as it was made
The proposer of the bill had to run
For his life. The ship-building programme:
If you're poor and you want a job, you vote yes;
If you're rich and pay ship-tax, you vote no;
If you're a farmer ... you vote no anyway.
Nothing stays the same for two days on end.
One minute you hate the Corinthians
And they hate you; next minute they're allies,
And you're busting a gut to be nice to them.
You think fools are brilliant, brilliant men are fools.
Quick! Wasn't that a *policy* just now?
Too late, it's gone: we threw the proposer out.

SECOND WOMAN (*as a man*).
The fellow's talking sense.

(*in a normal voice*)

How was that?

FIRST WOMAN.
Just right.

PRAXAGORA.
People of Athens ... *gentlemen* ... it's all your fault.
You all talk grandly about 'our common aim',

But when you come down to it, it's each man for himself.
What's the answer, did you say? I'll tell you:
Women. We must hand over the affairs of state
To women. They run the home; let them run the state.

CHORUS.
Hear, hear! Yes, yes! Hurray! Go on! More, more!

PRAXAGORA.
Women are better than men. I'll give you
Examples to prove it. Here's one: every day
They wet their wool the *usual* way –
No new-fangled methods. And what do we do,
We men in the Assembly? We're *always*
Experimenting, always playing about.

When they bake, they *squat*, like mother did;
They carry a *pot*, like mother did;
They have holy *days*, like mother did,
And funny *ways*, like mother did;
They henpeck us and wear us away
Like mother did;
They have lovers in day after day
Like mother did;
They adore honey-bread,
And drinking, and *bed* –
Oh, most of all, bed! –
Just like mother did.

So, gentlemen, there's nothing to discuss,
No need to ask what their policies are.
We should let them get started right away,
Put the state in their hands and let them rule.
You *know* it makes sense. Take the army first:
Each soldier has a Mum, who loves her son,
Looks after him, and sends his favourite food.
Financing expeditions? No problem:
They're not like us, you know: easy come, easy go –
They've been used to getting what they want, from birth.

What more need I say? Vote for my motion now,
And kiss hard lives goodbye – for evermore!

FIRST WOMAN.
Brilliant!

SECOND WOMAN.
Superb!

THIRD WOMAN.
Praxagora, *darling*!
Where did you learn to speak like that?

PRAXAGORA.
Oh, during the Troubles my husband and I
Lived over there, behind the Assembly-place.
I listened to the speakers then, and learned.

SECOND WOMAN.
No wonder you're so good at politics.
If your plan works, and we get power today,
We'll elect you our leader on the spot.

FIRST WOMAN.
But what about Kephalos? If he stands up
And starts insulting you, what will you do?

PRAXAGORA.
The potter? I'll say he's mad.

FIRST WOMAN.
They know that already.

PRAXAGORA.
Depressive mania.

FIRST WOMAN.
They know that, too.

PRAXAGORA.
All right. I'll ask them if they'll really let
A man so ... *potty* ... run the state to ... *pot*.

FIRST WOMAN.
What if Neokleides rolls his eye at you?

PRAXAGORA.
I'll tell him to roll it ... up a dog's behind.

SECOND WOMAN.
But suppose they start knocking you?

PRAXAGORA.
Knocking?
I know about knocking. I'll see to them.

THIRD WOMAN.
Suppose those big ... tough ... *brutal* policemen
Come and grab you ... and *squeeze* you ... ?

PRAXAGORA.
I'll squeeze *them.*
Make their eyes water. That'll deal with them.

SECOND WOMAN.
And we can help! We can do our bit!

FIRST WOMAN.
But there's another thing. How do we vote
When the motion's called? With our arms like this ...
Or this ... ? I've never done it like a man.

PRAXAGORA.
It *is* a problem. We'd better practise now.
Take the *right* sleeve in the *left* hand, and pull
It back. Then hold out the bare arm ... That's it.
Now then, hitch up your dresses, out of sight.
Boots on. Come on, you've all seen your husbands
Getting ready to go out. Now, the beards ...
Make sure they're straight. Cloaks next. You've all
Managed to get one? Good. Pull them right round.
Now, lean on your walking sticks, like a choir
Of greybeards singing the good old songs.
They'll think we're farmers, in town for the day.

THIRD WOMAN.
Lovely!

SECOND WOMAN.
Come on. Let's go in front.

FIRST WOMAN.
There *are*

Some ladies coming from the country. They said
They'd go straight to the Assembly, and meet us
there.

PRAXAGORA.
Is everyone ready? Come on, then.
You know the rule: the Assembly starts at dawn,
And if you're late, no pay. Not one bent pin.

FIRST WOMAN.
All right, *men*. Let's be on our way.
Remember you're men, all through today.
Do nothing odd, cause no surprise.
We'll win the prize; we'll show those guys.

CHORUS.
Come on! Look sharp! Be quick!

SECOND WOMAN.
In the middle of the night
Long before the morning light
Get up, get dressed, let's go.
If we're not there at the start
They won't let us play our part,
And we want to steal the show.

THIRD WOMAN.
Get inside and find a place.
Folded arms and frowning face.
Fight hard! Support the cause.
When our leader states her plan –
No, *his*, now she's a man –
Give her cheers and loud applause.

CHORUS.
Come on! Be quick! Look sharp!

FIRST WOMAN.
Push the others aside.
Get the best seats inside.
Don't hesitate or cower.
This Assembly doesn't need
Men's laziness and greed:

It needs *us* – women in power.

SECOND WOMAN.
The old-timers were proud,
A self-disciplined crowd
(Each brought his own packed lunch);

THIRD WOMAN.
They were manly and firm,
Didn't fidget and squirm
(Like this pathetic bunch).

CHORUS.
Look sharp! Be quick! Come on!

Exeunt. Enter BLEPYROS, *dressed in women's clothes.*

BLEPYROS.
I don't understand it. Where can she have *gone*?
It's not dawn yet, and there's no sign of her.
No sign of my clothes and boots either. And me
Lying there tossing and turning, dying for a ...
I mean, you get to feeling you're going to *burst* ...
In the end I had to put on her dress,
Her shoes, and come out here to find a place to ...
But where? Not here ... it's a bit public ...
Oh, I don't know, though. It's dark. Who's to see?

He squats.

Why did I have to take a wife, at my age?
Where's she gone? What's she up to? Ah well,
No time for that now. I've other things to do.

Enter PHEIDOLOS, *dressed in women's clothes.*

PHEIDOLOS.
Who's there? What are you doing? Heavens, Blepyros.

BLEPYROS (*jumping up*).
That's right ... neighbour.

PHEIDOLOS.
What's that – a yellow dress?
Have you had an accident?

BLEPYROS.
What? No. It belongs to my wife.
I snatched it up ... I had to come out
In a hurry.

PHEIDOLOS.
But where's your cloak?

BLEPYROS.
I couldn't find it, could I?

PHEIDOLOS.
Why didn't you ask your wife?

BLEPYROS.
I couldn't find her, either! She's gone ...
Slipped out ... disappeared. She's up to something.

PHEIDOLOS.
Well, that's amazing! It's just the same with me.
My wife's disappeared as well ... with *my* cloak.
I wouldn't have minded that, but she took my shoes
As well. She must have done: these are all I could find.

BLEPYROS.
I know how you feel. Just look at these.
Well, I was in a hurry. I had to wear *something*.
It was these or stay in ... and we've just put on
Clean sheets. What *can* they be up to? D'you think
They've gone to some kind of breakfast-party?

PHEIDOLOS.
Mm ... probably. It can't be anything else.
I mean, you know my wife – she's not the type.
What's wrong? Are you practising a dance?
Well, never mind. It's time for the Assembly.
If only I could find my *clothes* ...

BLEPYROS.
You go on. I'll come when I'm ready. *If* I'm ready.
I should never have eaten those hard-boiled eggs.

PHEIDOLOS.
It's a meeting to settle that big blockade.

Exit.

BLEPYROS (*muttering*).
Don't talk to *me* about big blockades.
What am I going to do? I've got to eat ...
Where will I find the *room*? I should never
Have bolted those eggs ... I'm really bolted now.
Ladies and gentlemen, is there a doctor
In the house? Or a plumber, perhaps?
Perhaps it's Amynon I need. Someone
Who knows his way around back passages.
You know Amynon. You know his motto,
'Go anywhere, do anything'. God, it's no joke.
I'm in agony. Hera, Artemis, help ...
Send me a midwife ... don't just leave he here.
What d'you think this is? The Battle of the Bulge?

He squats. Enter CHREMES, *in his own clothes.*

CHREMES.
Hello, what are you doing? Having a – ?

BLEPYROS.
No, no, good heavens no.
I'm ... well, I'm standing up.

CHREMES.
That's your wife's dress you're wearing.

BLEPYROS.
I *know* that!
It was all I could find in the dark.
What are *you* doing here, anyway?

CHREMES.
I've just come from the Assembly.

BLEPYROS.
Is it finished already?

CHREMES.
You're not joking. Right on the stroke of dawn.
You should have seen us: out before we were in.

BLEPYROS.
Did you get paid?

CHREMES.
I wish I had. I arrived too late.
The shame of it! I couldn't get in.

BLEPYROS.
Couldn't get in? No pay? That's not like you.

CHREMES.
There was a crowd of strangers there.
Odd-looking, pale-faced strangers. *Very* pale ...
We decided they were bakers.

BLEPYROS.
Eh?

CHREMES.
The flour.

BLEPYROS.
Oh.

CHREMES.
The whole place was full of them. Rows and rows,
Like buns on a shelf. There was no room for us.

BLEPYROS.
No point me going, then?

CHREMES.
You wouldn't
Have made it at cock-crow ... never mind now.

BLEPYROS.
Ye gods! Such dreadful news! Oh me, oh my!
I'll not get paid! I'm broke! I'm going to cry!
You saw that play too, didn't you? Years ago.
Aeschylus? Something about Achilles ... ?
Never mind. What did they want, all those bakers?

CHREMES.
Aha, you wait and see. The day began
With a debate on the Safety of the State.
Well, the first speaker was Neokleides.

BLEPYROS.
The one who squints?

CHREMES.
Exactly. He fumbled his way
To the speaker's platform, and the crowd roared,
'How can *he* see where we ought to go?
He can't even see the end of his own nose!'
He blinked at them a bit, and shouted back,
'All right, *you* tell me what to do!'

BLEPYROS.
That's easy.
A clove of garlic, crushed up in vinegar;
Stir in a handful of Spartan mustard,
And bung it in your eye when you go to bed.
That's what I'd have told him.

CHREMES.
The next speaker was Evaion.

BLEPYROS.
That bare-faced liar?

CHREMES.
Bare-faced, nothing. He arrived today
Stark naked. Or so we all thought. *He* swore
It was just that the body politic was full of holes.
'And that's the point,' he said. The crowd loved it.
'There's only one way to save the state: the rich
Must be robbed, to give to the poor. A cloak
In winter, to save the state from catching flu;
Then anyone who hasn't a blanket or a sheet
Gets taken to the cleaner's. That's fine for him –
And a fine for them, if they don't pay up.'

BLEPYROS.
Brilliant! We could really make a meal of it,
And make every grocer give a good square meal
To anyone who needs it – especially
That fellow down the road, who gives short change.

CHREMES.
After that, a young man jumped up . . . very pale,
Pretty . . . a bit like that pansy Nikias.

His proposal was that we hand over all
The affairs of state to women. At once
All those bakers started cheering and clapping ...
Mind you, the farmers didn't like it. They groaned.

BLEPYROS.
They always do.

CHREMES.
But they didn't groan loud enough.
He shouted them down, and gave us a list
Of all the good qualities women have,
And all the bad ones *you* have.

BLEPYROS.
Me?

CHREMES.
Yes, you. He said you were a pig ...

BLEPYROS.
Who, me?

CHREMES.
Yes, you. A selfish pig.

BLEPYROS.
Who, me?

CHREMES.
Yes, you. A selfish, mean old pig.

BLEPYROS.
Who, me?

CHREMES.
Yes, you. And all of *them* as well.

He gestures at the audience.

BLEPYROS.
We can't argue with that, at least.

CHREMES.
Women were stuffed (he said) with business sense
And brains, and keeping their secrets to themselves.
Men hold a meeting, and blab all over town.

BLEPYROS.
Mm. True.

CHREMES.
And women are generous (he said):
They lend each other clothes and jewels and cash
(And drinking cups); they always pay them back
Quietly, without a fuss. No lawyers,
No witnesses. Men *always* make a fuss.

BLEPYROS.
Mm. True.

CHREMES.
There are no women master-criminals
Or traitors or spies (he said); women are nice ...
They're good for you, and ... oh, lots more like
that.

BLEPYROS.
What was his motion?

CHREMES.
That we give the state
To women to manage – he said it was
The only thing we'd never tried.

BLEPYROS.
And did we?

CHREMES.
We did.

BLEPYROS.
So women are in charge now, not men?

CHREMES.
Exactly.

BLEPYROS.
My wife goes out to work instead of me?

CHREMES.
And buys the food and pays the rent.

BLEPYROS.
Who groans and staggers out of bed at dawn?

CHREMES.
She does. Your groaning days are gone for good.
You roll over and fart and go back to sleep.

BLEPYROS.
But just one minute. There *is* one snag.
We're not as young as we used to be. Suppose,
Now the women are on top, they demand –

CHREMES.
What?

BLEPYROS.
Demand their oats. What if ... we can't?

CHREMES.
Simple: they'll cut our provisions off. If food
Means oats and oats mean food, you'll have to try.

BLEPYROS.
But fancy being *made* to ... It's going to be hard.

CHREMES.
A good citizen does what must be done.

BLEPYROS.
It's like what my old grandad used to say:
'You can't cross an omelette ...'

CHREMES *and* BLEPYROS.
'When the stable door's bolted'.

CHREMES.
Let's hope he was right.

Noise of WOMEN, *off*.

Hey up. I'm leaving.

BLEPYROS.
Wait for me.

Exeunt. Enter WOMEN *and* CHORUS.

FIRST WOMAN.
Come on, be quick.

SECOND WOMAN.
Are we being followed?

THIRD WOMAN.
Any *men* around?

FIRST WOMAN.
Be careful. Walls have ears.

SECOND WOMAN.
And cobblestones have eyes.

FIRST WOMAN.
Tread firmly, like men.

THIRD WOMAN.
Don't let them find out.

SECOND WOMAN.
That would never do.

CHORUS.
Keep your cloaks pulled tight.
Look right. Look left. Look out.
Hurry up.
We're nearly there,
Back where it all began.
Our leader's house – Praxagora
Who made the plan and fooled the men.

Get rid of the beards. Don't hang about.
If they see us, they'll know.
Quick!
Into the shadows
And change. Our leader's here.
We don't want her to see
Men's clothes and beards. Get changed.

They start changing. Enter PRAXAGORA.

PRAXAGORA.
That's right. Everything's gone exactly right,
Exactly the way we planned. Quick, now:
Before any men come past and see,
Get rid of the cloaks, take off the boots,
Throw the walking sticks away.

(*to some of the* WOMEN)

You gather them up, get rid of them.
I want to slip into the house
Without *him* seeing me,
And put his clothes back
Just where they were before.

FIRST WOMAN.
Whatever you say. Your word is our command.

THIRD WOMAN.
You're so *clever*, darling. You know *just* what to do.

PRAXAGORA.
No, no, no. Everyone here was essential.
You know the law: one ... *man* ... one vote.

Enter BLEPYROS *and* CHREMES.
BLEPYROS *is still in women's clothes.*

BLEPYROS.
Ha! Praxagora. Where have *you* been?

PRAXAGORA.
What business is that of yours?

BLEPYROS.
What business of mine? Oh, very nice!

PRAXAGORA.
You think I've got a lover, don't you?

BLEPYROS.
What, just one?

PRAXAGORA.
Can't you tell?

BLEPYROS.
What? How?

PRAXAGORA.
Take a sniff. Go on. Where's the perfume? Well?

BLEPYROS.
Can't a woman go making love without?

PRAXAGORA.
I never do – as you should know.

BLEPYROS.
All right, then. Where *have* you been?
Sneaking out at dawn. And in my clothes, too.

PRAXAGORA.
I was with a friend. All night. A woman friend.
A pregnant woman friend. Her pains had begun.

BLEPYROS.
Why didn't you tell me before you went?

PRAXAGORA.
I should have asked her to hold on, I suppose?

BLEPYROS.
It's no way to behave. You should have said.

PRAXAGORA.
Don't you understand, I had to *hurry*?
The message was urgent. She couldn't wait.

BLEPYROS.
Well, why couldn't you go in your own clothes,
Instead of leaving me here in this nightie?
A wreath and a candle, I'd look like a corpse.

PRAXAGORA.
It was cold, love. You know how your poor little wife
Feels the cold. I needed your nice warm clothes.
You had all those blankets. You were all right.

BLEPYROS.
That doesn't explain the boots ... the walking stick.

PRAXAGORA.
I was afraid of being robbed on the road.
I thought, if I clatter along in *his* boots ...
If I rattle *his* stick on the cobble-stones ...

BLEPYROS.
You cost me a day's pay. A whole day's pay,
Because I couldn't get to the Assembly.

PRAXAGORA.
Well, never mind. It went exactly right.

BLEPYROS.
What. The Assembly?

PRAXAGORA.
No darling. The baby.
But *was* there one? An Assembly, I mean.

BLEPYROS.
Of course there was. I told you yesterday.

PRAXAGORA.
Oh yes. So you did.

BLEPYROS.
And you know what's been decided?

PRAXAGORA.
No.

BLEPYROS.
Huh! It's all right for *you* now. It's all yours.

PRAXAGORA.
What, dear? The mending?

BLEPYROS.
The State!

PRAXAGORA.
What? Ours?

BLEPYROS.
The State's all yours, to govern as you please.

PRAXAGORA.
Well now, isn't that lucky?

BLEPYROS.
Eh?

PRAXAGORA.
Well, just *think*!
We can start again. No more criminals,
No more lawyers, no more courts . . .

BLEPYROS.
I *like* courts.

CHREMES.
Hush, man. Your wife's talking. The lady of the house.

PRAXAGORA.
No more envy, no more greed; no poverty,
No despair; no pay-up-or-else, no arguments ...

BLEPYROS.
Fantastic! Lovely! I should live so long!

PRAXAGORA.
Oh darling, don't you believe me? All right ...
I'll prove it to *you*, and I'll prove it to *him*.

CHORUS.
From a pool of intelligence deep and vast
With dedicated concentration
Give a dazzling demonstration
Of the goodies you're bringing, success built to last.

A brilliant new programme, a dazzle of light,
A master-stroke, a revelation
To stun us into admiration
And startle this watching audience tonight.

PRAXAGORA.
It *is* startling. Quite brilliant, and new.
If you'll drop the old ways, branch out ...
Make experiments ... try something new ...

CHREMES.
Oh, don't worry. You know what we're like.
We love change. We'll try anything once.

PRAXAGORA.
Well then, listen and don't interrupt,
Or ask questions, or argue or fuss
Till I've finished. My programme is this:
ALL OUR WEALTH TO BE PUBLICLY OWNED.
PRIVATE PROPERTY: BANNED. NO MORE RICH,

NO MORE POOR, NO MORE MILLIONAIRE
SQUIRES, NO MORE BEGGARS. NO
BUSINESS TYCOONS AND NO FAILURES,
EQUALITY RULES.

BLEPYROS (*interrupting*).
All share equally – ?

PRAXAGORA (*furious*).
Shit!

BLEPYROS.
Not for me, thanks.

PRAXAGORA.
I didn't mean *that*!
I said *listen*, and *don't interrupt*.
Once all property's public – all land
And all money – we'll give you a grant
And supply you with all that you need,
Using feminine knowhow and thrift.

CHREMES.
Yes, that's fine – for the wealth you can *see*.
But supposing a man makes his cash
By invisible earnings, like shares . . . ?

PRAXAGORA.
He'll declare them, like everyone else,
Or be guilty of fraud.

BLEPYROS.
Just like now.

PRAXAGORA.
But he won't *need* his money –

CHREMES.
Why not?

PRAXAGORA.
Because all that he wants will be *free*:
Bread, fish, cakes, cloaks, wine, crowns, dried
peas –

There's no reason for hoarding your cash,
And no reason for cheating the state.

BLEPYROS.
Did they ask for a reason *before*?

PRAXAGORA.
But those days and those laws are all gone!
In a communal state, who needs cash?

BLEPYROS.
If you fancy a pretty young girl,
Will the Common Purse give you a grant
To buy presents and take her to bed?

PRAXAGORA.
There's no need: you can sleep with her for free.
My new system, called SEX-ON-DEMAND
(GO-TO-BED-AND-MAKE-BABIES) is law.

CHREMES.
But what if we all want the *same*
Pretty girls? Does your law cover that?

PRAXAGORA.
Yes. The girls make an organised queue,
And you sleep with the ugliest first.

BLEPYROS.
But look, what about old men like me?
If it's ugliest first, I won't *last*
Till I've got to the end of the queue.

PRAXAGORA.
Oh, don't worry. They won't *all* insist.

BLEPYROS.
I don't get it.

PRAXAGORA.
Exactly: you don't.

CHREMES.
It's a good law for females: there won't
Be a stone left unturned. But it's no
Good for males. All the he-men get girls,
And the rest of us nothing at all.

PRAXAGORA.
Yes you will, if you watch them and wait.
When the tough guys and he-men go out
To the new Common Tables, you pounce
On their girls. It's the same law for them:
IF YOU WANT THE WINE, THEN SQUEEZE
THE GRAPES.

BLEPYROS.
Ha! Lysikrates looks like a grape –
He'll be squeezed?

PRAXAGORA.
It's the law of the land.
Democratic and equal. Just think
Of the scene: Mr Big's with a girl,
Showing off all his money and charm –
And a down-at-heel weed comes along
And takes over and says, 'Stand aside!
When I've finished, I'll pass you the cup.'

CHREMES.
But if that's how we're going to live,
When a baby's born, how will it know
Who its Daddy is?

PRAXAGORA.
Simple: it won't.
There'll be hundreds of Daddies: all those
Who were adult and there at the time.

CHREMES.
No, that's not going to work. If the young
Treat their fathers the way they do now
When they *know* who they are, when they *don't*
They'll be dropping us right in the –

PRAXAGORA.
No,
It's not *like* that. You don't understand.
In the old days, you kept out of fights
When they didn't concern you; but now,

When we're one great big family, we'll fight
In a massive great family row.

BLEPYROS (*pointing into the audience*).
Just a minute! There's *him* ... and there's *him* ...
What if *they* call me Daddy? No thanks!

CHREMES.
It could be even worse.

BLEPYROS.
What d'you mean?

CHREMES.
Aristyllos the Armpit comes up
And says 'Daddy!', and gives you a kiss.

BLEPYROS.
That old dung-heap? He'd suffer.

CHREMES.
No, *you* would.

PRAXAGORA.
There's no chance of that. He's too old.
He won't kiss you. He knows his own Dad.

BLEPYROS.
Thank god. Have you *smelt* the man's breath?

CHREMES.
Then there's farmland. If nobody owns
Any fields, who's to dig them and plough?

PRAXAGORA.
Slaves. You've only one duty to do:
When it starts to get dark, you get dressed
And slip down to the table for dinner.

CHREMES.
But who'll make new clothes? We'll need new clothes.

PRAXAGORA.
When you wear out the old ones, the State
Will provide, out of public funds.

CHREMES.
Public funds? Ah. Suppose you're in court
And you're fined. Who'll pay that – public funds?

PRAXAGORA.
There won't *be* any courts.

BLEPYROS (*aside to* CHREMES).
Whoops! You're out of a job.

CHREMES (*aside to him*).
So are you.

PRAXAGORA.
We just don't need them now.

BLEPYROS.
What d'you mean?
They're essential. Non-payment of debts –

PRAXAGORA.
There won't *be* any payment of debts.
There won't *be* any debts. All our cash
Is community property now:
There'll be no need to borrow or lend.

CHREMES.
Very clever.

BLEPYROS.
But what about this?
A community dinner ends up in a fight
And the drunk beats you up. Well, who pays?

PRAXAGORA.
Ah! He'll have all his rations cut off,
And his belly will teach him good sense.

CHREMES.
No more thieves?

PRAXAGORA.
You can't steal what you own.

BLEPYROS.
If you go out at night and get mugged,
And they steal all your clothes –

CHREMES.
Sleep at home. They won't mug you in bed.

PRAXAGORA.
That's no problem: the clothes
Are *their* property too. If they ask,
Hand them over; next morning, go down
To the communal tailor's for more.

BLEPYROS.
No more ... *gambling*?

PRAXAGORA.
No money: no point.

CHREMES.
It's a new kind of life.

PRAXAGORA.
Public life.
The whole city one communal house ...
No more barriers ... freedom for all ...

BLEPYROS.
We will *eat* ... ?

PRAXAGORA.
We'll convert all the courts
Into communal dining-rooms –

BLEPYROS.
What?
With those hard wooden benches?

PRAXAGORA.
Ideal.
When the banquets are over, a choir
Of young children will stand up and sing
All the old songs, the ones we like best –

CHREMES.
Very nice. And the urns ... ?

PRAXAGORA.
We'll put those
In the market place. Then, every day,

We'll draw lots for our tables and food:
A: vegetarian,
B: honey-cakes,
C: fish
D . . .
D . . .

BLEPYROS (*sarcastically*).
D.licious. And what about M?

PRAXAGORA.
What about it?

BLEPYROS.
Em for Empty, you know.
They get nothing.

PRAXAGORA.
Of course not. There's plenty for all.

BLEPYROS *and* CHREMES *dream together*.

CHREMES.
Oh yes, plenty for all.
You'll get up from the table . . .

BLEPYROS.
Drunk, wearing your crown . . .

CHREMES.
You'll grab a torch, and go . . .

BLEPYROS.
And they'll be waiting for you,
Waiting in the shadows by the road.

CHREMES.
Hello, handsome. Got the time?

BLEPYROS.
Over here, lover-boy. Try me.

CHREMES.
And from an upstairs window:
Come upstairs if you like
Honey, peaches and cream . . .

BLEPYROS.
But Mummy comes first.
You'll have to try me first.

CHREMES.
Yes, and weedy old men
Will mock handsome young boys ...

BLEPYROS.
Not so fast! Hold your horses!
Put her down. I saw her first.

CHREMES.
Before she drinks the wine
She has to squeeze the grapes ...

BLEPYROS.
So get a grip of yourself, and wait!

PRAXAGORA.
You're beginning to get the idea?

BLEPYROS.
Oh yes.

PRAXAGORA.
Now, I have to go down to the market-place.
There's so much to do since I was elected
Chief Executive: check all incoming goods,
Hold auditions for Town Crieress,
Set up all the communal dining rooms
Ready for the feast ...

BLEPYROS.
There's a feast already?

PRAXAGORA.
Tonight. And then there are the prostitutes:
They've got to be stopped.

BLEPYROS.
Why?

PRAXAGORA.
These ladies here:
We want to save all the handsome boys for them,

Not for prostitutes. No slave is allowed to shave herself
Or wear perfume or seductive dresses
Like her mistress. Slaves must sleep only with slaves.
We call it free love, because it's *for* the free.

BLEPYROS.
Go on, then. I'll walk beside you.
Then people can point me out and say,
'Look! The General's husband. What a man!'

Exeunt PRAXAGORA *and* BLEPYROS.

CHREMES.
I'm going to take all my goods and property
Down to the communal market-place. First
I want to go through them and make a list.

He goes in. Music, dance. Then he comes out again, calling back inside in a coaxing way, as if to a pet.

Come on, little sieve. That's it ... out you come.
Go over there, ready to lead the procession.

A SLAVE *brings out a sieve, and lays it on the ground. Other* SLAVES *fetch the other items as* BLEPYROS *names them.*

There we are. Aren't you holy? Just what we need
For a civic procession. Now then, who's next ...
Who'll carry the litter? The rubbish pail,
Of course. Oh my dear, you might have washed!
Have you been with Lysikrates, that dirty old man?
I think we'll have a soap-dish next ... that's right,
And the water-cock ... And now, behind them ... ?

The SLAVES *bring in a rooster, followed by a beehive.*

Hello, old cock! You going to sing for us?
Hello, honey! You spread yourself just there.
A vase, a three-legged stool, a vinegar-pot ...
Ladles and jelly-spoons, bring up the rear ...

He starts piling the things on a handcart, ready to take out. Enter PHEIDOLOS, *muttering.*

PHEIDOLOS.
Hand over my property? I'd have to be mad.
I'll have a good look round first, and see
How the land lies. I'm not an idiot:
I'm not throwing away a lifetime's toil
Till I find out what's going on.
Ow! What's this in aid of? Are you moving house?

CHREMES.
No, I'm –

PHEIDOLOS.
Going to the pawnshop?

CHREMES.
No, I'm –

PHEIDOLOS.
A jumble-sale?

CHREMES.
No, I'm handing them in to the common store,
To the market-place, as the new law says.

PHEIDOLOS.
You're doing *what*?

CHREMES.
That's right.

PHEIDOLOS.
You're crazy.

CHREMES.
Why?

PHEIDOLOS.
Just look.

CHREMES.
You mean I'm crazy to obey the law?

PHEIDOLOS.
Poor old thing – what law?

CHREMES.
The new one, of course.

PHEIDOLOS.
That proves it. You're off your head.

CHREMES.
Off my head?

PHEIDOLOS.
You're nutty. You've flipped. You're round the twist.

CHREMES.
To do as I'm told?

PHEIDOLOS.
And where will it get you?

CHREMES.
It's common sense.

PHEIDOLOS.
Cha! It's nonsense.

CHREMES.
Aren't you going to hand in yours?

PHEIDOLOS.
Not yet, I'm not.
I'm waiting to see what the rest of them do.

CHREMES.
They'll be handing them in.

PHEIDOLOS.
I believe you.

CHREMES.
But everyone says so.

PHEIDOLOS.
Says so, eh?

CHREMES.
They promised they would.

PHEIDOLOS.
Promised, eh?

CHREMES.
You don't believe *anything*.

PHEIDOLOS.
Anything, eh?

CHREMES.
Oh, go to hell.

PHEIDOLOS.
To hell, eh?
D'you really imagine they mean what they say?
This lot? They're takers, not givers-away.
Even the gods want a hand-out, round here:
If you want any favours, you grease their palms.

CHREMES.
For heaven's sake, leave me in peace. I'm busy.
I've got to get this lot strapped up. Where's that cord?

PHEIDOLOS.
You're really going through with it?

CHREMES.
Why else would I tie up a three-legged stool?

PHEIDOLOS.
But it's daft!
Just wait, till you see what the rest of them do.

CHREMES.
Then what?

PHEIDOLOS.
Well then ... wait a bit longer, of course.

CHREMES.
For what?

PHEIDOLOS.
An act of god ... a fire ... a flood ...
A black cat crossing the path ... *anything*
That might persuade you to give it up.

CHREMES.
I'm not hanging round to come in *last*.

PHEIDOLOS.
Don't worry: you won't be last.

CHREMES.
What?

PHEIDOLOS.
I've told you. This lot here. They're *always* last.

CHREMES.
They'll hand them in.

PHEIDOLOS.
And if they don't?

CHREMES.
They will.

PHEIDOLOS.
And if they don't?

CHREMES.
We'll beat them up.

PHEIDOLOS.
And if we don't?

CHREMES.
We'll run.

PHEIDOLOS.
And if we don't?

CHREMES.
Oh, go to hell.

PHEIDOLOS.
And if I don't?

CHREMES.
Oh nuts!

PHEIDOLOS.
You're quite determined? You'll really hand them in?

CHREMES.
Oh yes. And look . . .

He points into the audience.

They're getting the idea too.

PHEIDOLOS.
Getting the idea? Look at him. Antisthenes.

He won't move. If he sat on the pot for a month,
He wouldn't move.

CHREMES.
There are plenty of others.

PHEIDOLOS.
Like the manager, you mean? Think *he'll move?*

CHREMES.
Well, I've never *seen* him move . . .

PHEIDOLOS (*to the audience*).
It's no good:
He's really going through with it.

CHREMES.
Of course I am.

PHEIDOLOS.
Have you forgotten what happened *last* year?
The *last* government fiasco? All that salt?

CHREMES.
Well, yes.

PHEIDOLOS.
And devaluation – remember that?

CHREMES.
Will I ever forget it? I'd sold my grapes:
I got a good price for the whole harvest,
A bag of silver. I went into town
To buy a sack of corn. I put the bag down –
And they laughed in my face. 'Silver? Hard luck:
From yesterday, we're only accepting gold.'

PHEIDOLOS.
And that brilliant new tax they tried – the one
Supposed to put us in the black for good?
Remember that? A tax on bits of string.
A knotty problem: they never tied it up.

CHREMES.
But things are different, now that women rule.
They'll get a grip on things.

PHEIDOLOS.
They won't grip *me*.

CHREMES.
You're babbling. Slave, come here. Take the pole.

Enter TOWN CRIERESS.

TOWN CRIERESS.
People of Athens, citizens, lend me your ears.
A communiqué from the commanderess.
NOW IS THE TIME FOR ALL GOOD MEN TO COME
TO THE PARTY. THE TICKETS ARE FREE. FROM ME.
STATE OF THE LARDER: GOOD. TABLES: GROANING.
CUSHIONS AND PILLOWS: SOFT. BOWLS: FULL OF WINE.
WAITRESSES: READY AND WAITING. FISH: BATTERED.
HARE: SPITTING. CAKES: BAKED. CROWNS: WOVEN.
EVERYTHING'S READY, FROM SOUP TO NUTS.

(*in a confidential aside*)

Even Geron's ready: wrinkled boots and baggy cloak
Changed for party clothes and dancing pumps.
The cooks (young and pretty) are personally guaranteed
By Smoios: old cunning-tongue's tasted every single dish.

(*back to the main announcement*)

THE BREAD'S READY. COME AND GET STUFFED.
MESSAGE ENDS.

Exit.

PHEIDOLOS.
Well, excuse me.
No point standing here, when duty calls.

CHREMES.
Where are you going? You've handed nothing in.

PHEIDOLOS.
I'm going to the party.

CHREMES.
You have to hand in first.

PHEIDOLOS.
Oh, I'll hand in.

CHREMES.
When?

PHEIDOLOS.
Afterwards.

CHREMES.
What?

PHEIDOLOS.
And I still won't be the last. You wait and see.

CHREMES.
You're going straight to the party?

PHEIDOLOS.
I know my duty. When my country calls ...

CHREMES.
They won't let you in.

PHEIDOLOS.
I'll go round the back.

CHREMES.
They'll still throw you out.

PHEIDOLOS.
Let them try. I'll sue.

CHREMES.
They'll laugh in your face.

PHEIDOLOS.
I'll make a stand ...

CHREMES.
A stand?

PHEIDOLOS.
A stand. Behind the door. And pinch
The goodies as they pass me by.

CHREMES.
Just mind.
You don't pinch mine. Hey, Sikon, Parmenon,
Pick up the things, and come with me.

PHEIDOLOS.
I'll help.

CHREMES.
Oh no you won't. You'll get down there, and tell
The Generaless they're yours. I'll manage, thanks.

Exit with his SLAVES, *taking the property.*

PHEIDOLOS.
H'm. Better think of something else. Fast.
I've got to get to the party, and still keep my stuff.
I've got it! Just a minute ... Yes, that's it!

He picks up an object at random from the stage – perhaps the statue of Hermes from beside CHREMES' *front door.*

One party-ticket. Quick ... no time to waste.

Exit. Choral interlude. Then enter FIRST HAG.

FIRST HAG.
Where have all the young men gone? Or *any* men?
Surely I plastered enough makeup on ...
They could hardly miss me in *this* dress.
I've a song in my heart ... I'm ready for love ...
And where *are* they? You can't grab what isn't there.
O Muses, come down here, into my mouth,
And find me some really sexy songs ...

GIRL (*from an upstairs window*).
So you slipped out first for once, you old prune!

What are you hoping to do – squeeze *my* grapes?
Go on, I'm listening. Anything you can sing,
I can sing sweeter ...

(*to the audience*)

What do you mean, *boring*?
This is live theatre ... you'll find it very nice.

FIRST HAG (*mocking*).
This is live theatre ... you'll find it very nice.
Where's the flute-player? Come on, sweetheart,
Get hold of your instrument. I'm going to sing.

Music. She sings and dances.

If you want a good time
Just ge *me* into bed.
Don't sample *her* wine:
Try my vintage instead.
A young girl never understands;
She won't be true.
What you need are experienced hands:
I'll stick to you.

GIRL (*to a different tune*).
Fly into my nest
If you're seeking the best,
Cool caresses, soft breasts, luscious legs;
Not vinegar dregs
And a beard and bad breath –
Sex with her is like sleeping with Death.

FIRST HAG.
When you're panting with lust
May your bed-frame go bust
And your legs get the staggers and shakes;
When you pucker and kiss
May your lovers all hiss
And turn into a bedful of snakes.

GIRL.
Where's my lover-boy gone?

Why's he taking so long?
Am I lonely and left on the shelf?
Now that Mummy's away –

(*aside, to the wings*)

Do I *have* to go on with this?

No answer. She continues:

Now that Mummy's away
And I'm ready to play,
Must I lie back and do it myself?

FIRST HAG.
Oh, you're so out of luck!
You're so itchy to fuck
And you've got to play patience instead.

GIRL.
You won't chase me away,
For whatever you say
I'm much younger ... and better in bed.

FIRST HAG (*spoken*).
Puss, puss, puss! Miaow all you like,
They won't come for you, they'll come for me.

GIRL.
With a hearse, I suppose?
Heard that one before?

FIRST HAG.
A hundred times.

GIRL.
You've heard them *all* before.
Poor ... *old* ... thing.

FIRST HAG.
Don't you worry about my age.

GIRL.
All that makeup ... like plaster on a wall.

FIRST HAG.
What's got into you?

GIRL.
Nothing. What's up with *you*?

FIRST HAG.
I've got a boyfriend. Epigenes.

GIRL.
Old Father Time, you mean.

FIRST HAG.
Epigenes: you wait and see.

GIRL.
He's coming for me, not you.

FIRST HAG.
Poor little pussy!

GIRL.
Dirty old bag!

FIRST HAG.
Why not stick your head in, and wait and see?

GIRL.
I will if you will.

FIRST HAG.
I've nothing to lose.

They hide. Enter EPIGENES.

EPIGENES.
I'll curl up with a *girl*,
Not a bag or a hag
With one foot in the grave.
I'm a man, not a slave.

FIRST HAG (*aside to the audience*).
Well, he won't get *that* ride.
He'll be sorry he tried.
And he'll pretty soon learn
It's democracy's turn.
Even so, I'd better keep an eye on him.

EPIGENES.
I'm drunk with her, on fire for her. Oh gods,
I can't wait to get her on her own. Ohh . . . *gods*!

GIRL (*from the window, aside to the audience*).
I've shaken her off. She's gone. Daft old bat!
She really believed me. Eek! Epigenes!

(*singing*)

Oh, darling, come quickly,
Let's hurry to bed.
I'm dying to fondle
Your nice curly head.
I want you, I want you,
Oh take me to bed.

EPIGENES.
Oh darling, come quickly
And open the door.
I'm panting for kisses
And desperate for more.
I need you, I need you,
Oh, take me to bed.

GIRL.
Oh yes, my love,
That's right, my love,
My sweet, my love,
My lovely love –

EPIGENES.
Please stop singing and open the door.

GIRL.
My honey-bee,
My piece of cake,
My magic wand,
My crown, my jewel –

EPIGENES.
I'm going crazy. Please open the door.

FIRST HAG (*coming forward*).
No need to knock. I'm over here.

EPIGENES.
Ergh! What?

FIRST HAG.
So impatient! You'll hammer it down.

EPIGENES.
Oh god . . .

FIRST HAG.
What a torch. Do you . . . want anything?

EPIGENES.
Er . . . I was . . . I was looking for a man.

FIRST HAG.
A *man*?

EPIGENES.
Yes. Er . . . you haven't seen him, have you?

FIRST HAG.
Now don't be silly. I *know* what you want.

EPIGENES.
Yes . . . but . . . not over a hundred . . . I can't,
I just *can't*. I was hoping . . . sort of, *twenty*?

FIRST HAG.
Poor darling! That was yesterday. Today
It's twenty last, and over-a-hundred first.

EPIGENES.
But, I mean . . . the law of supply and demand . . .

FIRST HAG.
Exactly. *I* demand . . . and *you* supply.

EPIGENES.
But *this* is the door I was knocking on.

FIRST HAG.
I'm sorry: you have to knock on my door first.

EPIGENES.
I want a woman, not a sack of flour.

FIRST HAG.
Oh, you're just saying that. I know you love me.
You're shy, out here in the street. Never mind:
Pucker up, there's a good boy.

EPIGENES.
But your lover ...

FIRST HAG.
Eh? Who?

EPIGENES.
What's his name? You know ... that sex ...
Er ... sex ... that *sexton*! Dug your grave years ago.

FIRST HAG.
I know what you want.

EPIGENES.
I know what *you* want.

FIRST HAG.
The law says you're mine.

EPIGENES.
You're crazy! Put me down.

FIRST HAG.
You're very hot. I'll take you up to bed.

EPIGENES (*aside to the audience*).
Don't bother with nails or hooks or glue. Use *her*!

FIRST HAG.
Flatterer. Come on, lover. Come home with me.

EPIGENES.
Oh, I forgot. I can't. Quite impossible.

FIRST HAG.
What?

EPIGENES.
The law. Ha-ha! Yes, the new law.
I can't give anything to you:
I have to give it to the State.

FIRST HAG.
That's quite all right.
I'm an official collector: you can give it to me.

EPIGENES.
But I haven't got it *with* me!

FIRST HAG.
Look: see this?

EPIGENES.
Erp! What is it?

FIRST HAG.
I thought it might change your mind.

EPIGENES.
What *is* it?

FIRST HAG.
Just listen. You'll see.

She unrolls it, and reads.

BY ORDER OF THE WOMEN. SUBJECT: SEX.
SEX BETWEEN A YOUNG MALE AND A YOUNG FEMALE
IS PERMITTED ONLY IF EVERY ELDERLY FEMALE
IS SATISFIED SHE HERSELF HAS BEEN SATISFIED
BY SAID YOUNG MALE. PENALTY FOR NON-SATISFACTION:
SAID MALE'S PRIVATE PARTS TO BE PLACED
IN THE HANDS OF A RECEIVER (OFFICIAL, ELDERLY, FEMALE).
BY LAW.

EPIGENES.
That's stretching things a bit.

FIRST HAG.
And that's the law.

EPIGENES.
Can't one of my neighbours stand bail for me?

FIRST HAG.
No standing, no bail. This thing's in your own hands.

EPIGENES.
Suppose I'm unfit?

FIRST HAG.
You can't withdraw.

EPIGENES.
Supposing I *won't*?

FIRST HAG.
You'll get a long stretch.

EPIGENES.
What *can* I do?

FIRST HAG.
Come home with me, to bed.

EPIGENES.
There's no escape?

FIRST HAG.
No hiding-place. Come on.

EPIGENES.
All right, then. Go and get everything ready:
The perfumed oil, the clean white sheets, the flowers,
The candles, the pot of water by the door –

FIRST HAG.
What are you talking about? Bed or a funeral?

EPIGENES.
It's hard to say. You may not stand the strain.

Enter GIRL.

GIRL.
Just a minute! Where are you taking him?

FIRST HAG.
Home.

GIRL.
You can't do that. You, go to bed with *him*?
You're old enough to be his mother.
What d'you think this is, *King Oedipus*?

FIRST HAG.
Bitch! You're just jealous. Is that what you think
Of the law? You'll be sorry. You wait and see.

Exit.

EPIGENES.
Oh, thank you, darling ... thank you. Pff!
Saved ...
In the nick of time ... a fate worse than death.
Take me upstairs, quick. I want to ... say
thanks ...
I want to show you my ... gratitude.

Enter SECOND HAG.

SECOND HAG.
Hello, hello, hello. Taking liberties,
Are we, dearie? He's to sleep with me first.
That's the law round here.

EPIGENES.
Oh golly, she's even worse.
Where did they dig you up, you walking corpse?

SECOND HAG.
Walk this way.

EPIGENES (*to* GIRL).
Don't just stand there. Do something.
She wants me to walk that way.

SECOND HAG.
The *law* wants you to walk this way.

EPIGENES.
Put me down! What are you, a vampire bat?

SECOND HAG.
Aren't you the cheeky one? Come on ... this way.

EPIGENES.
Quick! Fetch me a potty! I want to ...

SECOND HAG.
It's all right. I've a lovely one ... upstairs.

EPIGENES.
There isn't time for that! I'll send you up
A couple of my friends ...

SECOND HAG (*to* GIRL).
Excuse me, dear.

Enter THIRD HAG. *The* GIRL *runs inside.*

THIRD HAG.
Ha-HA! Caught you! Just where
Are you going with her?

EPIGENES.
I'm not! It's rape!
Oh please, please, whoever you are, help me.
Kind lady, don't let me be –

He sees her face.

Aaaaaargh!
Oh Herakles, Pan, Castor and Pollux,
Don't let it get me! It's worse than them all.
What is it? The Missing Link? The Living Dead?

THIRD HAG.
Never mind that. Come here.

SECOND HAG.
Come *here*.

THIRD HAG.
Don't worry. I won't let you go.

SECOND HAG.
Neither will I.

EPIGENES.
Leave me alone. You're pulling me in two.

SECOND HAG.
Do as the law says, then, and come with me.

THIRD HAG.
Not if an uglier old hag turns up.

EPIGENES.
And what about *her*? That pretty girl in there?

By the time you've done, there'll be nothing left
For her.

THIRD HAG.
That's her problem. And *this* one's mine.

EPIGENES.
All right, all right. I give in. Which one first?

SECOND HAG.
Me, of course. Come on.

EPIGENES.
She's got to leave me alone.

THIRD HAG.
It's my turn first.

EPIGENES.
Tell that to her, not me.

SECOND HAG.
I'm not giving up my turn.

THIRD HAG.
Neither am I.

EPIGENES.
Oh god!
I'm not a fucking WISHBONE!

SECOND HAG.
Pardon?

THIRD HAG.
Eh?

EPIGENES.
What good will it do, to pull me in two?

SECOND HAG.
Oh.

THIRD HAG.
Ah.

SECOND HAG.
Don't fight it. You're mine.

THIRD HAG.
I tell you he's mine.

EPIGENES.
It's like being on the rack. STOP PULLING THAT!
How can I paddle two canoes at once?

SECOND HAG.
Take some iron tablets. Quick. We're nearly there.

EPIGENES.
Oh my god, she's winning. We're nearly there.

THIRD HAG.
STOP!
It's all right. I know just what to do.
We'll *all* go in. We'll all three go to bed at once.

EPIGENES.
Oh no, no *please*! Not all at once! I *can't*!

THIRD HAG.
You've got to, lover. Don't make such a fuss.

EPIGENES (*to the audience*).
Don't sit there and laugh. It's tragedy, not farce.
I'll be treading *her* grapes half the night, and half
Making toad in the hole with *her*. Don't laugh.

(*to the sky*)

Zeus, what have I done? Was it something I said?
I'm a man, not a keeper in a zoo.
I'm in your hands ... oh please, look after me.
If I ... don't make it ... to the other side ...
Bury my corpse there ... by the exit sign ...
And erect ... erect a memorial stone
In my memory ... an angel, weeping tears
Of grief ...

(*in a different voice*)

... or two old crows, like HER and HER!

The HAGS *pursue him out. Short interlude. Then the* TOWN CRIERESS *comes in, tipsy.*

TOWN CRIERESS.
Ladles and jellymen ... what a nice time
We're having ... one and all ... especially me.
Friends, neighbours, countrymen,
Lend me your glasses. *The quality of wine*
Is not strained; it droppeth ... oh, it droppeth,
How it droppeth ... in jugs and jugs and jugs ...
What a lovely bouquet ... what a pert little wine ...
I think you'll be amused by its ... go on,
Pour yourself another. The night is young,
And these our revels now ... are just begun.

Has anyone seen Himself? I'm looking for
Himself ... the General's husband. Mr Boss.

CHORUS.
Stay here and wait. He won't be long.

TOWN CRIERESS.
That's right.
Ooh look, here he is. I think he's on his way.

Enter BLEPYROS.

Sir ... Mr General ... oh sir, aren't you lucky?

BLEPYROS.
Me?

TOWN CRIERESS.
Yes. There's no one else I'd rather be.
There's no one luckier.

BLEPYROS.
Why?

TOWN CRIERESS.
It's a great big town ...
Hundreds and hundreds and hundreds of people.
At least.

BLEPYROS.
So what?

TOWN CRIERESS.
Out of all those hundreds

And hundreds and hundreds, you're the only one
Not at the party.

CHORUS.
Lucky? That's *lucky*? How is it lucky?

TOWN CRIERESS.
Now where are you going?

BLEPYROS.
To the party, of course.

TOWN CRIERESS.
All right. But you're going to be the last, you know.
Everyone else is there. The Generaless
Told me to fetch you ... and these young ladies ...
There are a few bottles left, if you hurry ...

(*gesturing to the audience*)

Bring these nice people ... they're not *all* asleep.
Let's all go ... all go to the party.

BLEPYROS (*to the audience*).
Well, did you enjoy that? A lovely speech.
She meant it, too. There's plenty to eat
For every one of you – when you get back home.
I'm going to the party. I'll just get my torch.

TOWN CRIERESS.
Don't waste time, then. Go on. Take *them* with you.
While you get ready, I'll say a few words
To whet their appetites. Is the music ready?

Exit BLEPYROS. *Music.*

A little idea for the judges.
Did you like the plot? Give *us* first prize.
Did you like the jokes? Give *us* first prize.
Have you got all that? Give *us* first prize.
I know we had to come on here first,
But that's the fault of the draw, not us.
Remember us through all the other plays:
Don't act like third-rate whores, who forget
Every client they've had except the last.

(*to the* CHORUS)

Ladies, it's time. It's time, dear friends,
To pick up your feet and dance.
It's party time. Listen. Pick up the beat.

A rhythmic dance begins.

What's for dinner? There's

Mussels and oysters and crayfish
And winkles and scallops and lobster
And haddock and herring and salmon
And whiting and pilchards and coley
And mullet and turtle and CRAB;

Then there's

Chicken and turkey and pheasant
And woodcock and peacock and partridge
And pigeon and plover and heron
And song-thrush and lapwing and blackbird
And cygnet and rabbit and DUCK;

Then there's

Cherries and peaches and apples
And raisins and cheese and NUTS.

That's right, NUTS.

What was that? You want more?
Well, then, give us the prize,
And good eating ...

Good clapping ...

GOODNIGHT!

Exeunt omnes.

MENANDER

The Woman from Samos
(*Samia*)

translated by J. Michael Walton

Characters

MOSCHION, adopted son of Demeas
CHRYSIS, the woman from Samos
PARMENON, Demeas' slave
DEMEAS, a well-to-do Athenian
NIKERATOS, Demeas' neighbour
A COOK
PLANGON (non-speaking), Nikeratos' daughter
MYRRHINE (non-speaking), Nikeratos' wife
ATTENDANTS
CHORUS (indicated in the text only by a stage-direction)

Some of Menander's text from the early part of the play is missing. To provide the continuity of a complete piece, the present translator has filled in the gaps with invented material of about the right length. All such material appears in brackets.

ACT 1

Athens. The adjacent houses of DEMEAS *and* NIKERATOS. *Enter* MOSCHION.

MOSCHION.
(Heavens, what a business. What on earth am I going to do? After all, it's not really my fault. Well it is, but everything's become rather complicated. Her father won't be happy, that's for sure. Nor will mine, if it comes to that, however long the pair of them are away. Yes, it's my father Demeas who'll be the real problem. Not being my natural father he's more strict than if he were. You see, my own father died when I was a baby and I never knew my mother either. Demeas adopted me, though he's a bachelor, and brought me up as his own son. I'd do anything rather than upset him.)

But what's there to get upset about? It's regrettable, yes. I was in the wrong, I admit it. Look. Gentlemen. I think it would be best if I were to tell you the whole story, beginning with the sort of man my adoptive father is.

I look back on my childhood as comfortable. Nothing more to say except that at the time I didn't realise how comfortable. At eighteen I was registered as a citizen in the ordinary way, 'nem con' as they say, though between ourselves my origins are somewhat humble, God knows. Comfortable! Now look at me. My situation could hardly be more uncomfortable.

As a theatre patron I could afford to make a bit of a splash, if I say so myself, and in charity work too. Demeas kept hounds for me, horses – in the services I held a distinguished cavalry commission. A friend in need could always turn to me. Thanks to my father, I was a man. And I did thank him, by always behaving in public as a gentleman. Then it happened. Well, I might as well make all our affairs public. I'm not in any hurry.

There was this woman, you see, from Samos, called Chrysis, not a citizen so she was a courtesan. Demeas fell in love with her: that's human nature, after all. But he tried to conceal it, from shame, perhaps, I don't know. He certainly didn't want me to find out, but I did. I reckoned that if he was going to keep younger rivals at bay, she would have to become his full-time mistress. As I say, he wasn't keen on that, probably because he thought he would be setting me a bad example.

(He's a man of principle, you see but, like most men of principle, he's a stickler for keeping up appearances. His pride is important to him and I couldn't admit to knowing about the woman. Instead, I confided in our neighbour Nikeratos, who lives here next door with his wife Myrrhine and his daughter Plangon. Nikeratos has always been as poor as my father's rich but he's not afraid to speak his mind. And Plangon . . . but more of her in a minute. Nikeratos confronted Demeas and told him that he'd been seen with this Samian woman and how they'd seemed fond of one another. And what with one thing and another and Demeas being a bachelor, why not invite Chrysis to share his house with him. They couldn't marry, of course, that's the law, but there are no laws against being happy.

Finally Demeas agreed, on condition, as he told Nikeratos and Chrysis, that there could be no question of children because any child would be illegitimate. And anyway, I was his sole heir. He asked my blessing too which I willingly gave, though I had to pretend that the whole affair was a great surprise to me.

For a few months all went well. Then Demeas was called abroad on business. Rather than travel alone he invited Nikeratos to accompany him. He was sad to leave Chrysis but at least he knew she was safe in his house. Tearful farewells all round. Then, the day before they're due to leave, what happened? Chrysis announced she was pregnant. True to his word and, love her or not, Demeas' parting words were, 'Get rid of it or else'.

Are you with me so far? Father abroad. Mistress pregnant with a child she can't keep. Nikeratos also abroad leaving behind his daughter Plangon. Now Plangon's a beautiful girl, but in an awkward position because Nikeratos can't afford to give her a dowry.)

With the two men away, Plangon's mother became close friends with my father's mistress, Chrysis. In and out of one another's houses all the time. One day I happened to come back unexpectedly from the estate to find Plangon and Myrrhine with a number of other women at our house celebrating the Adonis festival. There was lots of eating and drinking and fun and games – you know how it is – and because I'd just come home, I couldn't resist going to have a look. I wouldn't have been able to sleep anyway with the racket they were making. The roof was decorated with fruit and flowers and the women were up there in ones and twos dancing the night away.

I'm not sure I want to tell you what happened next. Quite disgraceful, of course. But it's a bit late to worry about that. Still, I admit I am ashamed of myself. The girl got pregnant. There, I've told you the result. You can fill in the bit in between yourself. I don't deny it. It was all my fault and I went straight to Plangon's mother and swore to marry the girl as soon as her father returned home with my father. The baby was born recently and I brought it to our house. As it happened – a fortunate coincidence really – Chrysis had given birth to her child (only a week or two earlier but that baby died. She knew that Demeas had wanted her to get rid of it but she had hoped somehow that, once he had seen the baby and once he had seen her again, she would be able to win him round to letting her keep it. The question never arose but, having so recently lost a baby of her own, Chrysis agreed to act as wet-nurse to Plangon's. This way no one outside the family would know of Plangon's disgrace until, that is, her father returned from abroad. Then Plangon and I could get married and take the child back as our own.

So far so good. The problem will be with my father who won't be happy about me marrying a girl without a dowry. And if he catches sight of Chrysis with a baby he thinks is hers, there's no knowing how he'll react.

Now Parmenon tells me that father's ship has been sighted and should be landing today. I sent him off to the harbour for news but, whatever happens, I'm expecting a rough passage. Father's bound to think I've let him down. And after all that he's done for me. I think I'd better head down there myself and see what the slave's found out.

Exit MOSCHION. *Enter* CHRYSIS.

CHRYSIS.

What a sweet child. I could almost believe he is mine. I'm still not sure if we're doing the right thing. Demeas is a dear man and he's been good to me, but he'll have to know the truth sometime. I don't know how he'll take it. He's so strait-laced. And he does have a temper. If we can win him round to Moschion marrying Plangon, then he's bound to accept that all Moschion did was jump the gun a little. Didn't he? And if the worst comes to the worst, I can always continue to say the child is mine, whatever he said before he left. But then, what about Plangon? I don't know. I wonder what the news will be from the harbour.)

Oh, here they come and in a hurry. I'll hang on and listen to what they have to say.

Enter MOSCHION *and* PARMENON.

MOSCHION.
Did you actually see father, Parmenon?

PARMENON.
I told you. You don't listen, do you?

MOSCHION.
Nikeratos with him?

PARMENON.
They're both here.

MOSCHION.
That's something to be thankful for, I suppose.

PARMENON.
Be a man, can't you? All you have to do is tell them about the marriage the moment you see them.

MOSCHION.
How can I? Now it's staring me in the face, I've lost my nerve.

PARMENON.
What are you talking about?

MOSCHION.
I can't face my father. I'm too ashamed.

PARMENON.
Think of the girl you wronged. And her mother. You great softy, you're trembling like a leaf.

CHRYSIS.
Why are you shouting at him, you silly man?

PARMENON.
Is that you, Chrysis? You want to know why I'm shouting at him? That's funny, that is. I'll tell you what I'm shouting about. I want there to be a marriage, right? I want this . . . this . . . I want him to stop blubbing all over the porch. And I want him to start remembering that he swore an oath: sacrifices, garlands, wedding-cake. He's trying to wriggle out of it. Now, have I got something to shout about?

MOSCHION.
I'll do it. Everything. What have I got to say?

CHRYSIS.
There, there. Of course you will.

MOSCHION.
The baby belongs to Chrysis and she's bringing it up because it's hers. That's it, right?

CHRYSIS.
Yes, why not?

MOSCHION.
Father's going to be so angry.

CHRYSIS.
And after a while he'll stop being angry. Why? Because, my dear, he loves me. He's a man in love and he can't help himself, any more than you can. 'Love hath the better of temper'. There. Besides I'd put up with anything rather than see the poor mite in some slum foster-home.

(MOSCHION.
What about Plangon?

CHRYSIS.
Plangon can bide her time. As she doesn't have the baby, she needn't tell her father anything until you've seen him and confessed.

MOSCHION.
He'll be furious too.

CHRYSIS.
Not when he hears you're asking for her hand. Particularly if you ask to marry her before you tell him she's already had your baby. Besides, he's a poor man. He should be glad to get her off his hands.

MOSCHION.
That's the other problem.

PARMENON.
What is?

MOSCHION.
My father. He'll never agree to my marrying someone without a dowry. You know what he's like about money.

CHRYSIS.
He couldn't have been more generous to you. He knows Nikeratos and he respects him. They've been travelling companions for the best part of a year. He's not going to turn round and forbid you to marry Plangon on financial grounds. Especially when you've already fathered a child on her.

MOSCHION.
I'll never be able to tell him that. I won't have the nerve. He'll be furious.

CHRYSIS.
There'll be nothing for him to be furious about until it's too late. For the present, the baby's mine and if he's going to be furious with anyone, he'll be furious with me. Parmenon, come inside. If they've docked already we need to get ready. He could be here any time.

Exeunt CHRYSIS *and* PARMENON.

MOSCHION.
I'm in such a muddle. Who do I tell about what

baby? And when? I'm going to make a terrible mess of everything and everyone will be cross with me. I wish we'd never started this.)

What if I went and hanged myself? If only I was better at talking to people. Perhaps I'll go off somewhere quiet and rehearse what I'm going to say. 'What can't be cured must be endured.' I'll have to make the best of it.

Exit MOSCHION. *Enter* DEMEAS *and* NIKERATOS *with slaves and luggage.*

DEMEAS.
What did I tell you? It's fine to be back. You can feel the difference. After that frightful place.

NIKERATOS.
The Black Sea. What's it add up to? Stupid old men; endless fish; unrewarding business. As for Byzantium, a nasty taste in the mouth. And that's it. But back home, Lord, everyone as honest as the day is long. A poor man's paradise.

DEMEAS.
Dear old Athens. Blessings upon you. I wish you everything you deserve. We who love our city are the most fortunate people in the world. Oy, you (*to slaves*). Get inside. Don't stand there gawping. What's the matter with you?

NIKERATOS.
You know what I could never get used to, Demeas? The sun. Most of the time you never saw it. Everything shrouded in fog.

DEMEAS.
There was nothing worth looking at. That's how they manage with so little illumination.

NIKERATOS.
God knows, you're right there.

DEMEAS.
Our problem no longer. Now. That other little

matter we were talking about. What do you want to do?

NIKERATOS.
Marrying my daughter to your boy, you mean?

DEMEAS.
Yes.

NIKERATOS.
I still feel the same. Let's take the bull by the horns and name the day.

DEMEAS.
You really think so?

NIKERATOS.
Absolutely.

DEMEAS.
Splendid. It's what I've been hoping for all along.

NIKERATOS.
Give me a call when you're thinking of going out.

Exit NIKERATOS.

(DEMEAS.
What a match. He's such a proud man, I thought he wouldn't agree. That's one of the reasons I took him away with me. So he could see that as far as I'm concerned money is not that important. Poor Nikeratos. So worried that he'd never find a husband for Plangon because he couldn't afford a dowry. Why should I care? He's a good man. She's a nice enough girl. Moschion's all I have. Even if he's not my flesh and blood, he's never wanted for anything and he won't now. Who cares about a dowry? As long as Nikeratos agrees to sign over everything he has to Moschion the moment he dies, that's good enough for me. But how do I break it to Moschion? He's a conventional sort of boy. Likes to go about things in the proper way. I wouldn't wish to upset him. I'm not sure he ever accepted Chrysis. I know he said he did but he was a bit funny about it. I've missed her so much in the last

months. I can't put it off any longer. I have to go in and see her. Do excuse me but there's a group of dancers coming up the street. They'll keep you entertained till I get back.

Exit DEMEAS.

CHORAL INTERLUDE.

ACT 2

Enter DEMEAS.

DEMEAS.
That does it. That's it. What was the first thing I said to her when she entered my house? 'No children'. What was the last thing I said before I left and she told me she was pregnant? 'Get rid of it'. And she agreed. She agreed. What do I find? I come home after months abroad and what's the first thing I see? Chrysis, nursing a baby. Would you credit it? Why, here's Moschion. He looks distracted about something.

Enter MOSCHION.

MOSCHION.
I got all the way out of the city, sat down to plan what I was going to say and started daydreaming, planning the wedding instead. I made the sacrifices, sent invitations to the wedding-breakfast, ordered the libations. Then I cut the cake and started to hum the wedding-song. Silly of me. When I'd had enough of that . . . goodness, there's father. I hope he didn't hear what I've been saying. Father. Welcome back.

DEMEAS.
Moschion, my boy. I'm overjoyed to see you.

MOSCHION.
You don't look overjoyed. Whatever's the matter?

DEMEAS.
The matter? Only that I hadn't realised my mistress thinks she's my wife.

MOSCHION.
Thinks she's your wife? How could she? What are you talking about?

DEMEAS.
Apparently she's had a baby, my baby. To hell with the both of them. She can clear out and take the bastard with her.

MOSCHION.
You can't do that.

DEMEAS.
Can't I just? What do you expect me to do? Bring up a child that's illegitimate? Not my style. Oh no, not my style at all.

MOSCHION.
Illegitimate? Who's legitimate, for God's sake? Any man born might be illegitimate.

DEMEAS.
It's just a joke to you, isn't it?

MOSCHION.
I'm perfectly serious, I swear it. I can see no distinction between being of one race or of another. To anyone who believes in justice, if a man's good, he's legitimate, and if he's bad, he's a bastard.

(You always claim to do what's right and proper, but how do you *know* what is right and proper? Is it right and proper to throw Chrysis out of your house for having a baby when you love her and she loves you?

DEMEAS.
I gave strict instructions . . .

MOSCHION.
Would you marry her if you could?

DEMEAS.
The question doesn't arise.

MOSCHION.
But would you? Because, if so, the child is as good as legitimate.

DEMEAS.
Perhaps I'm being too hasty. Not that I agree with you, mind.

MOSCHION.
Then you won't tell her to leave and she can keep the baby?

DEMEAS.
I'll think about it. But, in return, there's something you can do for me.

MOSCHION.
Anything you want, Father. You know that.

DEMEAS.
I've been giving the matter some thought and it seems to me it's time you got married.

MOSCHION.
Married?

DEMEAS.
I never did. And look at the result. I find myself in the position of being a father when I can't be a father.

MOSCHION.
But I don't want to get married. Or rather I do want to get married.

DEMEAS.
I've found the ideal girl for you. Of course, she's not entirely ideal.

MOSCHION.
Who do you have in mind?

DEMEAS.
Nikeratos' daughter, Plangon.

MOSCHION.
Plangon?

DEMEAS.
Oh, I know it takes a little getting used to. She hasn't got a dowry. But Nikeratos has agreed that he will bequeath his entire estate to you. He's older than I am so you shouldn't have to wait that long. I've got to know him well over the past few months. He's not clever, of course, and he's never made any money but he's a decent sort of a fellow.

MOSCHION.
Yes.

DEMEAS.
And she's a nice girl. Quite pretty really.

MOSCHION.
This is wonderful. You see, I already want to marry her. We've been waiting for you and Nikeratos to get back to ask for your permission.

DEMEAS.
You mean it?

MOSCHION.
I'm in love with her. I'm in love with Plangon. And we want the wedding to be as soon as possible.)

DEMEAS.
My boy. Why, that's splendid.

(MOSCHION.
There is a slight complication.)

DEMEAS.
Yes, of course. But if they're prepared to offer her, you're prepared to accept.

MOSCHION.
No question. You can see I'm serious, can't you?

DEMEAS.
You mean it? No question? Moschion, I understand. I can see what you're telling me. I'll be off to have a

word with Nikeratos. This minute. To tell him to get going.

MOSCHION.

We've already got everything ready. I'll go indoors and have a wash and offer a libation. Then I'll go and fetch the girl.

DEMEAS.

Wait till I find Nikeratos. I have to check that he's still happy.

MOSCHION.

He's bound to agree. I'll leave you. I'd just be in the way.

Exit MOSCHION.

DEMEAS.

Well, well. 'There's a divinity that shapes our ends', as they say, 'untalk'd of and unseen'. I never even knew he was in love.

(But then a lot can happen in nine months. What a splendid fellow he's turned out to be. So frank, so artless. The way he stood up to me over Chrysis and the baby. There's not an ounce of guile in him. And fearless with it. I have to confess that when Nikeratos first suggested the match I wasn't keen. But everything's worked out for the best. Ah, here he comes.

Enter NIKERATOS.

Not a moment to lose, Nikeratos. Everything under control? Good. Make haste. The wedding is on and today.

NIKERATOS.

What wedding?

DEMEAS.

Moschion's, of course.

NIKERATOS.

To whom?

DEMEAS.
To you, daughter. To Plangon.

NIKERATOS.
Oh, I'm not sure about that.

DEMEAS.
Not sure? It's all settled. We agreed.

NIKERATOS.
Her mother mightn't agree, though. Then there's Plangon.

DEMEAS.
What have they got to do with it? Don't you see? Moschion's in love with her. He told me so himself. If he wants to marry Plangon and we want him to marry Plangon, who else comes into it?

NIKERATOS.
It's Myrrhine. After you'd said what you said, and I agreed with what you said, I went straight in and told Myrrhine that I'd found Plangon a husband.

DEMEAS.
Well?

NIKERATOS.
She gave me a funny look.

DEMEAS.
Is that it?

NIKERATOS.
And then she said 'What's the hurry?'

DEMEAS.
So what did you say?

NIKERATOS.
I went and told Plangon.

DEMEAS.
And what did Plangon say?

NIKERATOS.
She didn't say anything. Just burst into tears and ran off.

DEMEAS.
What's wrong with Moschion, for heaven's sake? A finer boy never lived.

NIKERATOS.
No, of course. I quite agree with you. Only they don't know that it's Moschion.

DEMEAS.
Why don't they know?

NIKERATOS.
I forgot to tell them. I just said I'd found her a husband. It was the idea of a husband that seemed to upset them, not the idea of Moschion.

DEMEAS.
We can't be doing with this sort of nonsense. You approve of Moschion, don't you? Of course you do. Anybody would. The whole thing's ridiculous. So the wedding can be today. Agreed?

NIKERATOS.
I'm not at all sure. Wouldn't it be more sensible . . . ?

DEMEAS.
The sooner the better. If we're going to fix a day, what's wrong with today?

NIKERATOS.
There's a great deal to do.

DEMEAS.
I don't believe in hanging about. Particularly if the women are shilly-shallying. Parmenon! We're having a wedding. Where is that slave?

Enter PARMENON.)

Parmenon. Bouquets. Sacrificial victims. Sesame-seed cake. Off to the market and don't come back till you've bought everything.

PARMENON.
Everything? Right, master. Leave it to me.

DEMEAS.
Get a move on. This minute. And bring back a cook.

PARMENON.
Bring back cook. Buy everything else.

DEMEAS.
Yes, yes. Buy everything.

PARMENON.
I'll run and fetch some money.

Exit PARMENON.

DEMEAS.
Still here, Nikeratos?

NIKERATOS.
I'd better go in and tell my wife to make preparations. Then I'll follow him down to the market.

Exit NIKERATOS. *Re-enter* PARMENON.

PARMENON.
Don't ask me. I don't know anything except that I've got my order and I'm doing what I'm told.

DEMEAS.
He won't find it easy convincing his wife, that's for sure. You should never waste time explaining things to people. Parmenon. Don't hover, boy. Off you go. At the double.

Exit PARMENON.

(Why do people do it? Why do they let wives get away with it? As soon as a man decides on something, his wife dreams up a reason why not. He'd be much better off not telling her in the first place. Or be like me and not get married at all.

Enter NIKERATOS.

DEMEAS.
Well?

NIKERATOS.
I went in and told them that she was going to marry Moschion whether she liked it or not.

DEMEAS.
More tears?

NIKERATOS.
Not a bit of it. Smiles all round. I'll never understand them.

DEMEAS.
That's a relief. I'll go and see how Moschion's getting on and you'd better go back in before they change their minds.

Exeunt DEMEAS *and* NIKERATOS *to their own houses.*

CHORAL INTERLUDE

ACT 3

Enter DEMEAS.

DEMEAS.
I'm flabberghasted. Speechless.)

It was all plain sailing. Everything going swimmingly when, out of nowhere, a tornado. Smashes over the unsuspecting crew and sinks them without trace. That's me. There I was helping with the wedding preparations, sacrificing to the gods, all according to plan. Now, God in Heaven, I don't know if I can believe my eyes. Here and now I parade myself before you as an unequivocal booby. Would you believe it? Look at me. Am I in my right mind or out of it? Or beating my head with the wrong end of the stick?

What happened was this. I went indoors, quick as I could, to get on with the wedding preparations. Lined up all the slaves. Gave them their orders perfectly clearly, cleaning, cooking, getting the baskets ready. Everything was under control, though there was a certain amount of confusion with all the running about. Only natural. Someone had put the baby down on a couch where it wouldn't be in the way. Of course, it was yelling. And the women were all shouting at once. 'Flour. Water over here. Fetch the olive-oil. More charcoal'. I joined in to give them a hand. Which is how I found myself in the store-cupboard. I was quite a while in there, sorting things out and seeing what was what.

While I was in there this woman came downstairs into the room next to the store-cupboard. That's where the loom is kept and you have to go through it to get upstairs or to the store-cupboard. It was Moschion's nurse, quite elderly now and a free-woman though she used to be a slave. Seeing the baby left to cry and nobody looking after it, and not realising that I was in the store-room, she saw no reason to guard her tongue. She went up to the baby and said the sort of things they say to babies. 'Nice baby. What a good boy'. That sort of thing. 'Where's your mummy, then?' Then she picked it up and gave it a cuddle. So it stopped crying and she said to it 'Oh dear, oh dear. It doesn't seem yesterday I was nursing Moschion – you've got his eyes alright – now he's got a boy of his own (and nobody can be bothered with you, poor thing'. And more in the same vein) until some slip of a girl came rushing in. 'Here, the child needs changing', declares the old woman. 'What's the matter with you? You can't neglect a baby just because its father's getting married.' Immediately the girl hushes her up. 'Keep your voice down, idiot. *He's* in there.' 'He's not is he? Where?' 'In the store-cupboard.' Then she says loudly, 'The mistress is calling for you, Nurse. Run along, now.' And not so loudly, 'He won't have heard. Don't worry.' 'Me and my mouth,' the old woman mutters and off she trots, Lord knows where.

Out I came. I was calm. I was collected, as you see I am now, just as though I hadn't heard a word and hadn't begun to wonder if ... First thing I clap eyes on is my Samian with the baby, breast-feeding. The baby must be hers. That's obvious. But who's the father? It's mine. It must be mine. The alternative ... well, frankly, I'm not prepared to put it into words because I don't believe it. All I have done is present the evidence. I heard what I heard. I'm not upset. Not at all. Not yet. I know my boy, indeed I do. He's a gentleman, always has been, and respect for me ... absolutely. The only thing is that I did overhear that nurse. And she was his nurse once. And she didn't know I was there. And looking back at how fond of the baby Chrysis is, and how he persuaded me, against my better judgement, to keep it ... I'm altogether furious.

That's handy. Here's Parmenon back from market with the hired help. I'll let him take them indoors.

Enter PARMENON, COOK *and assistants.*

PARMENON.
God almighty, Cook. I don't know why you bother with cooking knives. You could mince anything with that tongue of yours.

COOK.
You don't know what you're talking about.

PARMENON.
Don't I?

COOK.
No, you don't. That's what I think. What if I need to know how many tables you're going to use, how many waitresses, the serving-time, what to do about a *maîre d'*, have you enough crockery, is it an outdoor kitchen? And there's another thing ...

PARMENON.
Chop, chop, chop. You're mincing me again.

COOK.
The hell with you.

PARMENON.
After you. You lot, get indoors.

Exeunt COOK *and attendants.*

DEMEAS.
Parmenon.

PARMENON.
Someone call my name?

DEMEAS.
Yes, me.

PARMENON.
Oh master there you are. Well, cheerio.

DEMEAS.
Get rid of your basket and come back here.

PARMENON.
Right you are. Happy to oblige.

Exit PARMENON.

DEMEAS.
Never misses a trick, this chap, I'm sure of that. He knows what's going on round here if anybody does. There's the door. He's coming.

Re-enter PARMENON.

PARMENON.
That's it, Chrysis. Everything the cook wants, but for God's sake, keep the old woman away from the dishes. Right, master, what can I do for you?

DEMEAS.
You can come over here for a start, away from the door. A bit further.

PARMENON.
Anything you say.

DEMEAS.
Now listen here, Parmenon. I swear to you, I do

really, that I don't particularly want to give you a thrashing.

PARMENON.
A thrashing? What did I do?

DEMEAS.
You're hiding something, I know you are.

PARMENON.
Me? What? No. I'm not. I swear I'm not. By anything you like, Dionysus, Apollo, Zeus, Asclepius ...

DEMEAS.
That'll do. No need for any swearing. I'm telling you.

PARMENON.
Never in ...

DEMEAS.
Just look. Over there.

PARMENON.
Right. I'm looking.

DEMEAS.
That child. Whose is it?

PARMENON.
Mmmm. Child.

DEMEAS.
I'll ask you once more. Whose is that baby?

PARMENON.
Ah, that baby. That's Chrysis'.

DEMEAS.
And who is the father?

PARMENON.
You are. According to her.

DEMEAS.
Now you are in trouble. Make a fool of me, would you?

PARMENON.
What did I do?

DEMEAS.
I know everything. I know the baby is Moschion's and I know that you know, and that it's for him that she's bringing it up.

PARMENON.
Who says so?

DEMEAS.
Everybody says so. Now, answer me. Am I right?

PARMENON.
Well, yes, master, but we didn't want it becoming common knowledge.

DEMEAS.
Common knowledge? Slaves. Where are you? Fetch me a whip, one of you, for this reprobate.

PARMENON.
No, please.

DEMEAS.
I'll mark you for life.

PARMENON.
Mark me?

DEMEAS.
Here and now.

PARMENON.
I really have had it.

Exit PARMENON.

DEMEAS.
Where do you think you're off to, you little devil? Grab him.

'Blow winds and crack your cheeks.
Rage. Blow.'

What are you on about, Demeas? You're raving, numbskull. Control. Get a grip on yourself.

There. Moschion has done nothing to harm you.

An enigmatic thing to say in the circumstances, you might think, gentlemen, but true. Had he done what he has done voluntarily, or in an uncontrollable passion, or even out of spite, he would still be in the same frame of mind and he would be trying to brazen it out. But he's obviously in the clear.

The proposed marriage delighted him, not, as I assumed at the time, because of love or anything like that, but so as to escape the clutches of this Helen of Troy of mine. Whatever happened, the fault was hers. No doubt about that. She'll have caught him when he was the worse for wear. 'Strong drink and young blood have much to answer for', especially with a little encouragement.

I still can't fathom how a lad who seemed so restrained and so reasonable with everyone else could treat his father like this. I don't care if he was adopted ten times over, natural son or not, it's character that counts. I look to nothing else. The woman's a whore, an infection. Well, what of it? She won't get round me. Be a man, Demeas. Govern your passions. Fall out of love. And as far as possible, hush up the whole business. For Moschion's sake. Pitch her out of the house. Oh my lovely Samian girl. To hell with her. You've got your excuse. She wouldn't get rid of the baby. That's all anyone needs to know. 'Though hard be the task, keep a stiff upper lip.'

Enter COOK.

COOK.
He must be out here, is he? Oy, Parmenon. Damn it, he's done a runner on me. Fat help he was.

DEMEAS.
Get out the way, will you?

Exit DEMEAS.

COOK.
Dear, oh dear. What's all this, then? Some mad old

fellow just rushed indoors. What's his problem? Why should I bother? Off his head clearly. Nothing wrong with his lungs though. Hang on. All my dishes are out. He'll smash the lot. Fine thing that would be. There's a door slamming. Oh, you can rot in hell, Parmenon, for bringing me on this job. Whew! I need a breather.

Enter DEMEAS *and* CHRYSIS.

DEMEAS.
Be off with you. Do you hear?

CHRYSIS.
Where on earth am I to go?

DEMEAS.
You can go to hell, as far as I'm concerned.

CHRYSIS.
This is terrible.

DEMEAS.
Terrible, yes. Tears too? Tragic. I'll soon stop you . . .

CHRYSIS.
Stop me what?

DEMEAS.
Nothing. You've got the child, you've got the old woman. Now, clear off.

CHRYSIS.
All because I kept the baby?

DEMEAS.
Amongst other things.

CHRYSIS.
What other things?

DEMEAS.
Because of that.

COOK.
So that's what all the excitement's about.

CHRYSIS.
I don't understand.

DEMEAS.
You didn't appreciate when you were well off, did you?

CHRYSIS.
Didn't appreciate? What are you talking about?

DEMEAS.
You came to this house with the clothes you stood up in. You know what I'm talking about. One thin frock.

CHRYSIS.
So?

DEMEAS.
I was everything to you. You were nothing.

CHRYSIS.
Who's nothing now?

DEMEAS.
Don't bandy words with me, Chrysis. You have your own things, You can keep the slaves and the jewellery. Now, out of my house.

COOK.
It's a very angry man we've got here. I'll have a word. Excuse me, sir . . .

DEMEAS.
Are you addressing me?

COOK.
Don't bite.

DEMEAS.
Any girl would jump at what I can offer and thank God for it.

COOK.
What's he on about?

DEMEAS.
You have a son. You have everything.

COOK.
Not been bitten yet. Try again. (*Interrupting them.*) All the same ...

DEMEAS.
If you say another word to me, I'll punch your head in.

COOK.
Quite right. Absolutely. Well, then. I'll be back off indoors.

Exit COOK.

DEMEAS.
Something special, are you? You'll soon find out how you rate in the city. Ten drachmas a go and a free dinner. Till you die of drink. If you don't like the idea of that, then starve. You'll learn. Nobody quicker. And you'll realise what a mistake you made. Just keep out of my way.

Exit DEMEAS.

CHRYSIS.
What a disaster. This is awful.

Enter NIKERATOS.

NIKERATOS.
That sheep will provide everything we require for the gods and goddesses: blood, nice gall-bladder, great big spleen, just what the Olympians ordered. I'll parcel up bits for my friends and I'll get what's left – the skin. Gracious me, what's this? That's never Chrysis standing by the door and in tears. It's her alright. Whatever's the matter?

CHRYSIS.
He's thrown me out. That precious friend of yours. That good enough for you?

NIKERATOS.
Good lord. Demeas has?

CHRYSIS.
Yes.

NIKERATOS.
Whatever for?

CHRYSIS.
Because of the baby.

NIKERATOS.
Heavens. Well yes, I had heard from the women that you had kept it and were going to bring it up yourself. Damn fool thing to do but, there you go, he's a good-natured fellow.

CHRYSIS.
He didn't seem to mind at first. Only later.

NIKERATOS.
Just now?

CHRYSIS.
One minute he was telling me to make wedding preparations for Moschion, the next he came rushing in like a lunatic and threw me out.

NIKERATOS.
He's sickening for something. An insalubrious place the Black Sea. Come on. We'll go and see my wife. Cheer up. Nothing to fret over. Give him a little time to think it all out and he'll come to his senses.

Exeunt NIKERATOS *and* CHRYSIS.

CHORAL INTERLUDE

ACT 4

Enter NIKERATOS, *talking to his off-stage wife.*

NIKERATOS.
Woman, you'll be the death of me. I'll go and see him this minute. I wouldn't have had this happen. Not for money, I wouldn't. Oh dear no. Right in the

middle of the wedding. It's not a good omen. This girl thrown out of his house, coming into mine. Then there's the baby. Tears. Commotion amongst the women. And Demeas. What a shitty way to behave. Lord knows, he'll regret being so thoughtless.

Enter MOSCHION.

MOSCHION.
Will the sun never set? How shall I put it? Night has forgot itself, seeming always afternoon. I think I'll have a shower. I've had two already. What else is there to do?

NIKERATOS.
Moschion. I'm glad I've found you.

MOSCHION.
Can we start the wedding? I met Parmenon in the market and he told me it's all set. Can I go and see your daughter yet?

NIKERATOS.
You don't know what's happened?

MOSCHION.
No. What?

NIKERATOS.
What indeed? Some unpleasantness, all quite inexplicable.

MOSCHION.
Heavens. What unpleasantness? I don't know anything about any unpleasantness.

NIKERATOS.
It's Chrysis. I'm sorry, dear boy, but she's just been hoofed out by your father.

MOSCHION.
That's dreadful.

NIKERATOS.
Nevertheless, it's what happened.

MOSCHION.
Whatever for?

NIKERATOS.
Because of the baby.

MOSCHION.
Where is she now?

NIKERATOS.
She's with us.

MOSCHION.
This is a terrible thing to happen. Unbelievable.

NIKERATOS.
If you think it's so terrible . . .

Enter DEMEAS.

DEMEAS.
Give me a stick and I'll give you something to weep about. What is all this nonsense? Why doesn't someone give a hand to the cook? Of course it's a lamentable bloody occasion. A great loss to the household. Obviously.

Lord Apollo, greetings. We ask thy blessing on this wedding and grant us thy benevolence. I intend going through with it, gentlemen, biting back my fury, but I am going through with the wedding.

And please, Lord, keep an eye on me and see I don't give the game away and let me sing the wedding-hymn without choking. Even though I'll never see her again.

NIKERATOS.
You first, Moschion. After you.

MOSCHION.
Yes, alright. Father. Father, why are you doing this?

DEMEAS.
Doing what, Moschion?

MOSCHION.
What do you mean 'what'? Why has Chrysis left? Tell me.

DEMEAS.
A deputation. This is too much. That's my business, damn it. It has nothing to do with you. What nonsense is this? It's dreadful. They're ganging up on me.

MOSCHION.
What did you say?

DEMEAS.
I was right. It's obvious. Or why take her side when he should have been relieved to get rid of her?

MOSCHION.
What do you think your friends will say?

DEMEAS.
My friends, Moschion, will, I expect ... Let me finish.

MOSCHION.
It would be inhuman to do so.

DEMEAS.
You think you can stop me?

MOSCHION.
Yes, I do.

DEMEAS.
This is beyond the pale. Before was bad enough. But this ...

MOSCHION.
'Anger and haste hinder good counsel'.

NIKERATOS.
He's right there, Demeas.

MOSCHION.
Nikeratos. Go on in and tell her to hurry back home.

DEMEAS.
Moschion. Will you allow me? Allow me,

Moschion. And for the third time. I know everything.

MOSCHION.
Everything about what?

DEMEAS.
I don't want to discuss it.

MOSCHION.
You have to discuss it, father.

DEMEAS.
Have to, do I? Am I or am I not master in my own house?

MOSCHION.
One favour, that's all.

DEMEAS.
What sort of favour do you fancy? How would it suit you if I were to leave home and let you two get on with it. Oh, I'll arrange the wedding to Plangon while I'm at it. Do, please, let me make the arrangements for the wedding.

MOSCHION.
Well, thank you. But we must have Chrysis there too.

DEMEAS.
Chrysis!

MOSCHION.
I'm doing this all for you.

DEMEAS.
Couldn't be more blatant. Ye gods, I told you it was a conspiracy. I think I shall explode.

MOSCHION.
What are you talking about?

DEMEAS.
You want me to spell it out to you?

MOSCHION.
Alright.

DEMEAS.
Come over here.

MOSCHION.
Tell me.

DEMEAS.
Very well, then. I'll tell you. The baby. I know it's yours. I heard everything from one of your co-conspirators. Parmenon. So don't play games with me.

MOSCHION.
Well, if I'm the father, what have you got against Chrysis?

DEMEAS.
Whose fault is it then? Yours?

MOSCHION.
I don't see where she comes into it.

DEMEAS.
Don't you? Have you no conscience, the pair of you?

MOSCHION.
What are you shouting about?

DEMEAS.
What am I shouting about? You blackguard. You dare ask me that? Tell me then. Do you accept the entire responsibility? Have you the nerve to look me in the eye and tell me that? Do I mean nothing to you?

MOSCHION.
Why are you saying that?

DEMEAS.
You have to ask?

MOSCHION.
Father, it's not that bad. Thousands of people have done it.

DEMEAS.
Brazen. Here, now, with witnesses present. Who is

the mother of that child? You tell Nikeratos if you don't think it's 'that bad'.

MOSCHION.
Of course it would be wrong to tell him like this. He'll be furious when he finds out.

NIKERATOS.
You monster, you. I'm beginning to work out what's going on. The hypocrisy of it.

MOSCHION.
Now I have had it.

DEMEAS.
Begin to see, do you, Nikeratos?

NIKERATOS.
What dreadful dole is here? The enseamed bed of Tereus, the stewed corruption of Oedipus, the nasty sty of Thyestes. Worse.

MOSCHION.
Who? Me?

NIKERATOS.
You dared do this dreadful deed, dare did you? Now, Demeas, put on the wrath of Amyntor and blind the brute.

DEMEAS.
It's your fault that he found out.

NIKERATOS.
Is anyone safe? Have you no self-control? And I'm expected to give you my daughter's hand? Why, I'd rather – I don't want to tempt providence – I'd sooner marry her to a bigamist. What an unmitigated catastrophe.

DEMEAS.
It's me who's been wronged, you know, but at least I kept it to myself.

NIKERATOS.
You've a slave mentality, Demeas. If it was my nest

he'd fouled, he'd never have done it a second time, and nor would his mate. If it had been a tart of mine, I'd have sold her off tomorrow and disinherited my son while I was at it. It'd have been the talk of the town in every barber's shop and every arcade. From dawn to dusk everybody would have been saying what a fine fellow Nikeratos was, putting his son on a murder charge.

MOSCHION.
Murder charge?

NIKERATOS.
I'd call it murder if someone treated me like that.

MOSCHION.
All this has worn me out, God help me. I'm numb.

NIKERATOS.
To cap it all, I've welcomed the perpetrator into my own home.

DEMEAS.
Then throw her out, Nikeratos, I beg of you. Share my shame, like a good friend.

NIKERATOS.
If I as much as set eyes on her, I'll explode. Why are you staring at me, you savage, you sex-starved Thracian? Get out of my way.

Exit NIKERATOS.

MOSCHION.
Father, for God's sake listen to me.

DEMEAS.
I will not listen to anything.

MOSCHION.
Not even if I tell you that none of this is what you think. I've just realised what's happening.

DEMEAS.
Not what I think?

MOSCHION.
It's not Chrysis who's the mother of that child she was nursing. She was pretending it was hers to do me a favour.

DEMEAS.
What are you talking about?

MOSCHION.
It's the truth.

DEMEAS.
In what way to do you a favour?

MOSCHION.
I didn't want to tell you, but 'The lesser fault the greater doth displace', as you'll see if you only let me explain.

DEMEAS.
You'll be the death of me if you don't.

MOSCHION.
The baby belongs to Nikeratos' daughter, to Plangon – and to me. That's what I didn't want to tell you.

DEMEAS.
But how?

MOSCHION.
It just happened.

DEMEAS.
Don't try and hoodwink me now.

MOSCHION.
You want proof? What'd be the point of lying about it?

DEMEAS.
None, I suppose. Ah, there's the door.

Enter NIKERATOS.

NIKERATOS.
Worse and worse and worse. I went into the house.

What spectacle confronted me? I came straight out again, struck to the quick by what I could least have expected.

DEMEAS.
What can he mean?

NIKERATOS.
I found my daughter with a baby, giving it her tit.

DEMEAS.
Really?

MOSCHION.
Father, you hear that?

DEMEAS.
Moschion. You were not to blame. It was my fault entirely for believing you capable of such a thing.

NIKERATOS.
Demeas, I appeal to you.

MOSCHION.
Time for me to be off.

DEMEAS.
Don't worry.

MOSCHION.
I'd sooner die than face him.

Exit MOSCHION.

DEMEAS.
Whatever's the matter?

NIKERATOS.
Giving the baby a tit.
I just saw her, my daughter, in my house.

DEMEAS.
Probably a joke.

NIKERATOS.
It was no joke. As soon as she saw me, she collapsed in a heap.

DEMEAS.
She probably thought . . .

NIKERATOS.
What's all this 'probably' all the time?

DEMEAS.
I feel that I'm responsible for this.

NIKERATOS.
What are you talking about?

DEMEAS.
It's hard to credit what you say.

NIKERATOS.
I saw it.

DEMEAS.
You must have made a mistake.

NIKERATOS.
Every word is true, I tell you. I'd better go back.

DEMEAS.
Most peculiar. Hang on a moment, old chap.

Exit NIKERATOS.

Oh, he's gone. What a turnaround. That has torn it. When he finds out the truth, God help us, he'll hit the roof, shouting and screaming. What an uncivilised fellow he is, a shit-taster, a real law unto himself.

How could I have entertained such an idea? What a filthy mind. Death's more than I deserve, I swear it. Lord, what a bellowing. That's Nikeratos alright. Calling for fire. Says he's going to barbecue the baby. My grandson and I'll see it toasted. Another bang on the door. The man's a whirlwind, a positive dervish.

Re-enter NIKERATOS.

NIKERATOS.
Demeas, it's a conspiracy. Chrysis is conspiring against me and doing all sorts of terrible things.

DEMEAS.
What do you mean?

NIKERATOS.
She's told my wife not to admit to anything. My daughter too. Now she's seized the baby and refuses to hand it over. So don't be surprised if I kill her with my bare hands.

DEMEAS.
With your bare hands?

NIKERATOS.
She knows everything.

DEMEAS.
Nikeratos, you can't.

NIKERATOS.
I thought I'd let you know in advance.

Exit NIKERATOS.

DEMEAS.
He's having a brainstorm. There he goes again. What's a fellow to do in a mess like this? I've never known anything like it. It's chaos. Plain, unvarnished truth, I think. That's the answer. God almighty. The door again.

Enter CHRYSIS *with the baby.*

CHRYSIS.
What can I do? How can I escape? He'll take the child from me.

DEMEAS.
Chrysis. Over here.

CHRYSIS.
Who's that?

DEMEAS.
Inside. Hurry.

Re-enter NIKERATOS.

NIKERATOS.
Where are you? Where've you got to?

DEMEAS.
Oh, Lord. Hand-to-hand combat this time, I think. Is there anything you want? After someone, are you?

NIKERATOS.
Now Demeas. Out my way. Let me have that baby and we'll start listening to what the women have got to say.

DEMEAS.
Absolutely not.

NIKERATOS.
You're threatening me.

DEMEAS.
Yes, I am. (*Hits him.*)

NIKERATOS.
Right, then. Take that. (*Hits him back.*)

DEMEAS.
Chrysis. Run. He's stronger than me.

Exit CHRYSIS.

NIKERATOS.
You hit me first. I've got witnesses.

DEMEAS.
What about you? Taking a stick to an independent woman and chasing her.

NIKERATOS.
Perjurer.

DEMEAS.
Same to you with knobs on.

NIKERATOS.
The baby. Bring me the baby.

DEMEAS.
Ha, ha. It's my baby.

NIKERATOS.
It is not your baby.

DEMEAS.
Mine.

NIKERATOS.
Help. Someone.

DEMEAS.
Shout your head off.

NIKERATOS.
I'm off indoors to murder my wife.

DEMEAS.
What am I going to do? This is frightful. I must stop him. Where do you think you're off to? Stay here.

NIKERATOS.
Take your hands off me.

DEMEAS.
Get a grip on yourself.

NIKERATOS.
You do me wrong, Demeas. It's perfectly obvious, you're in the plot too.

DEMEAS.
Then allow me to put you in the picture and don't take it out on your wife.

NIKERATOS.
That son of yours has made a fool of me, hasn't he?

DEMEAS.
What nonsense you do talk. He'll stick by the girl. It's not what you think. Come on. Walk with me a little.

NIKERATOS.
Walk?

DEMEAS.
And pull yourself together. Now, Nikeratos. You know that old play, don't you, where Zeus is transformed into a shower of gold and seeps through the roof so he can screw the girl?

NIKERATOS.
What about it?

DEMEAS.
That's just the point. Maybe we ought to anticipate any contingency. Maybe you should make sure that your roof hasn't got a leak.

NIKERATOS.
It's got dozens of them. What on earth has that got to do with anything?

DEMEAS.
That's Zeus, isn't it? Sometimes a shower of gold. Sometimes a shower of rain. You follow? That's the thing. Didn't take long to work that one out, did it?

NIKERATOS.
Are you kidding?

DEMEAS.
Absolutely not. Kid you? Me? You're no worse a man than Akrisios was, I think. And if Zeus found his daughter acceptable, then yours . . .

NIKERATOS.
Damn me if it isn't Moschion making me look an idiot.

DEMEAS.
He'll marry Plangon. Don't worry about it. But I'm telling you, this is a wonderful thing.

There are thousands of people who are wandering about in public whose fathers are gods. What about Chaerephon who's always at parties but never brings a bottle? Only the Almighty could get away with it.

NIKERATOS.
Perhaps you're right. Tell me what to do, I don't want to fight with you over something so trivial.

DEMEAS.
Good thinking, Nikeratos. Then there's Androkles.

How old must he be? Always jogging. Plenty of boyfriends. Not one grey hair on his head. He'd rather die with his throat slit than turn white. I'd call that divine, wouldn't you?

Off you go and say your prayers. Burn a bit of incense and have a sacrifice. Moschion will come and fetch Plangon presently.

NIKERATOS.
I suppose I have to ...

DEMEAS.
Of course you do.

NIKERATOS.
If she was taken ...

DEMEAS.
That's enough. Go and get ready.

NIKERATOS.
Yes. I'll go and get ready.

DEMEAS.
So will I.

NIKERATOS.
Yes. You get ready as well.

DEMEAS.
What a good idea.

Exit NIKERATOS.

And thank God that all my suspicions proved ill-founded.

Exit DEMEAS.

CHORAL INTERLUDE

ACT 5

Enter MOSCHION.

MOSCHION.
At first I was relieved just to be exonerated from a false accusation and thought how lucky I'd been to get away with it. Now I've had time to mull it over and see the implications, I'm absolutely fuming. It makes me furious that my father could even have suspected me of such behaviour. If it wasn't for the position in which Plangon finds herself and all the problems to which I've been subjected, ethical, physical, temporal and natural, he'd never get away with such an accusation. I'd be off, away from Athens, and join up as a mercenary somewhere like Baktria or Karia. But I can't do the brave thing and all because of you, dearest Plangon. I'm in love and love overrules better judgement.

I still can't get over the dishonourable, the disreputable, the despicable opinion of me he has demonstrated. I think I should put the wind up him a little, even if I only *tell* him that I'm going to leave the country. If nothing else, he'll think twice before levelling accusations at me in future. Here's Parmenon, the right man at the right time, for once.

Enter PARMENON.

PARMENON.
That was so stupid. Hell's teeth. What a brainless, childish thing to do. I hadn't done anything, but I ran away from my master because I got scared. And what crime have I committed? Let us investigate point by point. One. The boy Moschion does what he shouldn't with a free girl. You can't blame Parmenon for that. She gets pregnant. Not guilty. The baby comes into our house. He brought it, not me. A member of the household claims it as hers. What did Parmenon do wrong? Nothing. So why did you run off, you silly coward? It's pathetic.

He did threaten to mark me for life. Yes, that's what it boils down to. It makes no odds whether I'm in the right or not. One way or another, I'll catch it.

MOSCHION.
Hey.

PARMENON.
Hello there.

MOSCHION.
No messing about. Just get indoors, quick.

PARMENON.
What for?

MOSCHION.
Fetch my greatcoat and sword.

PARMENON.
A sword? You?

MOSCHION.
Get a move on.

PARMENON.
What for?

MOSCHION.
Do it. There's no need for a song and dance.

PARMENON.
What's going on?

MOSCHION.
If I have to get the whip . . .

PARMENON.
No, no. I'm on my way.

MOSCHION.
Then what are you waiting for?

Exit PARMENON.

Father will come out. Then, of course, he'll beg me to stay. I'll let him beg for a bit. Serve him right.

Then, at a moment of my choosing, I'll let him persuade me. I'll have to be convincing, though. I wish I were a better actor. There's the door. He's coming.

Re-enter PARMENON.

PARMENON.
You've been overtaken by events. Your information's totally out of date which is why you're getting into such a tizzy over nothing.

MOSCHION.
Haven't you got my things?

PARMENON.
Look, they're starting the wedding. The wine's mixed. Incense burning.
'Upon such sacrifices, my master,
The Gods themselves throw incense.'

MOSCHION.
What about my things?

PARMENON.
Everything's ready except you. They've been waiting for you for ages. Go and get the girl. It's all worked out fine. Nobody's annoyed with you. Cheer up. What more do you want?

MOSCHION.
Order me about, would you, you devil? (*Hits him.*)

PARMENON.
Ow. Moschion, what did you do that for?

MOSCHION.
Get inside and fetch me what I asked for. Fast.

PARMENON.
My lip's bleeding.

MOSCHION.
And you're still talking?

PARMENON.
I'm going. I'm going. I've landed in it this time.

MOSCHION.
You're still here.

PARMENON.
The wedding really is on, you know.

MOSCHION.
Still on about that? Tell me something new.

Exit PARMENON.

That'll bring him out. But what am I going to do, gentlemen, if he doesn't beg me to stay? What if he gets angry and lets me go? What'll I do then? He wouldn't. Would he? What if he does? Anything can happen and I'll look ridiculous.

Re-enter PARMENON.

PARMENON.
There. Coat. Sword. Take them.

MOSCHION.
Bring them here, then. Anybody ... notice you? Anybody inside?

PARMENON.
Nobody.

MOSCHION.
Ah, nobody. Nobody at all?

PARMENON.
I told you.

MOSCHION.
Why did you tell me that? To hell with you.

PARMENON.
Off you trot. Anywhere you want. You're making a fool of yourself.

Enter DEMEAS.

DEMEAS.
Well, where is he then?
Tell me. My boy. What is all this?

PARMENON.
Off you go. Get a move on.

DEMEAS.
Why are you wearing your coat? What's the matter? You're not leaving, are you?

PARMENON.
You can see he is. All ready for the road. I'd better go and warn the family. I'm on my way.

Exit PARMENON.

DEMEAS.
Oh Moschion. You're upset and I love you for it. I can't say I blame you when I made such a groundless accusation against you. I was wrong. All I can do is ask you to consider this. Even in bad times, I'm still your father. I took you in when you were a baby and I've brought you up. If your life has had some joy in it, give me credit for that and balance it against the pain I've caused, as a son should. I blamed you for something you never did. That was unfair. I shouldn't have done it. I must have been out of my mind. That's the way things go. I was trying to protect your reputation in the eyes of the world, so I confided in no one. And all along I had the wrong end of the stick.

But I never said a word that an enemy could gloat over. What you're doing is broadcasting this mistake of mine and telling the world what a fool I've been. That's not worthy of you, Moschion. Don't allow the one day in your life when I let you down drive out the memory of the past. There's more I could say but, never mind. Grudging obedience won't do, you know. A father needs respect.

Enter NIKERATOS.

NIKERATOS.
Don't hold me back. Everything's ready. Libations, sacrifices, ceremony. All we need is him, if he ever

deigns to come in, so the girl's got someone for me to give her to. What's going on?

DEMEAS.
I don't know. Damned if I do.

NIKERATOS.
How can you not know? That's his greatcoat. He's planning to leave. It's obvious.

DEMEAS.
That's what he says.

NIKERATOS.
Says that, does he? And who's going to let him go, a self-confessed fornicator, caught in the act? I'll bind you over, young man, and quick about it.

MOSCHION.
Yes. You tie me up. Try it.

NIKERATOS.
Oh, you do talk rubbish. Put your sword away, will you.

DEMEAS.
Do put it away, Moschion, I implore you. Stop getting him excited.

MOSCHION.
Oh, very well, then.
Seeing as you beg me. You win.

NIKERATOS.
Seeing as we beg you? Come here.

MOSCHION.
Are you going to tie me up?

DEMEAS.
No, no he isn't. Go and fetch the bride.

NIKERATOS.
Are you sure?

DEMEAS.
Yes. Yes, of course.

Exit NIKERATOS.

MOSCHION.

If you'd behaved like this in the first place, Father, we could have done without the moralising.

Re-enter NIKERATOS *with* PLANGON *followed by* CHRYSIS *and* MYRRHINE.

NIKERATOS.

You first. Out you go.

Before witnesses I bestow this child upon you for the procreation of legitimate children, with all my worldly goods as a dowry, but not until I'm dead, which may never happen if I live for ever.

MOSCHION.

I hold her. I accept her. I love her.

DEMEAS.

Now all that is left is Moschion's ablutions. Chrysis, fetch the women, a water-carrier and a flute-player. Someone bring a torch and garlands and we'll all join the procession.

MOSCHION.

They're here already.

DEMEAS.

A garland for your head. Now smarten yourself up a bit.

MOSCHION.

Anything you say, Father.

DEMEAS.

Handsome boys, young men and old, gentlemen of the audience, your applause, please, that lovely sound which signifies the favour of Dionysus. And may the blessed goddess, Victory incarnate, judge of our splendid drama competitions, look with favour on my choruses, now and always.

END

EURIPIDES

Cyclops

translated by J. Michael Walton

Characters

SILENUS, an old man, father of the Satyrs
ODYSSEUS, King of Ithaca
CYCLOPS, the one-eyed giant Polyphemus
CHORUS of Satyrs
CREWMEN of Odysseus

In front of a cave on Mount Etna.

Enter SILENUS.

SILENUS.

Dionysus! It's your fault I'm still as full of aches and pains as when I had a young man's body. Hera drove you crazy then and you ran off, abandoning your nurses, the mountain-nymphs. That was the first time. Then when I stood at your side, your companion-in-arms, in the battle with the earth-born giants: what a time that was. You remember, I smashed Enceladus right through the skull with my spear. Killed him, stone dead. What do you mean, I dreamt it? It wasn't a dream when I showed Dionysus the spoils. He'll take some bailing out this time, though. Listen. It was Hera again. She persuaded a gang of Tuscan pirates to take you on an extended sea-voyage, didn't she? As soon as I heard about it, I set sail with the lads to rescue you. There I stood at the helm, guiding the ship, while my boys strained at the oars, churning the blue sea white. We were looking for you, Lord. We hadn't quite reached Malea – we were close – when an east wind blew up and drove us onto the rocky shore of Etna where the sons of Neptune live, the Cyclopes, one-eyed cave-dwellers, man-eaters.

One of them captured us and forced us to become his slaves. The master we now serve is known as Polyphemus. No more Bacchic junketings for us. We are shepherds for this godless creature. They are down there now, my lads, no, over there at the foot of the mountain, minding the sheep. So young, poor things. My lads, that is, not the sheep. I stay here to top up the troughs and clean up his quarters and serve his Stygian stews. I must go and rake out all his filth ready to welcome them back, my master and his sheep.

There are my boys now. I can see them, driving the sheep. No, over there. Hey, what are they up to?

What's that clapping noise? I don't believe it. They're dancing. They're dancing the *sikinnis*. It's like being back at Althea's house dancing for Dionysus, playing, singing, camping about and I don't know what else.

Enter CHORUS *with sheep*.

CHORUS.

Get down here.
Your fathers were of high degree,
Your mothers have a pedigree.
D'you hear?

What's the rush?
Why're you heading for the heights,
When you'll find your grazing rights
Are just as lush

By the trough,
Where the breeze is fast asleep
And the water's running deep
For you to quaff?

Accursed flock!
While your desperate lambs are bleating
You can only think of eating.
Here's a rock,

Here's a brick.
Get down here, you brood of Cyclops
Or you'll get it in the lamb-chops
Double-quick.

Hear them bleat.
Little lambs left in the fold
By evening need a sucking-hold
Nose to teat.

Do it now.
You need milking. They need feeding,
They've been sleeping. You're not heeding.
You know how.

Come away
To your cave in Etna's deep.

The best grass will always keep
Another day.

So sad.
No more Bacchus, no more dances,
No more thyrsus-waving Bacchants.
No more cymbals' rowdy clash;
No more happy wine-jars' splash;
No more nymphs in headlong rush;
Where the springing fountains gush.
Too bad.

I call on Dionysus.
I sing to Aphrodite.
I hunt her 'midst the bare-foot Bacchants.
Where do you wander, my Dionysus?
Where do you shake your golden hair?
I serve Polyphemus.
I attend the one-eyed Cyclops.
I slave for him, tricked out in filthy goatskin.
Where do you wander, my Dionysus?
Starved of your love,
I would that I were there.

SILENUS.
Shush, lads. That's enough. Get the attendants to shut the sheep in the shelter.

CHORUS.
Off you go now. Shoo. What's all the rush, father?

SILENUS.
I can see a boat on the shore. And it's Greek. Lords of the oar, there on the shore. No, they're heading this way. And they've got their commander with them. What's that they're carrying? It looks like baskets. Empty baskets and pitchers. They're after supplies. Poor things. Whoever they are, they can't know who Polyphemus is, nor what sort of reception they'll get, or they wouldn't be heading for this cannibal cave. Quiet now, quiet. Let's at least find out who they are and how they happen to be in Sicily.

Enter ODYSSEUS *and his men.*

ODYSSEUS.
Strangers, friends. Do you have any running water round here? We're a little bit parched, I can't deny it. And I don't suppose there's anyone with a bite or two to spare? We'll pay, naturally. Aye, aye, what's all this? It looks as though we've happened in on the garden-city of Dionysus. Those are satyrs, that crowd over there by the cave. I'll address myself to the decrepit one. Hello, old man.

SILENUS.
Welcome, strangers. Who are you? Where do you come from?

ODYSSEUS.
I am Odysseus. King of the Cephallenians. Odysseus, from Ithaca.

SILENUS.
I've heard of you. Son of Sisyphus and a right rattle.

ODYSSEUS.
That's who I am. So less of the lip.

SILENUS.
Where did you set out for Sicily from?

ODYSSEUS.
From Troy. We've come from the Trojan War.

SILENUS.
Troy? You can't be much of a navigator if you're heading for Ithaca.

ODYSSEUS.
A force ten gale drove us here.

SILENUS.
Hard luck. The same thing happened to me.

ODYSSEUS.
Then you too were driven here unwillingly?

SILENUS.
We were chasing pirates who had kidnapped Dionysus.

ODYSSEUS.
What place is this? Does anyone live here?

SILENUS.
That mountain there, that's Etna, highest in Sicily.

ODYSSEUS.
There's no sign of walls or fortifications, as far as I can see. Is there a city near here?

SILENUS.
No. No people, so no city.

ODYSSEUS.
Who does the land belong to? Or is it the province of the wild beast?

SILENUS.
Cyclopes. And they don't live in houses. They live in caves.

ODYSSEUS.
Do they obey one man? Or do they favour democracy?

SILENUS.
They're a solitary lot. There's none of them pays no attention to nobody.

ODYSSEUS.
A predominantly cereal-crop economy, I imagine. How else would they live?

SILENUS.
Milk, cheese and mutton.

ODYSSEUS.
And they cultivate Dionysus, eh? Fruit of the vine?

SILENUS.
Not a drop. It's a rotten place. No drinking, no dancing.

ODYSSEUS.
A decent welcome for strangers, though, I expect?

SILENUS.
If they're juicy. They eat them.

ODYSSEUS.
Eat them? Do you mean they feast on human flesh?

SILENUS.
Yes, they eat them. Allcomers.

ODYSSEUS.
Where is this Cyclops? He's not in there, is he?

SILENUS.
He's out hunting on Etna with the dogs.

ODYSSEUS.
We'd better get a move on. Do us a favour.

SILENUS.
I don't know about that, Odysseus. Of course we'd like to help.

ODYSSEUS.
Sell us some bread. We've nothing left.

SILENUS.
Like I told you, there's only meat.

ODYSSEUS.
Only meat? Fine. Beggars can't be choosers.

SILENUS.
Cheese, we got, fig-juice, cheese and milk.

ODYSSEUS.
Fetch it out. We want to see what we're buying.

SILENUS.
How much have you got? In gold?

ODYSSEUS.
We don't actually have any gold. We do have a rather special vintage ...

SILENUS.
Wine? Oh, bless you, sir, bless you. That's been in short supply round here.

ODYSSEUS.
And this is rather special, as I said. A present from Dionysus' own son, Maron.

SILENUS.
Maron? Not Maron. Why, I used to nurse him in these very arms, so I did.

ODYSSEUS.
That's the one. Son of Dionysus.

SILENUS.
It will be back on board, I suppose. You wouldn't have it with you?

ODYSSEUS.
Yes, I do. Here it is. In this wineskin.

SILENUS.
In that? That is hardly a decent mouthful.

ODYSSEUS.
More than you think and twice enough to see you under the table.

SILENUS.
You're talking liquid pleasure.

ODYSSEUS.
You fancy a drop, do you? Neat, naturally.

SILENUS.
Oh, of course. Call it a buyer's sample.

ODYSSEUS.
The flask comes with matching accessory. Have a cup.

SILENUS.
Oh, that takes me back.

ODYSSEUS.
There, now.

SILENUS.
Oh, I say. Oh my. What a bouquet.

ODYSSEUS.
Take a look at that.

SILENUS.
It's a sniff of it I want.

ODYSSEUS.
Enough of this talk. What about a taste?

SILENUS.
Yes. Mmmm, yes. Feet, Dionysus says you gotta dance. Da, da, dee. Da, da, da.

ODYSSEUS.
And how did that lubricate your larynx?

SILENUS.
It's making my toe-nails curl.

ODYSSEUS.
Actually, we could offer cash.

SILENUS.
Forget the cash. Untie the skin.

ODYSSEUS.
We'll need some cheeses then. And a few lambs.

SILENUS.
Anything, anything. What's a Cyclops matter? Just one more mouthful or I'll go crazy. You can buy the flock, the whole lot, and I'll go and jump in the sea off the Leucadian Rock, so long as I can get tanked up to the eyeballs first. Anyone who doesn't like drinking must be . . . must be out of his mind. With a drink inside you, you can face the world, erect, grab yourself a fistful of tit and let your hands roam free over some of those soft acres. Bit of dancing. Begone dull care. Give me one more slurp at the skin and I'll tell that big, dumb Cyclops what he can do with his eye-socket.

CHORUS.
Here, Odysseus. Can we have a word?

ODYSSEUS.
Fire away. We are all friends here.

CHORUS.
Did you really capture Troy?

ODYSSEUS.
Certainly.

CHORUS.
And get Helen back?

ODYSSEUS.
We sacked Priam's entire domain.

CHORUS.
And when you got her, did you all give her a bang? Did you? Give her what she wanted? I bet she enjoyed it, did she? The bitch. One look at some fancy trousers and a gold medallion and, phht. 'Bye, 'bye, Menelaus. Poor little chap. They ought to abolish women, the whole lot of them. But leave a few for me.

SILENUS.
Oy, Odysseus. Here's your little lambs. Pick of the flock. A little bit of curd and a nice piece of cheese. Now, push off as quick as you like. Only leave me that luscious liquor. Oh lord, the Cyclops is coming. What are we going to do?

ODYSSEUS.
I think we're in trouble, old chap. Where can we run to?

SILENUS.
Get in the cave. You can hide there.

ODYSSEUS.
That's a terrible idea. We'd be trapped.

SILENUS.
It's not a terrible idea. There are plenty of hiding-places in there.

ODYSSEUS.
Hide? Never. Defeated Troy would weep to see me flee a single man. I who faced a thousand Trojans in the field.

If we should win, we gain eternal fame.
If die, at least we know we saved our name.

Enter CYCLOPS.

CYCLOPS.
Come on, shift yourselves. What's going on? You're not on your holidays. This all looks a bit Bacchic, a bit Dionysiac, to me. We'll have no Dionysus here, thanks very much. None of your ding-dongs and your rat-a-tat tats. How's my little lambs in the cave? Having a proper suckle? Are they snuggling up under their mothers like they should? Is there a full complement of cheeses in the wicker? Speak up. What do you say? Quick, or it'll be club and tears time. Head up. Don't look down.

CHORUS.
Right. Anything you say. We're looking up into the sky. Good heavens, stars. And Orion's belt.

CYCLOPS.
What's for breakfast?

CHORUS.
Here it is. I hope your taste-buds are primed.

CYCLOPS.
Are the milk churns full?

CHORUS.
You can drink a bucketful if you want.

CYCLOPS.
Sheeps' milk or cows', or half and half?

CHORUS.
Please yourself. Just don't swallow me.

CYCLOPS.
Not likely. It would polish me off, a tum full of tap-dancers. Hallo, what's this posse at the door? Has the country been overrun with crooks and cutthroats? Those are my sheep, from my cave. I can see them. All hobbled for off. Cheese presses. And the old fellow with his meat beaten by the looks of him.

SILENUS.
Oh, the pain. They murdered me. Oh, it does hurt.

CYCLOPS.
Who murdered you? Who punched your head in, old man?

SILENUS.
It was them, Cyclops, when I tried to stop them robbing you.

CYCLOPS.
Did they not know that I am a god? Like my father before me?

SILENUS.
I did tell them, naturally. They grabbed your stuff anyway, ate your cheese. And they were just making off with those lambs over there. There was nothing I could do. They said they'd put you in a pillory three yards high. And extract your entrails through your eye-socket. And give your back a good flaying. And tie you up to the rowing-bench on their ship and sell you off as a navvy or labour for the treadmill. That sort of thing.

CYCLOPS.
Is that a fact? Right. Be so good as to go and sharpen the cleavers and the carvers and get a nice big fire going. Then I can slit their throats and barbecue the best bits to take the edge off my appetite. Stew the rest. I'm fed up with mountain-meat. And, if I ever have to face boiled lion again . . . or stag . . . Time for man-chop.

SILENUS.
That's the ticket, master. Be adventurous. The old menu's so boring. It's a while since we've had visitors at this establishment.

ODYSSEUS.
Ah, Cyclops. Our turn, I think, for a few words. We arrived here at your cave from our ship, in need of food, which we fully intend to pay for. This individual did, in actual fact, barter these lambs in exchange for some wine. He was agreeable. We were agreeable. There was no question of coercion.

There's not one grain of truth in what he says. What has happened is that he has been caught out trading your belongings.

SILENUS.

Who me? You'll rot in hell, you will.

ODYSSEUS.

Only if I lie.

SILENUS.

Oh Cyclops, I swear to you, by your father Poseidon, by Triton, by Nereus and his daughters. And by Calypso. By the sacred waves of the sea and all the little fishes, dear handsome Cyclops, old friend, boss, what can I say? Would I sell your stuff? Let my lads come to a bad end if I tell a lie. And you know how much I love them.

CHORUS.

Hold on. Hold on. I saw you selling the stuff to the strangers. And if I tell a lie, let my father come to a bad end. There's no need to harm the strangers.

CYCLOPS.

I don't believe you. I trust him more than I'd trust Rhadamanthus. So he's right. And I've got a few words for the strangers. Where are you from? Where do you belong? Where were you brought up?

ODYSSEUS.

We're Ithacans by race, but we come from Troy. We were driven here, Cyclops, by contrary winds on the way home from sacking the city.

CYCLOPS.

Oh, you are, are you? You're the ones who trooped off to Troy beside Scamander after that dreadful Helen.

ODYSSEUS.

That's us. A brave bunch for a doughty deed.

CYCLOPS.

A bad business all round. Phrygia laid to waste and all for the sake of one woman.

ODYSSEUS.

God's will, you know. No blame attached to mortals. Be that as it may, most noble son of the sea-god, we do throw ourselves on your mercy, speaking as free men. Do not risk killing these men who have come to your home as friends and don't have them served up for lunch. It would not be seemly. At the far corners of the Greek world we have protected your father's holy places. The haven of holy Taenarus remains inviolate. The caves on Malea's Cape: silvery rock of sacred Athene at Sunium: sanctuaries at Geraestus; all safe and down to us. We never gave anything Greek to the Trojans – what a suggestion. We're in this together, you and us. This is part of Greece, here beneath Etna with its fire-breathing rock. And, if you respect these arguments, the moral law – bear with me, please – decrees that you should receive suppliants and seafarers in trouble, give them presents and clothe them, not push an ox-spit up them and kebab them for breakfast. Hasn't Priam's land bereaved poor Greece enough, draining the blood of war-torn corpses, robbing wives and silver-haired parents of husbands and favourite sons? If you're going to consume the left-overs for dessert, where can anyone turn? Hear me, Cyclops. Restrain those greedy molars. Choose the decent way, not this. Plenty of men have come to regret short-term gain.

SILENUS.

Take my advice, Cyclops. Don't leave a scrap of him. Swallow his tongue, then you'll become as big a bull-shitter as he is.

CYCLOPS.

Listen, pygmy. The clever man's god is money. Everything else is wind and words. That stuff about my father's shrines up and down the coast, forget it. All these words, who needs them? I'm not afraid of any thunderbolt from Zeus, friend, 'cos I've got no reason to believe he's any bigger a god than I am.

And *I don't care*. About anything. If it's raining, I go indoors where it's nice and sheltered. If I've an appetite, I serve it, a little bit of tasty, wild or tame. I lounge about massaging my belly, drinking milk by the gallon. And if Zeus thunders at me, I wank in his face. When the north wind brings snow from up in Thrace, I put on a fur-coat and stoke up the fire. Winter doesn't bother me. The earth provides the grass to feed my flocks – she can't help it. And I don't make a sacrifice to anybody – except me. The biggest of my gods is my stomach. Eat lots and drink lots every day, that's Zeus for the discerning, and no problem. And all those who want to decorate man's life with morals, stuff 'em. No skin off my soul if I eat you. But just in case there are rules of hospitality, so as to protect myself, as it were, I can offer you a fire and a cauldron of salty water, to boil the flesh off your bones nicely. Now creep off in there and show a little respect to my household god. Reverence the altar of me.

ODYSSEUS.

Woe. Alas. The pains I bore at Troy and on the sea only to be shipwrecked against the rude and inhospitable heart of this unruly creature. Pallas Athene, goddess born of Zeus, help me now. Now, Athene, for never was my extremity so pressing at Troy, no nor danger so profound. And you, Zeus, god of hospitality, sitting up there in the stars, take a look at this one. For, if you cannot see what's happening here, you're not much of a Zeus and that's a fact.

Exeunt ODYSSEUS, *his men and* CYCLOPS.

CHORUS.

Open up, Cyclops,
Your hungry throat, Cyclops.
Open up, Cyclops.
It's *table d'hôte*, Cyclops.
Stranger, grilled or in a stew,
For a gobble, gulp or chew,

While you're lounging in your coat,
Made of goat, Cyclops.

No thanks, Cyclops,
I'm not your guest, Cyclops.
No thanks, Cyclops,
While you digest, Cyclops,
A sacrificial feast
More fitting for a beast,
Going home, may I suggest,
Would suit me best, Cyclops.

On this we'll all agree, it's a pretty rotten host
Who will entertain a stranger and then serve him up on toast.
It's the sort of boorish manners I really can't abide
Notwithstanding the free offer of a salad on the side.

Enter ODYSSEUS.

ODYSSEUS.
Oh heavens. How can I say it? How can I tell of the terrible things I saw in the cave? More like a play than real life.

CHORUS.
What is it, Odysseus? Don't tell me that wicked Cyclops has slaughtered your companions.

ODYSSEUS.
Two of them, anyway. He had a good look and picked out the plumpest.

CHORUS.
You poor man. Tell us what happened.

ODYSSEUS.
As soon as we had entered that rocky place, Polyphemus lit a fire, throwing great logs from a lofty oak onto the hearth – three wagonloads at least. On the fire he placed his bronze cooking-pot and drew his pine-needle bed close to the flames. Then he milked his sheep, filling a hundred-gallon churn with the foaming liquid. Beside it he set an ivy bowl, four foot across, but more like six foot deep; and

thorn-spits, burnt to a point at one end and finished with a billhook: all Etna's sacrificial gear.

As soon as everything was ready, this hellish cook grabbed two of my men. In a single movement he bled one of them into the brazen pot and, holding the other by the ankle, cracked open his skull on a jagged bit of wall, so his brains spilled out. With his knife he chopped off the flesh to bake on the fire and put the limbs into the pot to boil. It was terrible. Tears pouring from my eyes, I approached and waited upon him. The others, like birds, were huddled in the recesses of the cave, white-faced.

Sated on the flesh of my companions, the Cyclops fell back with a vast belch. Then it came to me, a heaven-sent idea. I filled a cup with Maron's wine and handed it to him with these words: 'Cyclops, son of Poseidon', I said, 'take a look at this. Such wine you find in Greece. Dionysus' glory.' And he, though bloated with his filthy meal, snatched it from me and drained it off without pausing for breath. Then he lifted his hands in delight. 'Thanks,' he said, 'my dearest guest, for supplying a fine wine for a fine meal.' When I saw he really was delighted, I poured him some more, well aware that the wine would bewilder him and set him up for the fate he deserved. He started to sing. I just kept filling him up: warming his cockles and filling him up. There's the Cyclops singing away on one side, my sailors howling away on the other, all round the cave. What a row. So I popped out quietly to save myself and you too, if you want. Now, do you or don't you want to get away from this unconscionable creature, so that you can live your lives with the nymphs in the halls of Dionysus? What do you say? Your father inside says 'Yes', but he can hardly stand up from the drink and is glued to his cup, wings flapping like a bird trapped in lime. But you, you're young. Let's get away together and you can go and find your Dionysus, dear old Dionysus, a far cry from this ghastly Cyclops.

CHORUS.
Yes, oh yes, dear friend. Just to see the day when we escape from this ogre. My poor old prick's been in retreat recently. He could do with a nibble.

ODYSSEUS.
Right then. Here's my plan to avenge myself on this foul fiend and to effect your release.

CHORUS.
Hit me with it. You could play no sweeter music in Asia than 'Death and the Cyclops'.

ODYSSEUS.
He's got it into his head that he wants to hold a party with his brother-Cyclopses, so delighted is he with this draught of Dionysus.

CHORUS.
I get you. You're going to set on him when he's by himself in the woods, or shove him over a cliff.

ODYSSEUS.
Hardly. I prefer the subtle approach.

CHORUS.
What then? We always heard you were the wily one.

ODYSSEUS.
I'm going to stop him holding this party by telling him that a Cyclops shouldn't share his wine, but keep it all for himself. Then I'll wait until he's overcome and in a Dionysiac stupor. There's an olive-branch in there and my intention is to sharpen it with my sword and heat it in the fire. As soon as it is alight, I'll pick it out and plunge it into his eye-socket. That will sizzle his vision. And, just as a shipwright drives his drill with a double strap, I'll twirl my twig in his socket and recycle the Cyclops.

CHORUS.
Oh boy, oh boy. A wild idea. We love it.

ODYSSEUS.

And then we will all climb aboard my black ship, you, my friends and the old man, and get away from this land double-quick.

CHORUS.

Is there any way I could give a hand, especially with the red-hot gouging? I would like to give a hand with the gouging.

ODYSSEUS.

Certainly. It's a huge brand. All hands to the plough.

CHORUS.

I can lift a hundred cartloads, so long as I get to carbonize his eyeball, like a wasps' nest.

ODYSSEUS.

Quietly does it, now you know the plans. On the word go, follow your leaders. I have no intention of deserting my men by beating a retreat. Though, of course, I could, me being outside the cave. But it wouldn't be fair for me to desert my companions – we came here together after all – just to save my own skin.

CHORUS.

After me. Me first, not you.
Don't push, what's the rush? Form a queue.
To grasp the flaming flagpole
And shove it in his eyehole
And twiddle till his brains are seeping through.

Shhh. Quiet. Here he comes.

Under the influence, singing a song.
The tune's picayune
And it's ever so long.
Reeling he's roused from his revelling bunk.
We'll speed his arousal
We'll teach him carousal.
By the time that we've finished he'll end up blind
drunk.

Happy the man laid out with grapes in a bunch.
Happy the man engaged with a friend after lunch,
Getting happily laid.
Happy the man with a delicate girl in his bedding
Happy the man anticipating the wedding,
With the bridesmaid.

Enter CYCLOPS *with* SILENUS.

CYCLOPS.
La-di-da-di-da-di-da.
I'm crammed full of wine,
With feasting replete.
My tum's like a drum,
My cargo's complete.
Which reminds me I wanted to share with my fine kin
A paean Cyclopean
So pass me the wineskin

CHORUS.
With eye all-inflamed he parades from the hall.
Is it me that he loves? What a fate to befall.
The bridal torch is waiting
And she's ready for the mating
Inside that juicy hall.
Preparation's almost done.
For the groom it's just begun.
His crown still needs it's multi-coloured shawl.

ODYSSEUS.
Listen here, Cyclops. There's not much I don't
know about this Dionysiac stuff I gave you.

CYCLOPS.
Who is he, this Dionysus? Not a proper god, is he?

ODYSSEUS.
At giving mankind pleasure, he's the best.

CYCLOPS.
Oh, what a burp. Yes, very tasty.

ODYSSEUS.
That's the god exactly. Does no harm to anyone.

CYCLOPS.
Doesn't he mind living in a skin, being a god?

ODYSSEUS.
Just put him in there, not a care in the world.

CYCLOPS.
It's not right for gods to live in skins.

ODYSSEUS.
Who cares, as long as he makes you happy? What's your problem with the skin?

CYCLOPS.
I don't like wineskins. I just like what goes in them.

ODYSSEUS.
You stay here, then, and enjoy yourself, Cyclops.

CYCLOPS.
Shouldn't I offer a drop to my brothers?

ODYSSEUS.
Keep it to yourself. That's what you'd expect from someone with class.

CYCLOPS.
It would be more friendly to share it.

ODYSSEUS.
Parties always end in fisticuffs, I'm afraid.

CYCLOPS.
I'm so drunk, nobody could lay a finger on me.

ODYSSEUS.
Really, old chap. Home is the place when you're paralytic.

CYCLOPS.
It seems a bit silly not to go to a party when you've been drinking.

ODYSSEUS.
No, I assure you. 'The drunk who stays at home is no fool.'

CYCLOPS.
What are we going to do, Silenus? Do you think I should stay?

SILENUS.
Oh, I do, Cyclops. Who needs any more drinkers?

CYCLOPS.
Well, there you go. And the ground just here is like a feather bed made of flowers.

SILENUS.
It certainly is. It's nice to have a little drink in the sun. Stretch yourself out over there.

CYCLOPS.
What are you doing putting the bowl behind me?

SILENUS.
We don't want anyone spilling it.

CYCLOPS.
We don't want anyone drinking it. Pinching it, that's what you're after. Put it here in the middle. And you there, stranger, what's your name anyway?

ODYSSEUS.
My name is Nobody. And what have you to offer me in return?

CYCLOPS.
Of all the lot of you, I'll eat you last.

SILENUS.
That's a great boon you've given your guest there, Cyclops.

CYCLOPS.
Oy. What are you up to? Did you have a quick swig?

SILENUS.
Not a bit of it. It just kissed me, because I'm so pretty.

CYCLOPS.
You love wine. Wine doesn't love you. So watch it.

SILENUS.
Honest to god, it's fallen in love with me.

CYCLOPS.
Pour. To the top. Give it here.

SILENUS.
Have I got the blend right? I'd better check.

CYCLOPS.
You'll be the death of me. Hand it over.

SILENUS.
No, no. Wait till I put this garland round your head – and have a quick wet in the process.

CYCLOPS.
This cup-bearer's a villain.

SILENUS.
I am not. Oh, it is sweet, isn't it? There now, you'll need a wipe-down, so's you can have a proper drink.

CYCLOPS.
That's enough. My beard and moustache are both clean.

SILENUS.
You should just lean over onto your elbow, elegantly, then you drink. No. Watch me and drink like I do, or rather, like I don't.

CYCLOPS.
Ah, what are you doing?

SILENUS.
Down to the dregs. Lovely.

CYCLOPS.
Hey, stranger. You pour.

ODYSSEUS.
You'll find the wine responds to me. It knows me.

CYCLOPS.
Just pour.

ODYSSEUS.
Shut your mouth will you? I'm pouring.

CYCLOPS.
It's difficult shutting your mouth when you're drinking.

ODYSSEUS.
That's right. Pick it up. Pour it down. Don't leave a drop. Waste not, want not.

CYCLOPS.
Whew. What a clever little tree that vine must be.

ODYSSEUS.
If you pour a nice big drink on top of a nice big meal, then your thirst will be slaked and you can have a nice little sleep. Leave one drop and Dionysus will desiccate you.

CYCLOPS.
Oh wow. I nearly drowned. Unbelievable. Whoops. Heaven seems to be getting muddled up with the earth. There's the throne of Zeus and the glory of the gods. It's divine. Shall I make love to the lot of you? Don't tempt me, Graces. No I'll make do with my Ganymede here. I'll have a better jiggle with him than with all the Graces put together. I'd rather have little boys than women any day.

SILENUS.
I realise that you're Zeus, Cyclops, but you're not casting me as Ganymede, are you?

CYCLOPS.
The one I stole from Dardanus, yes you are, by Zeus.

SILENUS.
Oh boys, I've had it. He's going to do unmentionable things to me.

CYCLOPS.
Any objections? I may be drunk, but I'm not that drunk.

SILENUS.
Oh lord. This is going to leave a nasty taste in the mouth.

Exeunt CYCLOPS *and* SILENUS.

ODYSSEUS.

Right you are, sons of Dionysus, noble fellows. Your man is indoors. Before long, he'll vomit up the flesh out of his vile throat and pass out. Inside, the stake is smoking nicely, all set to scorch the Cyclops' eye-hole. Courage now. Be men.

CHORUS.

Our resolve is like granite. In you go now, before our father gets more than he bargained for. Everything's ready out here.

ODYSSEUS.

Now Hephaestus, Lord of Etna,
Cauterise the eye
Of this thy revolting neighbour
And rid thyself of him,
Once and for all.
And thou, Sleep,
Offspring of sable Night,
Launch thyself upon this heathen creature,
Irresistibly.
And after our famed Trojan tribulations,
Destroy not Odysseus and his crew
At the hands of one who cares
Naught for men,
And less for gods.
Else we must think
That Heaven is ruled by Luck
And Lucky Dip more powerful than the gods.

CHORUS.

We're singing songs
Of savage tongs
Ready to nobble a
Guest-gobbler.

With a blazing light
To scramble his sight
This stock of oak
Ready to poke.

No time to shirk.
Come, wine, do your work.
Let the Cyclops rue
Your powerful brew.

How I miss you, Dionysus,
Ivy-kissing Dionysus.
Oh let me bid farewell
To this Cyclopean hell.
Shall I ever see you more, my Dionysus,
And dwell with you in bliss, my Dionysus?

ODYSSEUS.
Quiet, for god's sake, you animals. Hush now. Shut your faces. Don't hawk, don't spit, don't breathe, don't even blink. On pain of rousing that devil and missing out on the Cyclops-gouging.

CHORUS.
We're perfectly silent, holding our breath.

ODYSSEUS.
Let's go then. Inside and all hands to the brand. It's well alight.

CHORUS.
Do you think you should tell us the batting order? Who holds the stake and where for the eye-burning? So we all get a share. Because some of us are a bit of a long way from the door for actually pushing the flame into the eye. And I've just turned my ankle. Funny you should say that. I think it's broken. I was standing over there and I just felt it go. Me too. No idea why.

ODYSSEUS.
Just felt it go!

CHORUS.
Oh, dust in my eye. Ash, probably.

ODYSSEUS.
You pifflers. A fine help you turned out to be.

CHORUS.
Just because I don't want to damage my back – I've got a bad back – and have my teeth knocked out of my head, suddenly I'm a coward. I do know a wonderful magic song which will make the brand jump up all by itself and sear the skull of this one-eyed son of the soil.

ODYSSEUS.
I might have known how much use you'd be. Now I know even better. I'll have to use my trusty crew inside. If you are too feeble to lend a hand, at least give them a bit of encouragement. Sing them a song or something.

CHORUS.
That's what I'll do. We'll take the risk, but by proxy. You do the blinding. We'll call the tune.

Exit ODYSSEUS.

CHORUS.
Twist it, be firm with it.
Give him a perm with it.
Wind it and twine it,
Try to refine it.
Now anticlockwise and just watch him squirm with it.

Exercise, exorcise. Make his eye water.
Pulverise, cauterise. Give him no quarter.
Miserable animal,
Man-mangling cannibal
Grind up his cornea with pestle and mortar.

CYCLOPS (*inside*).
Ahhhh. My eye's incandescent.

CHORUS.
That's music. Bravo. Sing me some more, Cyclops.

Enter CYCLOPS.

CYCLOPS.
Ahhh. I'm assaulted. I'm destroyed. But nobody's getting out of this cave with a smile on his face. I'll stand at the entrance and block it with my hand.

CHORUS.
What's the problem, Cyclops?

CYCLOPS.
I'm dead.

CHORUS.
You do look dreadful.

CYCLOPS.
I feel awful.

CHORUS.
Did you fall in the fire while you were pissed?

CYCLOPS.
Nobody's done for me.

CHORUS.
No harm done then.

CYCLOPS.
Nobody has blinded my eye.

CHORUS.
Then you can't be blind.

CYCLOPS.
Take a look, can't you?

CHORUS.
How could nobody blind you?

CYCLOPS.
It's not funny. Where is Nobody?

CHORUS.
Nowhere, Cyclops.

CYCLOPS.
That stranger. It's the stranger has done for me. Do you follow? That rotten devil that gave me the wine to drink.

CHORUS.
It's a terrible thing though, the drink. Two falls and a submission, soon as you like.

CYCLOPS.
Good god, they've got away. Or are you still inside?

CHORUS.
They're over there by the rock, sheltering in silence.

CYCLOPS.
Which side?

CHORUS.
Right.

CYCLOPS.
Oh, right. Where?

CHORUS.
By the rock. Got them?

CYCLOPS.
Ouf. One damn thing after another. I've split my head open.

CHORUS.
They're getting away.

CYCLOPS.
Where? Over here?

CHORUS.
No. I told you.

CYCLOPS.
Then where?

CHORUS.
Turn round. There, now, there, by your left hand.

CYCLOPS.
You're mocking me. I'm just a butt.

CHORUS.
No, of course we're not. He's standing in front of you.

CYCLOPS.
You devil you. Where are you?

ODYSSEUS.

Out of your reach. And taking good care that Odysseus stays that way.

CYCLOPS.

What's that? That's a different name.

ODYSSEUS.

Yes, Odysseus. It's the name my father gave me. And you've paid the price for your deplorable dinner. A fine thing it would have been to incinerate Troy, but not avenge the murder of my companions.

CYCLOPS.

I knew it. The old oracle was right. It said you would come from Troy and leave me blind. But you'll have to pay a price too. Years more drifting about at sea.

ODYSSEUS.

And you can stuff all that. I've kept my word. I'm off to the shore to launch my ship into the Sicilian sea and aim for home.

CYCLOPS.

That's what you think. I'll tear off a rock and hurl it at your shipmates. I'm off up the mountain through the back door of the cave, even if I am blind.

Exit CYCLOPS.

CHORUS.

We'll join you on board, Odysseus and for the rest of our lives, we'll serve nobody but Dionysus.

Exeunt omnes.

EURIPIDES

Alkestis

translated by J. Michael Walton

Characters

APOLLO
DEATH
SERVANT
ADMETUS, King of Pherai
ALKESTIS, his wife
EUMELUS, their son
DAUGHTER (non-speaking)
HERAKLES
PHERES, Admetus' father
SECOND SERVANT
SERVANT TO PHERES (non-speaking)
CHORUS OF PEOPLE OF PHERAI

Before the palace of ADMETUS, *King of Pherai. Enter* APOLLO.

APOLLO.
Home of Admetus, I salute you.
Here, god though I am, I humbled myself
To eat at slavery's table.
Zeus was the cause, I cannot deny it, killing my son,
My Asklepius, with a lightning-bolt through the heart.
Distraught, incensed, I in my turn slew the Kyklopes,
Fashioners of that flame.
To atone, my father bound me servant to a mortal man.
That's how I came here, herdsman to Admetus,
A stranger then, but deserving my protection.
A god myself, I found a god-fearing man,
In Admetus, son of Pheres. So I have preserved him,
Cheating the Fates to keep Death at bay.
Those goddesses allowed that, should he find a substitute,
A surrogate to die on his behalf,
Admetus might avoid his own impending death.
He tried everyone, his family in turn,
His father, even his aged mother.
No one could he find willing to leave this life,
And pass from light to dark for him –
Save one, his wife Alkestis.
Now she lies propped up in his arms,
Gasping out her last remaining breath.
This is the day when he was doomed to die,
The very day when she must face the grave instead.
I may not taint myself here at such a time.
Dear as it is, I now must leave their home.
Here, right on cue, comes the minister of the dead,
Here's Death, her escort to the underworld.
Punctual as ever.
He's been waiting for her, waiting for the day.

Enter DEATH.

DEATH.
Apollo! You, here!
What are you up to now?
Why do you still loiter here,
Violating my rights, depriving me of my due?
Was it not enough to extricate Admetus,
Devising some means to cheat the Fates?
Now you fancy fighting me off, do you,
To protect the wife too?
She pledged herself to us the moment she released her husband.
Alkestis, daughter Pelias, is mine.

APOLLO.
No cause for concern. I ask for justice. What is fair, no more.

DEATH.
Your justice needs your bow, does it?

APOLLO.
I always carry it. You know that.

DEATH.
To do this house a favour, flouting natural law.

APOLLO.
The man's a friend. Let me grieve on his behalf.

DEATH.
By stealing another corpse from me?

APOLLO.
There was no coercion last time.

DEATH.
Then how's he up here, instead of underground?

APOLLO.
His wife took his place: it's her you have come for.

DEATH.
Exactly. And it's her I'm taking down.

APOLLO.
Go on then, I cannot expect to convince you, I realise that.

DEATH.
Not to take those whose time has come? But that's my function.

APOLLO.
It is. But only when they're ready.

DEATH.
So that's your argument. And you believe it.

APOLLO.
Is Alkestis never to see old age?

DEATH.
Quite impossible. I too have rights.

APOLLO.
Young or old, you can only take a life once.

DEATH.
The younger the victim, the greater respect for me.

APOLLO.
As an old woman she'd have an expensive funeral.

DEATH.
One law for the rich, Apollo! Is that what you propose?

APOLLO.
What are you talking about? What are you trying to imply?

DEATH.
That you would condone the wealthy buying old age.

APOLLO.
So you offer me nothing?

DEATH.
Nothing. You know how I operate.

APOLLO.
Feared by men and loathed by gods.

DEATH.
You may never have what you must not have.

APOLLO.
Savage as you are, you may yet give way.
A man is coming to the house of Pheres,
Bidden by Eurystheus to fetch a team of horses
From wintry Thrace. Such a man,
Welcomed here in Admetus' home,
Will recover Alkestis from you by force.
You'll get no thanks from me for this
But lose respect just as you lose her.

DEATH.
Say as much as you like. No good will come of it.
The woman comes to Hades with me.
I'll fetch her now, my blade at the ready.
One lock of hair snipped off
And she is fast bound to the gods below.

Exeunt DEATH *and* APOLLO. *Enter* CHORUS.

CHORUS.
Why the silence before the door?
Not a word from the house. Why?
No friend in sight.
No one to tell us
Whether we should be mourning the queen.
Or whether Alkestis, daughter of Pelias,
Still lives.
Finest of women,
As we know,
As everyone knows.
What a wife!

Can anyone hear weeping in there?
Or beating of hands?
A sound of grief to say that all is over?
No servant attends the door as yet.
Oh Apollo, healing god,
Would that you were here
To guide us through this storm.

It would not be so silent were she dead.
She'll be dead.
Still indoors, though.
Why so? I cannot tell. What makes you so sure?
Admetus would hardly have committed to the grave
So noble a wife without her proper due.

There's no sign before the door
Of springwater. You'd expect
Some offering if she's gone.
No lock of hair either,
Cut off to mark a grief.

And not a sound of servant-girls in tears.
It is today, isn't it?
What do you mean?
When she's due to pass on . . . go below.
You wring my heart. You wring my very soul.
All decent folk must mourn a virtuous life.

Travel however far we might,
To Lykia,
Or Ammon's desert sands,
Nowhere could we find
A key
To free this woman's soul.
Her fate stands close,
Relentless.
I know no god to supplicate,
No sacrifice to help.

One only was there, once.
If Phoebus' son, Asklepius,
Still saw the light of day,
He'd help her flee the shadows
Shrouding Hades' door.
Alive he raised the dead
Until Zeus' thunderbolt
Blasted him to ash.
What prospect now for life?
What hope for her redemption?

The king has done all he can.
No god stays unpetitioned,
No altar dry of sacrificial blood.
There is no cure.

Enter SERVANT.

Here comes a servant from the house.
She's in tears. What is she going to tell us?
We understand your grief. It's natural
If something has happened to your masters.
It's your mistress, isn't it? Is she alive?
Or has she passed away? Tell us, please.

SERVANT.
Living, you could say: and dead.

CHORUS.
How can she be dead at the same time as being alive?

SERVANT.
Too weak to raise her head but breathing still.

CHORUS.
That's dreadful. What a man and what a wife to lose.

SERVANT.
He doesn't realise yet, nor will he till he's suffered.

CHORUS.
Is there no hope for her?

SERVANT.
This is the day. There's no fighting it.

CHORUS.
If there's anything we can do . . .

SERVANT.
She's all decked out for her husband to bury.

CHORUS.
At least she knows she dies
The finest, noblest wife who ever lived.

SERVANT.
The noblest wife? Who would argue with that?
What would it take to be a better wife?

How could a wife show respect for her husband
Greater than dying for him of her own free choice?
The whole city knows that. That's public
  knowledge.
Now to make you marvel more,
Let me unveil the private face of grief.
When she realised the fatal day was here,
She bathed her pallid skin in water from the stream.
Then, after bathing, took a dress and ornaments
From her cedarwood chest and put them on.
Standing before the altar at the hearth
She prayed to Hestia, patron of the home:
'Mistress, this is the last time I shall pray to you.
I am leaving now to go beneath the earth.
Look after my children. For my son
Find a loving wife; for my daughter a decent
  husband.
And let them not die like their mother,
Prematurely, but live a happy life,
Prospering in the land they call their own.'
Next she visited every altar in Admetus' house,
Adorning each with a wreath and myrtle she herself
  had picked,
Bowing before them.
Never a tear, not as much as a sigh,
No outward sign to mar her beauty
Or warn of ill to come.
At last she reached their bedroom.
Throwing herself on the bed, now finally came the
  tears.
'Dear bed,' she wept, 'where I gave my virginity
To the man for whom I now give my life.
Goodbye, bed. I don't hate you.
It's only me that's dying.
It was that or betray you and my husband too.
Some other wife will possess you,
No truer than me, but perhaps more fortunate.'
Prostrate she kissed it, wetting the coverlet
With tears that now flowed uncontrollable.
Exhausted finally with so much crying,

She pulled herself up and staggered to the door,
Only to turn back time and time again
To throw herself down onto her bed once more.
The children were weeping too, hanging from her dress.
And she took each in turn in her arms,
As someone condemned to die will do, and cuddled them.
All of us servants could only stand round weeping too,
Consumed with pity. She offered us each her hand,
With a word for everyone, however humble.
That is how great a calamity strikes Admetus' home.
Had he died, that would be it. Full stop.
In his escape there'll be no forgetting.

CHORUS.
And Admetus? Is he not a party to all this grief?
Deprived in such a way of such a wife?

SERVANT.
He's weeping all right, clasping his beloved in his arms,
Begging her not to leave him. Useless really,
With her wasting away before his eyes.
She's sinking fast, too weak to lift a hand.
Breathing still, though barely, she wants
A last look at the sun's bright light,
One more time, one last time.
I'll go on in and tell her that you are here.
Not everyone is so inclined
To offer support when times are bad.
You've always been a friend to the masters here.

Exit SERVANT. *The* CHORUS *remain.*

CHORUS.
Lord Zeus, is there no solution,
No light at the end of this dreadful tunnel?
Who's to know? Is this the right time
For cutting our hair
And putting on mourning?

I think it is. We must.
Praying, though, to the gods
Whose power is greater than ours.
O healing Lord Apollo,
Devise some means to help Admetus.
Contrive, as once you found a way,
Contrive to loose Death's grip
Check Hades' bloody power.

Grief, all grief.
Oh son of Pheres,
What have you done?
The loss of such a wife.
Could a man not slit his throat for this
Or choke it in a noose
And hang there?
He shall see his loving wife,
No, the most loving there ever was,
This day, before him, dead.

Enter ADMETUS *with* ALKESTIS *on a couch and the two children, a boy and a girl.*

She's coming, look.
Her husband's bringing her out here.

Cry out, land of Pherai,
Cry lamentation for the finest of women,
Fading fast,
Carried by sickness beneath the earth.
Never again will I claim
That marriage brings more joy than woe.
I think about the past,
And in the present moment see
A king with the best of wives.
And for the future
Only a long, bleak stretching out of time.

ALKESTIS.
The sun. Daylight.
The clouds are racing in the sky.*

*Until line 280 the exchanges between Alkestis and Admetus are in lyrics similar to those of the main choruses.

ADMETUS.

The sun sees us both, both you and me,
Two sufferers who never deserved your death.

ALKESTIS.

My country now and my home
Where marriage brought me from my own Iolkos.

ADMETUS.

Be strong, Alkestis. Don't leave me.
Pray pity from the gods.

ALKESTIS.

The boat's coming. I can see it
With its twin oars.
There's Charon at the helm,
The ferryman, calling to me.
'What are you waiting for? Come on.
You're wasting my time.' —
He wants me to hurry.

ADMETUS.

A terrible voyage for all of us too.
Ah, how we suffer.

ALKESTIS.

Someone grips me by the hand. Can you not see?
The threshold of Hades.
Dark. Dark brows and wings.
What do you want? Leave me alone.
This path frightens me.

ADMETUS.

Pity your loved ones. Pity me most.
And the children sharing my grief.

ALKESTIS.

Let go. Let me go now.
Lay me down. I've no more strength to stand.
Death's at my side.
My eyes are growing dark.
Children, where are you, children?
Say goodbye. Your mother's leaving now.
Farewell. The sun is yours.

ADMETUS.
These words tear me apart.
Worse than any death.
Please god, you must not leave me.
Don't leave your children motherless.
Be strong. Fight back.
If you die, there'll be nothing left for me.
For you we live, without you die.
We worship you.

ALKESTIS.
Admetus, you can see how things are with me.*
Before I die, I want to say something to you.
I need to tell you what is on my mind.
I have chosen to die out of respect for you,
Valuing your life higher than my own.
I could have married any man in Thessaly
And lived comfortably, just by saying no.
But I wasn't prepared to live without you,
Without the father of our children.
I chose to give up youth and happiness.
Your father and mother made their choice,
Though an honourable death was what
They could look forward to, saving their only son.
Their hope of further children faded long ago.
Had I lived, you would not face the future alone.
The children would not have to grow up motherless.
Well, that's god's will. So be it.
In return, there is something you must promise me.
Not much – what could be? – in return for a life,
But fair, you will agree.
I trust you love these children no less than I do.
Make sure they are heirs to our home.
Never marry again. Don't force on them a step-
  mother
Who knows she'll be no better wife than I
And take out her jealousy on the children.

*Alkestis now reverts to the more prosy iambics of most dialogue scenes.

Promise me you won't do that.
Stepmothers always hate a first wife's family
Like poison.
For a boy a father's his tower of strength
To talk with and receive advice
But what about a daughter? What about you, my child?
What would a father's new wife mean for you?
She might choose to tarnish your reputation,
Spoiling your youthful hopes of marriage.
There'll be no mother to dress you for your wedding.
No one to give support in childbirth
When your mother's what you need.
I'm going to die. Not tomorrow or the day after.
Now, here and now. Alkestis, the late wife.
Be good. Be happy.
You can boast, my dear, you had the noblest wife.
You, children, that your mother had no equal.

CHORUS.
No need to worry. I can vouch for him.
Any right-minded man would do as you ask.

ADMETUS.
Of course. Of course. Don't think about it.
There was no one but you while you lived.
In death you'll remain my only wife.
In all Thessaly none will claim your place,
However well-born, however beautiful.
These children are enough. God grant me joy of them
As I must forfeit all my joy in you.
My mourning for you will not last a year
But a lifetime. That I swear, dear wife,
In hatred for my mother and my father,
Who professed their love until the time to act.
But you gave everything, your life for mine.
In losing you have I no right to grieve?
I'll give up company. Hold no more parties here.
Abandon fine clothes and ornament.

There'll be no music. This house was filled with music.
Never again will I pick up my lyre
Or raise my spirits playing on the flute.
With you gone all my joy in life is dead.
I'll have a statue made by some rare master,
Beguiling Nature of her custom.
As she lies in our bed I'll fall upon her
Clasp her in my arms and call your name.
A widower, I'll seem to hold my wife,
Cold comfort, perhaps, but consolation.
You could come to visit me in my dreams.
It's good to see a loved one in one's dreams,
However brief the vision. Had I the voice
Of Orpheus or his tunes, I'd charm Demeter's daughter,
Or her husband, and hale you out of Hades with my song.
The hound of Hell would not stand in my way
Nor Charon, the ferryman of dead souls,
Till I had restored you to light and life.
Wait for me, though, until I do die.
Prepare a home for us where you can live with me.
I'll have myself buried in the same grave,
My corpse laid out beside your bones.
In death I'll not be parted from my own true wife.

CHORUS.
As friend to friend we'll share your grief,
The best we may. She deserves it.

ALKESTIS.
You heard all that, children,
Your father's promise never to remarry,
Never to supplant you or replace me.

ADMETUS.
I've said so and I'll keep my word.

ALKESTIS.
In that case take the children from me.

ADMETUS.
I accept this your precious gift.

ALKESTIS.
You must now be mother to them too.

ADMETUS.
Of course. They'll no longer have you.

ALKESTIS.
My dears, I'm leaving you, when I most need to stay.

ADMETUS.
How will I ever manage without you?

ALKESTIS.
Time's a great healer, the dead are nothing.

ADMETUS.
Take me with you. Please take me too.

ALKESTIS.
It is for you I die but one death's enough.

ADMETUS.
God in Heaven, what a wife you've taken.

ALKESTIS.
My eyes are growing heavy. How dark it is.

ADMETUS.
Don't go. I can't face your leaving.

ALKESTIS.
No more. There's nothing left.

ADMETUS.
Look at me. The children . . .

ALKESTIS.
Goodbye, my dears. I have no choice.

ADMETUS.
Look at them. Please.

ALKESTIS.
Nothing left.

ADMETUS.
Don't go. You mustn't go.

ALKESTIS.
Farewell.

ALKESTIS dies.

ADMETUS.
Damned. I'm damned.

CHORUS.
She's dead. Admetus' wife is dead.

EUMELUS.
Fate takes its course. Mother's gone.
Father, she's no longer here,
No longer here in the sun,
Leaving us desolate.
An orphan life begins.
Look in her eye, her lifeless eye.
See her hands, nerveless.
Hear me, mother, only listen
As I beseech you,
With a little boy's kiss.

ADMETUS.
She cannot see or hear you.
We've a heavy load to bear, you and I.

EUMELUS.
I'm young to be abandoned,
Father, so early on my journey.
I'm not sure I can manage.
And you, dear sister,
How will you survive?
What a pointless marriage, father,
Pointless when you must face old age alone.
She died, before her time.
When you went away, mother,
You left our house empty.

CHORUS.
Admetus, you must face up to the inevitable.
You're not the first of men – you will not be the last –

To lose an admirable wife. Only one thing's sure
That death will claim his due from each of us.

ADMETUS.

I know that. This was not unheralded.
I've known long enough that it was coming.
All the same . . . it's time to bury the dead.
Please, wait. Stay and grieve with me.
Let's sing a hymn for that remorseless god below.
I declare a period of mourning throughout Thessaly,
For all my citizens to share my grief for this my wife,
Shaving their heads and clothed in black.
Trace-horses and single mounts
To have shorn mane.
No lyre, no flute in the city
For a period of twelve full months.
I'll never bury anyone so dear
Nor one who loved me dearer.
All honour to her who died that I might live.

Exit ADMETUS *and the children with the body of* ALKESTIS.

CHORUS.

Alkestis, daughter of Pelias,
We offer our last farewell
As you head for your sunless new home.
Let the black-locked lord of Hades
And the time-worn escort Charon
Know it's the finest of wives
He rows to the Acheron shore.

Poets with seven-stringed lyre,
Or unaccompanied,
Will sing your praises,
Under night-long Spartan moon
In the month of Karneia,
Or in Athens in all her glory.
Legend in song is your legacy.

Were it in my power –
Would that it were –
To light a path from Hades,

To take up an oar
And row you home
Across that fatal river.
You, the only one,
You alone, prepared to choose
Death to save your husband's life.
May the dust lie light, good lady.
And should that husband choose another wife,
Let him feel the burden of contempt
From me and from the children, his and yours.

A mother would not take his place,
Nor a father willing to bury
An aged body for a son,
Their white hair for the child they bore.
Young as you were,
You parted from this life.
What a partner in marriage!
Would I might find a gift so rare,
To guarantee a lifelong harmony.

Enter HERAKLES.

HERAKLES.
Friends. People of Pherai, you're locals, I assume.
Can you tell me if Admetus happens to be home?

CHORUS.
Why, Herakles, yes. Admetus, son of Pheres is here.
Tell me what brings you this way again,
To Thessaly and this town of Pherai?

HERAKLES.
Some job I have to do for Eurystheus of Tiryns.

CHORUS.
Where are you headed? Is it another long journey?

HERAKLES.
Thrace. The four-horsed chariot of Diomedes this time.

CHORUS.
How will you manage? You've not encountered him before, I take it?

HERAKLES.
No, never. I've never been to Bistonia.

CHORUS.
You'll not win those horses without a fight.

HERAKLES.
I'm not a man to let that stand in my way.

CHORUS.
Win or lose. Life or death.

HERAKLES.
Well, it won't be the first time.

CHORUS.
If you do kill their master, what then?

HERAKLES.
I'll drive them back home for Eurystheus.

CHORUS.
You'll have to bridle them first.

HERAKLES.
Just so long as they don't breathe fire.

CHORUS.
They do feed on human flesh.

HERAKLES.
They're horses, you know, not wolves.

CHORUS.
They say their mangers are caked in blood.

HERAKLES.
The man who reared them – what's his background?

CHORUS.
His father's Ares, lord of the Golden Shield of Thrace.

HERAKLES.
Just another labour for me. My destiny.
It's a hard path I travel, always uphill.
Always another son of Ares to fight.
First it was Lykaon, then Kyknus, now a third of them

To face, Diomedes and his horses.
Still, there's not a man alive can say
Alkmene's son would flinch before the foe.

Enter ADMETUS *in mourning.*

CHORUS.
Here's Lord Admetus now coming from the house.

ADMETUS.
Greetings, Herakles, son of Zeus, from Perseus' line.

HERAKLES.
Admetus, King of Thessaly. I hope you're well.

ADMETUS.
I wish I were. I know you mean it kindly.

HERAKLES.
You're in mourning. Hair cut short. Why's this?

ADMETUS.
We have a funeral here today.

HERAKLES.
Please god, none of the children.

ADMETUS.
No, they're fine, both here indoors.

HERAKLES.
Your father was a good age, if it's him.

ADMETUS.
No, he's still alive, Herakles. So is my mother.

HERAKLES.
It cannot be your wife, can it? Not Alkestis?

ADMETUS.
There's no one answer to that question.

HERAKLES.
What are you talking about? Is she dead or isn't she?

ADMETUS.
She's here, but she isn't, you see. That's why I'm upset.

HERAKLES.
I haven't any idea what you're talking about.

ADMETUS.
Do you not know what is going to happen?

HERAKLES.
I know she agreed to die in your place.

ADMETUS.
How can I call her alive when she agreed to that?

HERAKLES.
Well don't start mourning yet. Wait till she does die.

ADMETUS.
If you're destined to die, you're dead, that's all.

HERAKLES.
They're not the same thing at all.

ADMETUS.
You see things one way, Herakles, I another.

HERAKLES.
Well, who are you mourning at the moment? Some friend?

ADMETUS.
A woman. Some woman whose memory we honour.

HERAKLES.
Family? Or no relation?

ADMETUS.
No relation. But close to us.

HERAKLES.
How did she come to die in your house?

ADMETUS.
As an orphan. Her father was dead.

HERAKLES.
That's a shame. I'm sorry to find you so upset.

ADMETUS.
Why in particular?

HERAKLES.
I'll seek lodging somewhere else.

ADMETUS.
No, really. I couldn't allow that.

HERAKLES.
You don't want a guest in a house of mourning.

ADMETUS.
The dead are dead. Please, come inside.

HERAKLES.
It can't be right to be entertained by friends who grieve.

ADMETUS.
You can have a guest-room away from the main house.

HERAKLES.
I'll go. My thanks, all the same.

ADMETUS.
You shall not go to anyone else's house.
(*To a* SERVANT.) Hey you. Show him the far guest-rooms.
Tell the steward to provide some decent food
And plenty of it. Close off the courtyard doors.
We can't have guests upset.
By the sound of weeping.

Exit HERAKLES *and* SERVANT.

CHORUS.
What are you doing? Admetus, at such a time as this
You think of entertaining? Are you insane?

ADMETUS.
So you think I should send him packing,
A guest in our city and in my house?
You'd have commended that, would you?
How could I? It would hardly ease my pain
To add discourtesy to personal disaster.
More problems, as if I hadn't enough,
To be branded inhospitable.

He's always been the perfect host to me
Whenever I've visited that desert Argos.

CHORUS.
Perhaps so, but why call him a friend and
Hide from that friend the fate you've suffered?

ADMETUS.
He would never have entered this house
Had he any idea what has happened.
Oh, I know, there'll be some who will criticise me
For what I've done. I'm sorry but no house of mine
Will ever reject a guest. It's a matter of honour.

Exit ADMETUS.

CHORUS.
A house of welcome, we commend that,
A friendly home,
Where Apollo himself was once happy to stay.
Apollo, lover of music,
Living here as a humble shepherd,
Serenaded his sheep with wedding songs,
Caressing the glen with pure melody.

Dappled lynxes joined in for joy.
Lions, a bloody pride,
Stole in from the dale of Othrys
And stayed, enchanted,
Poised to watch a fawn slip from the sheltering firs,
High-stepping with dainty foot
To Apollo's dancing notes.

Which is why by the edge of our lake Boibeïs
The flocks of this prosperous household
Are all but too vast to count.
Fertile fields stretch westwards
As far as the Molossian mountains,
Gloomy stable to the setting sun:
And in the east to harsh Aegean shore,
Deep down below Mount Pelion.

And now, once more, his door is open
To receive this guest, though his eyes are filled with tears
For a wife who lies inside, dead.
Decency may be taken to the limit.
What the good do must be wise.
Though I sometimes nurse doubts,
In my heart I feel sure
That the god-fearing man must prosper.

Enter ADMETUS *and a funeral procession with the body of* ALKESTIS.

ADMETUS.

Your witness is appreciated, people of Pherai.
The servants will escort the body
In the proper way to the grave, then to the pyre.
As is the custom, please make your pronouncements
For her final journey.

CHORUS.

I can see your father heading this way.
He walks like an old man. There are servants with him
Carrying grave-offerings for your wife.

Enter PHERES.

PHERES.

I've come to offer support, my boy.
She was a good woman, your wife. No one will dispute that.
A decent woman, that's what you've lost.
But, there you are. What will be, will be.
You can't argue with Fate. You just have to put up with it.
There's an ornament here. Take it and bury it with her.
We should pay proper respects to the body of someone
Prepared to die to save your skin, eh, son,
And to preserve me from a childless and miserable
Old age? Her life's a shining example to any woman.

It was a brave thing to do. Noble. A noble thing to do.
Dear Alkestis, saviour of my son, prop to me
To save me from collapse, farewell, and may you fare well down there.
I tell you, a marriage like that, it's all a bonus.
Otherwise, don't get married at all, I say.

ADMETUS.
I never invited you to this funeral.
You do not belong amongst my friends.
Alkestis will never wear a gift from you.
She takes nothing of yours to her grave.
Sympathise! You should have sympathised when I was dying.
You stood aside then sure enough, old man,
To let a young man die instead. Crocodile tears.
Were you really my father?
And what about my so-called mother?
Son of a servant, am I, a behind-closed-doors child
Transferred to your wife's breast in secret?
Put to the test, you showed your colours soon enough.
I disown you as a father.
For sheer cowardice you have no rival.
The age you are, at the far end of life,
And unwilling, no, too frightened rather,
To die for your own son. You'd let her die instead,
An outsider, not of our blood, but a woman
Who is now my only family, father and mother.
The honourable thing would have been for you
To face up to dying for your son.
There's little enough life left to you as it is.
Then I could have lived out my life with her
And not been left deserted to my misery.
You have had everything the happy man could ask:
Still young when you became king,
In me a son and heir to inherit your house,
And save it from some outsider's grasping fingers.
Nor can you ever accuse me of failing to honour

Your age or station. That excuse for letting me die
Won't wash. I showed you respect.
And this is how you repaid me, you and that wife of yours.
You'd better get breeding again
If you want looking after in your dotage,
If you want a son to lay you out and see you off.
I'll not soil my hands by burying you.
As far as you're concerned, I am dead.
If I'm alive through finding someone else
Who cares enough to take my place,
Then that is where my duty and my love belong.
The old are always asking for a 'blessed release'.
Grumbling about the tedium of old age. Oh yes!
One glimpse of death and no one wants to die.
Suddenly old age no longer seems so bad.

CHORUS.
Stop. That's enough. And at a moment like this.
This is not the time to provoke your father.

PHERES.
Who do you think you're talking to, boy?
Some Trojan slave bought with your pocket-money?
I'm a Thessalian, remember. My father was a Thessalian.
And a free man. Remember?
How dare you talk to me like that! Youth's no excuse.
You don't hurl insults and simply walk away.
I brought you up and made you master here.
It's not my job to die for you too.
There's no family custom I'm aware of
That says fathers should die for children. It's not Greek.
Good luck or bad, that's your problem.
All my dues I've paid.
You rule a huge kingdom. I'll leave you land,
Acres of it. That's what I received from my father.
What did I do wrong? What did I deprive you of?
Don't die on my account. And I won't die for you.

So you like life. You don't think your father likes life?
You're dead a long time, you know.
Life's short and sweeter for it.
You pulled no punches in your fight for life.
It's you who's cheating death to live,
And killing your wife to do it.
You accuse me of cowardice? Letting your wife die instead?
What a brave figure you cut. So young too.
It's a clever scheme you've worked out, I must admit.
How to cheat death, permanently. All you have to do
Is marry yet another wife and she'll do your dying for you.
Then you can always blame the family, can't you,
For refusing to do what you're too frightened to?
Don't talk to me. Just consider this.
If you're so fond of your life, aren't the rest of us?
Home truths. That's what you'll get for abusing me.

CHORUS.
You've both said far too much already.
Don't talk to your son like that.

ADMETUS.
No. Go on. I've had my say. You shouldn't try to hurt me
If you can't face the truth.

PHERES.
I'd have hurt you more if I'd died for you.

ADMETUS.
You think death the same for young and old?

PHERES.
Once we live. Not twice. Once.

ADMETUS.
And you would live longer than Zeus.

PHERES.
You've suffered nothing at our hands. Why curse your parents?

ADMETUS.
So eager to prolong your lives.

PHERES.
It's your place she's taking in the coffin.

ADMETUS.
A monument to your cowardice.

PHERES.
Her death has nothing to do with me. You cannot say that.

ADMETUS.
My god! I hope there's a time when you need me.

PHERES.
The more you marry, the more you can kill off.

ADMETUS.
Some taunt when it's you that wouldn't die.

PHERES.
I'm glad to be alive, to see god's light. Why deny it?

ADMETUS.
It's beneath contempt for a man to speak like that.

PHERES.
You'll not goad these old bones into their grave.

ADMETUS.
When you do die, you die in disgrace.

PHERES.
Why should that bother me when I'm dead!

ADMETUS.
That's terrible. What a shameless old man you are.

PHERES.
She wasn't shameless, of course. Just stupid.

ADMETUS.
Go away. And leave me to bury my dead.

PHERES.

Oh, I'm going. Let her killer get on with burying her.
Her family may come asking questions, of course.
If he doesn't avenge a sister's blood
Akastus is not the man I took him for.

ADMETUS.

Get away from me, you, and take that wife of yours with you.
Grow old and grow old, childless, as you deserve.
I will not have you stay under the same roof.
If a proclamation would divorce me from my parents
I'd do it now, kick them out the house.

Exit PHERES.

But for us here, we have our sombre task.
It's time to go. To escort her to her grave.

CHORUS.

Alkestis. Such courage. So brave.
A remarkable woman. Wonderful.
Farewell, Alkestis,
May Hermes, guide of the soul,
And Hades welcome you.
And may you win your just reward
To sit by Hades' bride.

Exit the funeral procession and the CHORUS.
Enter a SECOND SERVANT.

SERVANT.

We've had guests before. Plenty of them. From all over the world. All sorts. Coming here to Admetus' palace. And I've given them their dinners. But never. Never ever. Never anyone more trouble than this one. He marched in. He could see the master was in mourning. In he came. No shame. How did he respond to our hospitality? Not like a gentleman. He knew how we . . . he knew what had happened. Everyone's upset. It was potluck, of course, but if we missed a single thing, anything, he demanded we go and fetch it, instantly. And drink. He never lets go of the ivy goblet. Fills it up and swills it down. Red wine, 'the dark mother'. Neat. So now, of course, he's become . . . overheated. Myrtle-leaves in his hair. And he's singing. Like a tone-deaf dog. It's awful in there. Howling wherever you turn. On one side Herakles, oblivious to Admetus' problems. Servants on the other, crying their eyes out for the mistress. Oh, we made sure not to let Herakles see as much as one damp eye. Admetus' orders. Now I've got to go in there and feed him. Guest! Scoundrel more like. A marauding brigand. While she departs for ever from this house. And I can't even be there. I can't stretch out a hand, can't as much as grieve for a mistress who was more a mother to each and every one of us. She saved us countless times, when the master was in one of his tempers. So can you blame me, for saying this guest's a brute? I can't stand the man. He intrudes on private grief.

Enter HERAKLES.

HERAKLES.

Oy, you, why the long face? A servant shouldn't go all sulky in front of the guests. You need to be a bit more friendly. Smile a bit, can't you? What are you looking like that for? One of your master's friends and you look at me as though I was something the cat brought in. It's not your funeral, you know. Here, come over here. I want to tell you something. Listen. Life, eh? What's it all about? Have you any idea? Have you any idea what life is? I haven't. I haven't a clue. And if I haven't a clue, what hope have you got? No, listen. Every single man, and woman, has got to die. That's their destiny. There's not one of them, not a single one of them can say for sure that they will live through tomorrow. Not one. It's a fact. Because Fate moves in a mysterious way. No one can teach us about Fate. We can't learn about Fate from experience. So, think about that. I'm telling you. Here's my philosophy. Enjoy yourself. Have a drink. Live in the present. Live from day to day and let

Fate take care of the rest. Have a bit of fun. A bit of love. A bit of passion. There's something you can worship. Aphrodite's your goddess. Forget everything else. Am I right? Of course I am. Take it from me. So cheer up. Don't be all upset. Have a little drink with me and stop worrying about Fate. Why not go and get a garland or two? I tell you. A drink'll take that scowl off your face. Splish-splash. Gurgle, gurgle. Down the hatch. You are human, aren't you? Then act human, for god's sake. You don't want to be one of these wet blankets, these po-faced puritans, do you? If you ask me. In my considered judgement, that's no life. No life at all. A calamity on legs, that's what you are.

SERVANT.
Yes. I know. I know. It's just that at the moment we are not in the mood for levity.

HERAKLES.
Because of . . . ? It's not as if she were one of the household, this dead woman. You can overdo grief, you know. It's not your masters, you've lost.

SERVANT.
Not a master . . . ? Do you not know what we've suffered here?

HERAKLES.
I think I do, unless Admetus lied to me.

SERVANT.
He's over-generous, that man. Too welcoming.

HERAKLES.
It's only some foreigner's funeral. Why cold-shoulder me?

SERVANT.
An outsider, yes. Too much of an outsider.

HERAKLES.
Has he been keeping something from me?

SERVANT.
Don't trouble yourself. Our master's problems are our affair.

HERAKLES.
There's more to this than concern for some 'outsider'.

SERVANT.
Well, yes. Or I would never have been so upset at your behaviour.

HERAKLES.
I've been wronged by my hosts, have I?

SERVANT.
You happened to arrive at the wrong moment. We're in mourning. You can see our hair. We're all in black . . .

HERAKLES.
Who's dead? Not one of the children, or the old man, his father?

SERVANT.
It's his wife. It's Alkestis, Admetus' wife.

HERAKLES.
What? Alkestis? And you've been entertaining me?

SERVANT.
He was too ashamed to send you away.

HERAKLES.
The poor man. What a wife to lose!

SERVANT.
We feel we've all died. Not just her.

HERAKLES.
I thought as much. When I saw his eyes fill with tears,
The hair, his face. But he convinced me.
This was some stranger's funeral, that's what he said.
Against my better judgement in I came,
And started drinking at my kind host's invitation,

While all this was going on. Rampaging around.
What a state I'm in. Garlands. And you never spoke out
When the whole house was on the rack.
Where are they burying her? Tell me. Where will I find her?

SERVANT.

Take the Larisa road. Go straight on
Till you see the stone tomb just outside of town.

HERAKLES.

Come now, brave heart and hand,
Show what Alkmene's son,
Her son by Zeus, can do.
For I must save her, save
The dead Alkestis,
Return her to her home
And redeem Admetus.
I go to watch for Death,
Black-cloaked keeper of corpses,
Who haunts tombs, lapping up the oblations.
There may I lie in ambush, jump out
And grab at Death, pin Death in my arms.
Once I hold Death, crushing rib to rib,
Nothing will break my hold until I win her back.
If I miss my prey there,
If blood proves poor bait,
Then I'll go down to the sunless underworld,
And demand her back from Hades and his wife.
I'll bring Alkestis back. I know I can.
Return her to my friend who welcomed me
And, at a time of raw adversity,
Declined to turn me from his door.
He concealed his feelings, good man that he is,
From respect for me. Where in Thessaly
Will you find that sort of courtesy? In what Greek home?
He deserves his reward.
He will not find such virtue misdirected.

Exeunt HERAKLES *and the* SERVANT.

Enter ADMETUS *and the* CHORUS.

ADMETUS.
Dreadful homecoming.
The sight of this house, lifeless, dreadful.
Where do I go? Where can I stay?
What do I say? What do I not say?
Would it were me that had died,
Fated from the moment of birth.
I envy the dead, I yearn to be with them,
Sharing that blackness.
There's no consolation wherever I look,
Not in sunlight, not underneath my foot.
Her life for mine
Death claimed his prize.

CHORUS.
Go in, Admetus, go in. Hide yourself indoors.

ADMETUS.
The pain!

CHORUS.
A fate to weep for.

ADMETUS.
It is. It is.

CHORUS.
I know. It hurts. I know.

ADMETUS.
I cannot face it.

CHORUS.
This is no help to her.

ADMETUS.
Do not say that.

CHORUS.
This may be harsh but you will never see
Your dear wife's face again.

ADMETUS.
Stop telling me this. Pain . . .
Is there anything worse a man can suffer

Than the loss of his loyal wife?
I wish we had never married.
I wish she'd never lived here in this house.
Single and childless, that's the man I envy,
The solitary soul, concerned only with himself.
But an ailing child,
Or marriage-bed with one side empty,
These are unbearable. Better none of them.

CHORUS.
It's the way it is. You can't argue with Fate.

ADMETUS.
Don't tell me that.

CHORUS.
You must keep a sense of perspective.

ADMETUS.
No!

CHORUS.
This is difficult to bear. For all that . . .

ADMETUS.
How can I bear it?

CHORUS.
You have to learn to live with it. You're not the only man . . .

ADMETUS.
What am I to do?

CHORUS.
Who ever lost a wife. It's a disaster, I know.
But we all face disaster at some time. That's life.

ADMETUS.
It has no end, the misery of grief
For those who die.
Why did you stop me? Why did you hold me back
When I would have thrown myself into her grave
To lie beside the finest woman who ever lived?
Twin faithful souls united in death
Crossing over to Hades, together.

CHORUS.
One of my family lost a son. An only son.
Died at home. He was such a lovely boy.
He learnt to live with it.
His hair turned grey and he can't walk straight.
And he faces his declining years,
Childless.

ADMETUS.
The very sight of this house! How can I go in there?
How can I live when the guardian angel's gone?
Nothing's the same any more.
I came here, I remember,
In a torchlight procession, torches of Pelian-pine,
Hand-in-hand with my bride, my beautiful bride,
Singing wedding-songs.
The wedding-party followed behind,
Cheering us on, showering blessings upon us,
As we linked two fine, two noble families.
Now she's dead.
For wedding-song, offer dirges,
For bridal white, black mourning,
My escort to a marriage-bed
With the ghost of my lost love.

CHORUS.
Misfortune took you unawares.
Innocent. A life untouched by grief.
Your life is saved. Now live it.
Your wife has died and you've found love lives on.
There's no novelty here, except for you.
Death's always been keen to claim a wife.

ADMETUS.
Friends, dear friends, this may seem strange to say.
My wife is luckier in her fate than me, I think.
No pain can touch her any more.
She has a blessed release from all her troubles.
It is I who should not be alive, I who live on time
Less borrowed than ransacked, the bitterer for that.
Till now I never realised, never knew till now.
How can I face the world indoors?

What conversation could I ever again enjoy?
Where am I to turn?
In there lives only loneliness to drive me out.
No one in her bed. Her chair empty. Cobwebs under the eaves.
The children falling down and crying for their mother.
Servants tearful for the mistress they've lost.
That's indoors. Outside?
There'll be weddings in Thessaly. Crowds of women.
And I'll suddenly see one who reminds me of Alkestis.
Enemies will sneer 'There goes the man who's still alive,
The coward without the nerve to die.
Who sold his wife and chased her off to Hell.
Do you call that a man? Condemns his parents
When he couldn't die himself.'
To crown it all, I've lost my name.
Is there anything left to live for, friends,
When I've branded myself a coward?

CHORUS.
I have searched in the arts,
I've let fancy fly free,
I've pored over thick books,
And all to no avail.
Nothing can outweigh Necessity.
Arcane tomes from Thrace,
Orphic utterances,
Apollo's own nostrums,
Pain-salving drugs for the sons of Asklepius:
None offers an antidote
To Fate.

Fate alone has no altar,
No image in wood.
She welcomes no sacrifice.
Keep at bay, I pray.
Don't encroach on my life, Necessity,

Any more than before.
Even almighty Zeus
Is powerless without you.
You can even tame iron down among the Chalybes,
There's none as remorseless
As Fate.

In steely grip, Admetus, that goddess holds you fast.
You must endure. The dead can never be restored
Through tears and mourning.
The gods' own children
Slip into Death's shadows.
She was a dear friend to us in life,
No less dear as a memory shall she be.
Finest of all women
Was Alkestis, your wife.

We shall not treat you, Alkestis, as some departed soul.
Your tomb must be a shrine. A place of reverence.
Your honour a god's.
The passing traveller
Stepping aside shall say
'Here lies the woman who died for her man.
We salute you, blessed guardian spirit,
Look kindly upon us.'
Such greetings will she hear.

Admetus, I think it's Herakles I can see
Heading this way, back to your house.

Enter HERAKLES *with a veiled woman.*

HERAKLES.
A friend deserves an honest response, Admetus,
Better that than some smouldering resentment.
I arrived at a time of personal disaster for you,
Believing I had some claim on your friendship.
You chose not to tell me that your wife lay dead.
Instead you offered your best hospitality,
Pretending you were upset over some stranger or other.
So I got all dolled-up in garlands,

Made free with the wine, blind to the world,
In your house, which happened to be a house of mourning.
I take you to task for that, for insulting me like that.
I have no wish to add to your grief, but I blame you.
That's why I have come back. I've something to say to you.
This woman here. I want you to take her in for me.
While I go to fetch these Thracian horses
And kill off the tyrant of Bistonia.
Should I fail to return . . . of course I will,
Then keep her as a gift to the household.
I did not win her easily, I can tell you.
I came across some competition these men were organising,
An athletic competition. There you are. She was the prize.
The runners got a horse. An ox for the boxers
And the wrestlers. And this woman.
It seemed a shame to turn it down, when I'd won.
So, like I said, you look after her, eh?
She's not kidnapped, you know. I won her fair and square.
You'll thank me one day, you see if you don't.

ADMETUS.

I meant no disrespect, Herakles, when I concealed
From you what had happened to Alkestis. Still less
To treat you as anything other than a friend.
I did not want to heap trouble on trouble
By packing you off to someone else's house.
I had enough to weep about as it was.
As for the woman, please, lord Herakles,
If you can, find someone else to take her in,
Someone in Thessaly who has not suffered such a loss.
You have plenty of friends in Pherai.
Don't remind me what has happened.
I'm afraid the sight of her about the house
Might make me cry. Don't make things worse for me.

Anyway, where could we put a young woman in this house?
She is young, I suppose, from the look of her clothes.
She can hardly live in a male household, can she?
Consorting with young men all day won't guarantee her purity.
It's not so easy to keep young fellows in check,
Herakles. It's you I'm thinking about.
There's only Alkestis' room. Oh no.
You cannot want me to give her Alkestis' room?
I'd be reproached from every side.
By my people for betraying my saviour
In slipping into some young woman's arms.
And by her, by Alkestis. She deserves respect.
It's her I have to think about.
Whoever you are, young woman . . . you're her height,
You have her natural posture, her figure.
Remove her from my sight, now piercing to my soul.
Chide me that I might say indeed
You are Alkestis.
She stirs my heart. My eyes are filled with tears.
Now, only now, Admetus, the real taste of pain.

CHORUS.
Though I cannot commend a fate like this,
You can only endure what the gods may send.

HERAKLES.
Would it were in my power to bring her back,
Back to the light from her underworld home,
A favour from me to you.

ADMETUS.
I know you would wish it. But how?
For the dead there's no way back.

HERAKLES.
Don't lose control. Bear up, now.

ADMETUS.
That's easier said than done.

HERAKLES.
You cannot mourn for ever. Where's the point in that?

ADMETUS.
I know. I know. My grief consumes me.

HERAKLES.
A loved one dead. Yes, that deserves your tears.

ADMETUS.
This has destroyed me. No words can say . . .

HERAKLES.
It's a good woman you've lost. Who would deny it?

ADMETUS.
There's no light left in my life.

HERAKLES.
Time's the great healer. Your grief's still young.

ADMETUS.
Time, you call it. Certainly, if time means dying.

HERAKLES.
A new woman will cheer you up. You'll see, when you get married again.

ADMETUS.
Don't say that. How could you think such a thing?

HERAKLES.
What? Never marry? No little wife in your bed?

ADMETUS.
I'll never sleep with another woman.

HERAKLES.
What use is that to your dead wife?

ADMETUS.
I must respect her memory, wherever she is.

HERAKLES.
I approve. Really. Most high-minded of you. But pointless.

ADMETUS.
Whatever you wish. You'll not see me married again.

HERAKLES.
Faithful for love. Well, I commend that.

ADMETUS.
I would rather die than break my word.

HERAKLES.
Take this woman in anyway to your respectable house.

ADMETUS.
I swear by Zeus, I cannot do it.

HERAKLES.
You're making a big mistake if you don't.

ADMETUS.
And it will torment me if I do.

HERAKLES.
Give in. As a favour to me. You owe me a favour.

ADMETUS.
For heaven's sake. I wish you'd never fought for her. Nor won.

HERAKLES.
You share the prize, that's all.

ADMETUS.
It's generous of you. But the woman must go elsewhere.

HERAKLES.
If she must, she must. But take a little look first.

ADMETUS.
If that's what it takes to prevent your being angry with me.

HERAKLES.
Trust me. I know what I'm doing.

ADMETUS.
You win. But I'm not happy about this.

HERAKLES.
The day will come when you'll be grateful. Believe me.

ADMETUS.
Fetch her indoors. If I have to receive her, so be it.

HERAKLES.
I'm not handing this woman over to any servant.

ADMETUS.
All right. Take her in yourself, if that's what you want.

HERAKLES.
Into your hands only.

ADMETUS.
I prefer not to touch her. The door's open.

HERAKLES.
I entrust her to your right hand and yours alone.

ADMETUS.
My lord, you compel me against my will.

HERAKLES.
Do not shun her. Nay, present your hand.

ADMETUS (*without looking at her*).
Like a man cutting off Medusa's head.

HERAKLES.
Are you holding her?

ADMETUS.
I'm holding her.

HERAKLES.
Then take care of her. And in future you can say
What a generous guest the son of Zeus has proved.
Take a look. Now, tell me if she resembles your wife a little.
And change sorrow to happiness.

ADMETUS.
What can I say? If this be magic.
Let it be an art lawful as eating.
Strike all that look upon with marvel.
Is this truly my wife I look upon
Or some god's illusion sent to mock me?

HERAKLES.
She's real. It is Alkestis.

ADMETUS.
Some phantom, maybe, stolen from the dead.

HERAKLES.
I'm not some witch-doctor you welcomed here.

ADMETUS.
How can I see my wife? I buried her.

HERAKLES.
It is her, strange as it may seem.

ADMETUS.
May I touch her? Speak to her as my wife?

HERAKLES.
Say what you like. Here is your heart's desire.

ADMETUS.
You have her eyes, her body. Dearest Alkestis,
I hold you in my arms when I thought
Never again to see your face.

HERAKLES.
Indeed you do. And I trust no jealous god is watching.

ADMETUS.
Noblest son of almighty Zeus, how can I thank you?
May your father protect you.
You have restored me, single-handed.

HERAKLES.
I battled for her life with the powers from below.

ADMETUS.
But where could such a fight with Death take place?

HERAKLES.
I ambushed him by the tomb.

ADMETUS.
Why does she not say anything?

HERAKLES.
You may not hear a word from her

Before purification from the underworld
When she is released on the third day.
Take her in, Admetus, and in future
Treat your guests as a good man should.
I'll say goodbye. I have a labour to perform
Set by Eurystheus, tyrant son of Sthenelus.

ADMETUS.
Wait. Stay here with us. Please.

HERAKLES.
Some other time. Now I have to hurry.

ADMETUS.
Good luck. Come back safe.

Exit HERAKLES.

Throughout our lands I declare a public holiday,
A thanksgiving festival of song and dance.
Let altars smoke with sacrifice and feast.
Now we look forward to a better life,
Blessed by fortune, as I'll not deny.

CHORUS.
However clear they may appear,
The gods are seldom what they seem.
Things rarely end as you expect,
Not when a god's at work.
And that's the lesson of this fable.

Exeunt omnes.

A Note on the Translators

KENNETH McLEISH's translations, of plays by all the Greek and Roman dramatists, Ibsen, Feydeau, Molière, Strindberg and others, have been performed throughout the world on stage, film, TV and radio. His original plays include *I Will If You Will*, *Just Do It*, *The Arabian Nights*, *Omma* and *Orpheus*. His books include *The Theatre of Aristophanes*, *Guide to Shakespeare's Plays* (with Stephen Unwin), *The Good Reading Guide* and *Guide to Greek Theatre and Drama*. He was Editor of the Drama Classics series for Nick Hern Books and a Fellow of the Royal Society of Literature. He died in 1997.

J. MICHAEL WALTON worked in the professional theatre as an actor and director before joining the University of Hull, where he holds the Chair of Drama. He has published four books on Greek theatre, *Greek Theatre Practice*, *The Greek Sense of Theatre: Tragedy Reviewed*, *Living Greek Theatre: A Handbook of Classical Performance and Modern Production* and *Menander and the Making of Comedy* (with the late Peter Arnott). He is Series Editor of Methuen Classical Greek Dramatists, edited *Craig on Theatre*, and, with Marianne McDonald, *Amid Our Troubles: Irish Versions of Greek Tragedy*. He has translated plays by Sophocles, Euripides, Menander and Terence, and was founder director of the Performance Translation Centre in the Drama Department at the University of Hull.

Methuen Classical Greek Dramatists

Aeschylus Plays: One
(Persians, Seven Against Thebes, Suppliants, Prometheus Bound)

Aeschylus Plays: Two
(Oresteia: Agamemnon, Libation-Bearers, Eumenides)

Aristophanes Plays: One
(Acharnians, Knights, Peace, Lysistrata)

Aristophanes Plays: Two
(Wasps, Clouds, Birds, Festival Time, Frogs)

Aristophanes & Menander: New Comedy
(Women in Power, Wealth, The Malcontent, The Woman from Samos)

Euripides Plays: One
(Medea, The Phoenician Women, Bacchae)

Euripides Plays: Two
(Hecuba, The Women of Troy, Iphigeneia at Aulis, Cyclops)

Euripides Plays: Three
(Alkestis, Helen, Ion)

Euripides Plays: Four
(Elektra, Orestes, Iphigeneia in Tauris)

Euripides Plays: Five
(Andromache, Herakles' Children, Herakles)

Euripides Plays: Six
(Hippolytos, Suppliants, Rhesos)

Sophocles Plays: One
(Oedipus the King, Oedipus at Colonus, Antigone)

Sophocles Plays: Two
Ajax, Women of Trachis, Electra, Philoctetes)

Methuen Student Editions

Jean Anouilh	*Antigone*
John Arden	*Serjeant Musgrave's Dance*
Alan Ayckbourn	*Confusions*
Aphra Behn	*The Rover*
Edward Bond	*Lear*
Bertolt Brecht	*The Caucasian Chalk Circle*
	Life of Galileo
	Mother Courage and her Children
	The Resistible Rise of Arturo Ui
Anton Chekhov	*The Cherry Orchard*
	The Seagull
Caryl Churchill	*Serious Money*
	Top Girls
Shelagh Delaney	*A Taste of Honey*
Euripides	*Medea*
John Galsworthy	*Strife*
Robert Holman	*Across Oka*
Henrik Ibsen	*A Doll's House*
	Hedda Gabler
Charlotte Keatley	*My Mother Said I Never Should*
Bernard Kops	*Dreams of Anne Frank*
Federico García Lorca	*Blood Wedding*
	The House of Bernarda Alba (bilingual edition)
John Marston	*The Malcontent*
Willy Russell	*Blood Brothers*
Wole Soyinka	*Death and the King's Horseman*
August Strindberg	*The Father*
J. M. Synge	*The Playboy of the Western World*
Oscar Wilde	*The Importance of Being Earnest*
Tennessee Williams	*A Streetcar Named Desire*
	The Glass Menagerie
Timberlake Wertenbaker	*Our Country's Good*

Methuen World Classics
include

Jean Anouilh (two volumes)
Brendan Behan
Aphra Behn
Bertolt Brecht (seven volumes)
Büchner
Bulgakov
Calderón
Čapek
Anton Chekhov
Noël Coward (eight volumes)
Feydeau (two volumes)
Eduardo De Filippo
Max Frisch
John Galsworthy
Gogol
Gorky
Harley Granville Barker (two volumes)
Henrik Ibsen (six volumes)
Alfred Jarry
Lorca (three volumes)
Marivaux
Mustapha Matura
David Mercer (two volumes)
Arthur Miller (five volumes)
Molière
Musset
Peter Nichols (two volumes)
Clifford Odets
Joe Orton
A. W. Pinero
Luigi Pirandello
Terence Rattigan (two volumes)
W. Somerset Maugham (two volumes)
August Strindberg (three volumes)
J. M. Synge
Ramón del Valle-Inclán
Frank Wedekind
Oscar Wilde

Methuen Contemporary Dramatists
include

John Arden (two volumes)
Arden & D'Arcy
Peter Barnes (three volumes)
Sebastian Barry
Dermot Bolger
Edward Bond (six volumes)
Howard Brenton (two volumes)
Richard Cameron
Jim Cartwright
Caryl Churchill (two volumes)
Sarah Daniels (two volumes)
Nick Darke
David Edgar (three volumes)
Ben Elton
Dario Fo (two volumes)
Michael Frayn (three volumes)
David Greig
John Godber (two volumes)
Paul Godfrey
John Guare
Lee Hall
Peter Handke
Jonathan Harvey (two volumes)
Declan Hughes
Terry Johnson (two volumes)
Sarah Kane
Barrie Keeffe
Bernard-Marie Koltès
David Lan
Bryony Lavery
Deborah Levy
Doug Lucie
David Mamet (four volumes)
Martin McDonagh
Duncan McLean
Anthony Minghella (two volumes)
Tom Murphy (four volumes)
Phyllis Nagy
Anthony Nielsen
Philip Osment
Louise Page
Stewart Parker (two volumes)
Joe Penhall
Stephen Poliakoff (three volumes)
David Rabe
Mark Ravenhill
Christina Reid
Philip Ridley
Willy Russell
Eric-Emmanuel Schmitt
Ntozake Shange
Sam Shepard (two volumes)
Shelagh Stephenson
Wole Soyinka (two volumes)
David Storey (three volumes)
Sue Townsend
Judy Upton
Michel Vinaver (two volumes)
Arnold Wesker (two volumes)
Michael Wilcox
Roy Williams
Snoo Wilson (two volumes)
David Wood (two volumes)
Victoria Wood